MATHEMATICS
for
BUSINESS
and
ECONOMICS

Rochid J. Elias
University of Maine at Augusta

D. VAN NOSTRAND COMPANY

New York   Cincinnati   Toronto   London   Melbourne

D. Van Nostrand Company Regional Offices:
New York   Cincinnati

D. Van Nostrand Company International Offices:
London   Toronto   Melbourne

Copyright © 1979 by Litton Educational Publishing, Inc.

Library of Congress Catalog Card Number: 78-62188
ISBN: 0-442-21757-9

Published by D. Van Nostrand Company
135 W. 50th Street, New York, N.Y. 10020

10 9 8 7 6 5 4 3 2 1

PREFACE

MATHEMATICS FOR BUSINESS AND ECONOMICS is an introductory text in applied mathematics for students in business and economics courses. Each chapter begins with sections that explain basic mathematical concepts that have applications in business and economics. Later sections are built upon previous ones to show how these basic mathematical concepts are used in economics. Examples are given to illustrate every concept, and many examples are accompanied by figures that enable the student to visualize the concepts. Every section is followed by a set of problems.

Chapter 1 introduces the idea that systematic relationships among variables can be described mathematically by using the concept of a function. It shows how functions are represented graphically and how the concept of slope enables the measurement of the rate of change and direction of change in a function. After discussing the intersection of linear functions, the text shows how this concept can be applied to problems of market equilibrium. Break-even analysis, the consumption function, and the multiplier are introduced. Determinants and the idea of the best-fitting line are subjects that can be studied at the instructor's discretion.

Chapter 2 presents the problems of nonlinear functions, their graphing, and ways in which they can be solved. The quadratic formula is discussed.

Chapter 3 gives an overview of algebraic functions, polynomials, the production function, and exponential and logarithmic functions.

Chapter 4 explains some fundamental concepts of calculus, restricting its treatment to a few basic functions that many students will find sufficient for understanding basic problems in business and economics. After defining the derivative of a function, the text focuses on the power rule as a method for finding the derivative of a function. The student is encouraged to make a connection between the derivative of a function and the concept of "marginal" in economics. The text shows how the derivative is related to some central aspects of economic theory: marginal propensities to consume and save, marginal cost and revenue, the marginal products of labor and capital. In the process, total cost, total product, profit maximization, and the production function are also discussed. The chapter also provides an introduction to integral calculus and shows how certain economic functions can be related to, or reconstructed from, their marginal functions.

Chapter 5 gives an introduction to the study of matrix algebra, which is essential to students in business and economics because of its diverse applications in accounting, economics, and computer programming.

Chapter 6 outlines basic concepts and formulas used to calculate simple and compound interest, the meaning of bank discounting, annuities, mortgage payments, and four methods of calculating depreciation.

There are three appendixes: Appendix A is an Algebra Review, which includes mathematical concepts, notations, laws, and techniques that have been used in the text. It can be taught as a brief refresher before the rest of the course, or it can serve as a handy reference for those whose skills need reviewing. Appendix B consists of tables for reference: logarithms, present and future value tables, and a table of the exponential function. Appendix C gives Answers to Selected Problems, including many line graphs. A set of answers is available from the publisher on request.

The author would like to thank the following professors who helped develop this text: William J. Carroll, Rutgers University; Henry A. Gemery, Colby College; Louis F. Bush, San Diego City College; Peter R. Kressler, Glassboro State College; J. Duvall, Mountain View College; Stanley M. Lukawecki, Clemson University; Eugene F. Krause, University of Michigan.

CONTENTS

2 SECOND DEGREE FUNCTIONS 77

3 ALGEBRAIC AND EXPONENTIAL FUNCTIONS 95

4 BASIC CALCULUS 123

5   MATRIX ALGEBRA   201

6   THE MATHEMATICS OF FINANCE   239

LINEAR FUNCTIONS

1.1 THE CONCEPT OF A FUNCTION

The concept of a function is fundamental in business and economics. The term "function" is used to describe relationships that exist between variables—for example, the price of a product and the quantity demanded for the item, the demand for a product and a seller's revenue, or a firm's production and its total cost of production. These relationships form the basis of much of the analysis in the first four chapters of this book. One of the major objectives is to move from the demand of a product to a firm's revenue, then to move the firm's cost function, and finally to obtain and maximize the firm's profit function.

What Is a Function?

If two variables—call them x and y—are so related that whenever a value is assigned to x, one value of y results according to some rule, then y is a function of x and is expressed symbolically as $y = f(x)$. x is called the *independent* variable and y the *dependent* variable. The set of values that x can assume constitutes the *domain* of the function; the set of values that y can assume constitutes the *range* of the function.

The variables x and y were arbitrarily chosen and more appropriate letters can be used when desired: TC for total cost, ATC for average total cost, I for income, Q for quantity, R for revenue, P for price, and so on. The functional notation $f(x)$ does not have to employ the letter "f" but can include any letter, lower- or uppercase: $y = G(x)$ is read as "y is a function of x."

Example 1: $y = f(x) = 2x + 4$ or simply $y = 2x + 4$ is a function, because it satisfies the definition of a function. Two variables, x and y, are present; a relationship of equality exists; and for each value of x a rule gives one value to y. The domain and range of the function consist of all real numbers.

Example 2: $a = H(b) = 2b + 4$ or simply $a = 2b + 4$ is the same function as that in Example 1, but different variables are used.

Example 3: $y = f(x) = 1/x$ or simply $y = 1/x$ is a function, but division by 0 is not permitted. Thus, the domain and range consist of all real numbers except 0.

Example 4: $y^2 = x$ is not a function, because for each x there is no unique y (for example, when $x = 4, y = +2$ or $y = -2$).

Example 5: Assume that a firm's total cost (TC) of production (x) is given by:

$$TC = 4x + 10$$

TC represents a function, because for any level of output there is a unique total cost. The domain of x excludes negative numbers, and the range of TC is numbers greater than or equal to 10. In the applied sense we must assume a reasonable maximum for x over a specified time period.

Example 6: Assume that the relationship between price (P) and quantity demanded (Q) for a particular product is given by:

$$Q = f(P) = 8 - 2P$$

In this example quantity demanded is a function of price, and specific units for Q, P, and time will be ignored. At various prices we can establish quantity demanded and determine the domain and range of $Q = f(P)$:

$Q = f(0) = 8$
$Q = f(1) = 6$
$Q = f(2) = 4$
$Q = f(3) = 2$
$Q = f(4) = 0$

These results are frequently presented in a table or a schedule:

Price (P)	Quantity demanded (Q)
0	8
1	6
2	4
3	2
4	0

All values of P fall within the domain of $Q = f(P)$. All values of Q fall within the range of $Q = f(P)$.

PROBLEMS 1-1

Answers to asterisked problems are given in Appendix C at the end of the book.

*1. Find the domain and range of the following functions:

a. $y = 2x - 3$ e. $y = x^4$ h. $y = \dfrac{2}{x - 2}$

b. $y = 2x^2$ f. $y = -x^4$ i. $y = \sqrt{x - 2}$

c. $y = \dfrac{1}{x}$ g. $y = \sqrt{x}$ j. $y = |x|$

d. $y = x^2 + 2$

*2. Given that $f(x) = 2x + 4$ and $g(x) = x^2$, find $f(0), f(3), f(-4), f(a), f(a + b)$, $f(x + \Delta x), g(0), g(-3), g(c), g(a + b), g(x + \Delta x)$.

3. Given that $k(x) = .25x - 6$, find $k(0), k(24), k(x + \Delta x)$.

4. Given that $h(x) = \sqrt{x}$, find $h(1), h(-1), h(4), h(16), h(a^2)$.

5. Given that $G(z) = \sqrt{z}$, find $G(1), G(-1), G(4), G(16), G(a^2)$.

6. Given that $D = f(p) = 100 - 20p$, find $f(0), f(1), f(2), f(3), f(4), f(5)$.

1-2   THE RECTANGULAR COORDINATE SYSTEM

The rectangular coordinate system is used to describe functions graphically. The system consists of a horizontal axis that represents the independent variable—x—and a vertical axis that represents the dependent variable—y. These axes are number lines that intersect at right angles at the origin of the axes. Any point in the plane can be described by the number pair (x, y), where y is the perpendicular distance measured from x. If y is positive, the point is measured above the x axis, whereas if y is negative, the point is measured below the x axis. Keep in mind that the independent variable x is listed first, and the dependent variable y is listed second in the notation (x, y). (See Figure 1-1.)

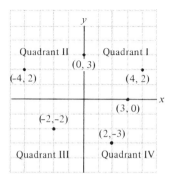

FIGURE 1-1

PROBLEMS 1-2

*1. If a point lies on the y axis, what is the value of the x coordinate? If a point lies on the x axis, what is the value of the y coordinate?

2. Locate the following points in the rectangular coordinate system: $(3, 6)$, $(-3, -7)$, $(-5, -4)$, $(0, 5)$, $(5, 0)$, $(-1, 5)$, $(5, -1)$.

1-3   LINEAR FUNCTIONS

A linear function can be written in the general form:

$$y = mx + b$$

This is considered the *explicit form* of the linear function, because y is given directly—explicitly—in terms of x. The several implicit forms of linear functions are reducible to the explicit form. The graphical representation of the linear function can be obtained by plotting any two points in the plane and drawing an extended line through the points. Remember that the x and y variables in the explicit form $y = mx + b$ are the same x and y variables as are found on the axes of the rectangular coordinate system.

With the exception of lines that are parallel to one of the axes, every linear function will cross the x axis, called the x-axis intercept, and the y axis, called the y-axis intercept. Finding the x- and y-axis intercepts are of major importance in mathematical economics and thus will be given special attention. Stating this more positively, *the single most important curve-sketching technique is the intercept technique*. Linear functions are straight lines (often called curves in economics); irrespective of the function, there are only two steps involved in finding the intercepts:

Step 1:   Let $x = 0$ and solve for y (the y-axis intercept).
Step 2:   Let $y = 0$ and solve for x (the x-axis intercept).

Example 1:   Sketch the graph of $y = 8 - 2x$ where y is the dependent variable and x is the independent variable (see Figure 1-2).

Step 1:   Let $x = 0$ and $y = 8$ (y-axis intercept).
Step 2:   Let $y = 0$ and $x = 4$ (x-axis intercept).

Example 2   Sketch the graph of $Q = 8 - 2p$ where Q is the dependent variable and p is the independent variable (see Figure 1-3). If Q represents quantity demanded and p represents price (over a certain time interval), then the graph of $Q = f(p)$ could represent a consumer's demand for a particular product. Units for p and Q are left arbitrary.

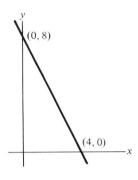

FIGURE 1-2

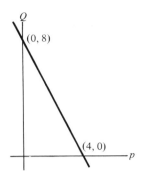

FIGURE 1-3

Step 1:   Let $p = 0$ and $Q = 8$ (the Q-axis intercept).
Step 2:   Let $Q = 0$ and $p = 4$ (the p-axis intercept).

For $Q = f(p) = 8 - 2p$, price is the independent variable and by mathematical convention belongs on the horizontal axis. Quantity demanded is the dependent variable and belongs on the vertical axis. In economics, however, this convention is reversed for $Q = f(p)$, and this will be considered shortly. *Unless a special note is made, we will assume that the independent variable will be located on the horizontal axis and the dependent variable will be located on the vertical axis.*

Example 3:   It is possible for a line to intercept only one axis. In plotting this and the following examples, plotting points gives the graphical representation. Plot the graph of $y = 3$ (see Figure 1-4). On the table we see that, for every x, y is always 3. This is a *constant function.*

x	y
0	3
1	3
2	3
.	.
.	.
.	.

$y = 3$

FIGURE 1-4

Example 4:   Plot the graph of $x = 3$ (see Figure 1-5). On the table we see that, for every y, x is always 3. The expression $x = 3$ *is not a function,* because for each x there is no unique y.

x	y
3	0
3	1
3	2
.	.
.	.
.	.

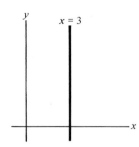

FIGURE 1-5

PROBLEMS 1-3

*1. Plot the graphs of the following lines; use the intercept technique when possible:

*a. $y = 5x + 10$ h. $y = .25x$ o. $x = 0$

*b. $y = -5x + 10$ i. $y = .25x - 6$ p. $-y = -x$

*c. $y = -5x - 10$ j. $y = -5$ q. $-y = x$

*d. $y = 5x - 10$ k. $y = 5$ r. $\dfrac{2}{y} = \dfrac{3}{x}$

e. $y = 5x + 20$ l. $y = 0$

f. $y = 5x - 20$ m. $x = -6$

g. $y = 5x$ n. $x = 6$

2. Plot the graphs of the following lines; use the intercept technique:

a. $2x + 4y = 8$ g. $-3x + 5y = 7$ k. $\dfrac{x}{8} + \dfrac{y}{12} = 1$

b. $2x - 4y = 8$ h. $-3x + 5y = -7$

c. $-2x + 4y = 8$ i. $\dfrac{2}{3}x + \dfrac{4}{3}y = 8$ l. $\dfrac{x}{8} - \dfrac{y}{12} = 1$

d. $2x + 4y = -8$

e. $-2x - 4y = -8$ j. $\dfrac{2x}{3} - \dfrac{5y}{2} = 13$ m. $3x - 5y = -22$

f. $3x + 5y = 7$

*3. Plot the graphs of the following:

*a. $y = |x|$ d. $y = |x| + 2$ g. $y = |3x + 1| - 2$

b. $y = -|x|$ e. $y = |x - 2|$ h. $x = |y|$

c. $y = |x + 2|$ f. $y = |3x - 1|$ i. $x = |y| + 1$

1.4   THE SLOPE OF A LINEAR FUNCTION

For the equation $y = mx + b$ the constant term, b, represents the y-axis intercept, and the coefficient of x—m—is the *slope* of the linear function. The slope of a function is of major importance in economics, and it is stated that *the single most important concept in mathematical economics is the slope of the linear function. The term "slope" as used in mathematics is synonymous with the term "marginal" as used in economics.*

What Is Slope?

Given that $y = mx + b$, m is the slope of the linear function and is defined as:

$$m = \frac{\text{change in } y}{\text{change in } x} = \frac{\Delta y}{\Delta x}$$

The uppercase Greek letter delta (Δ) means "change in."

It is important to recognize that this is the definition of the slope of $y = f(x)$, where y is the dependent variable. For any two points on the plane (x_1, y_1) and (x_2, y_2) the slope of y is found by evaluating:

$$m = \frac{y_2 - y_1}{x_2 - x_1} = \frac{\Delta y}{\Delta x}$$

A geometrical interpretation of the definition may be stated graphically (see Figure 1-6).

Example 1:   Find the slope of the line through the points $(1, 2)$ and $(4, 8)$. It makes no difference which point you select for (x_1, y_1) or (x_2, y_2). (See Figure 1-7.)

$$m = \frac{y_2 - y_1}{x_2 - x_1} = \frac{6}{3} = 2 \qquad \text{or} \qquad m = \frac{\Delta y}{\Delta x} = \frac{6}{3} = 2$$

Example 2:   Find the slope of the line between the points $(-1, 5)$ and $(3, -7)$.

$$m = \frac{\Delta y}{\Delta x} = \frac{-12}{4} = -3$$

Example 3:   Find the slope of the line between the points $(1, 4)$ and $(3, 4)$.

$$m = \frac{\Delta y}{\Delta x} = \frac{0}{2} = 0$$

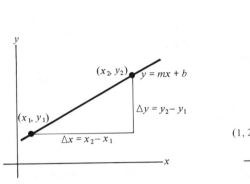

FIGURE 1-6   FIGURE 1-7

Example 4:   Find the slope of the line between the points (3, 2) and (3, 5).

$$m = \frac{\Delta y}{\Delta x} = \frac{3}{0} \quad \text{undefined}$$

In the above examples we found the slope of $y = f(x)$, which is $\Delta y/\Delta x$. The slope can be found directly if the expression of the line is given in the direct form: $y = mx + b$, read as: "y changes m times as fast as x." The slope tells us how fast y changes as x changes.

The slope of a linear function is a fraction, $m = \Delta y/\Delta x$, and thus can be positive, negative, 0, or undefined. The following illustrations bring out this important fact.

Positive Slope for $y = f(x)$

The change in y with respect to the change in x is positive. As x increases, y increases (see Figure 1-8).

Negative Slope for $y = f(x)$

The change in y with respect to the change in x is negative. As x increases, y decreases (see Figure 1-9).

Zero Slope for $y = f(x)$

When y does not change, the slope is 0 (see Figure 1-10). C is constant.

Undefined Slope for $y = f(x)$

When Δx is 0, slope is undefined, because division by 0 is undefined (see Figure 1-11).

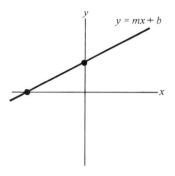

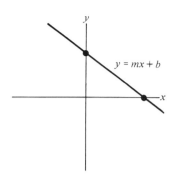

FIGURE 1-8   FIGURE 1-9

If a linear function is expressed in the explicit form $y = mx + b$, the slope of y is immediately given as m. If the linear function is expressed implicitly in a form such as:

$$ax + by + c = 0$$

then the slope can be found by solving the equation for y.

Example 5:   Find the slope of $2y - 4x - 8 = 0$. In order to find the slope of $y = f(x)$ the function must be solved for y:

$$y = 2x + 4$$

The slope of $y = f(x)$ is 2.

Example 6:   The slope of a linear function is frequently viewed from a table that represents points that lie on the line. Using such a table find the slope of $R = f(x) = 6x$. In this example R represents a firm's total revenue with respect to quantity sold X. The variables R and TR are frequently used interchangeably to indicate a firm's total revenue. The specific item manufactured, the time period, units for the variable X, and the domain of X will be ignored:

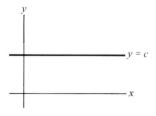

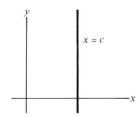

FIGURE 1-10   FIGURE 1-11

Quantity sold (X)	Total revenue (R)

$$\begin{array}{l}
0 \\
\quad \rceil \Delta x = 1 \\
1 \\
\quad \rceil \Delta x = 1 \\
2 \\
\quad \rceil \Delta x = 1 \\
3
\end{array}
\qquad
\begin{array}{l}
0 \\
\quad \rceil \Delta R = 6 \\
6 \\
\quad \rceil \Delta R = 6 \\
12 \\
\quad \rceil \Delta R = 6 \\
18
\end{array}$$

$\Delta R / \Delta x$ is always 6. In economics the term "slope" is replaced by "marginal." The slope of $R = f(x) = 6x$ is 6; thus, marginal revenue is 6.

Example 7:   Linear function $Slope\ of\ y = f(x)\!\left(\dfrac{\Delta y}{\Delta x}\right)$

$y = -5x$	-5
$y = -5x + 2$	-5
$-y = 3x + 7$	-3
$2x + y = -3$	-2
$-3x - 5y - 4 = 0$	$-\dfrac{3}{5}$
$y = 4$	0
$x = 4$	undefined
$\dfrac{y}{3} = \dfrac{x}{7}$	$\dfrac{3}{7}$

If the slope of $y = f(x)$ is given by $\Delta y/\Delta x$, then $\Delta x/\Delta y$ represents the slope of $x = g(y)$. For $y = mx + b$:

slope of $y = f(x)$ is: $m = \dfrac{\Delta y}{\Delta x}$

slope of $x = g(y)$ is: $\dfrac{1}{m} = \dfrac{\Delta x}{\Delta y}$

Example 8:   Linear Function $Slope\ of\ y = f(x)\!\left(\dfrac{\Delta y}{\Delta x}\right)$ $Slope\ of\ x = g(y)\!\left(\dfrac{\Delta x}{\Delta y}\right)$

$y = 5x - 7$	$\dfrac{5}{1}$	$\dfrac{1}{5}$
$y = -3x$	$-\dfrac{3}{1}$	$-\dfrac{1}{3}$
$y = 5$	0	undefined
$x = 5$	undefined	0

Example 9:   Assume that y represents price and x represents quantity demanded. $y = 12 - 3x$ means that the slope of price (y) is -3 and the slope of quantity

demanded (x) is $-1/3$. $y = 4$ means that the slope of price is 0 and that the slope of quantity demanded is undefined. $x = 4$ means that the slope of price is undefined and the slope of quantity demanded is 0.

The Point Slope Formula

We must now find the linear function that passes through any two given points. To solve this problem we use a technique for obtaining certain linear economic relationships. The formula for finding the line through two points is called the *point slope formula* and is derived immediately from the definition of the slope.

The expression that is used to determine the linear function that passes through a point (x_1, y_1) with slope m is:

$$y - y_1 = m(x - x_1)$$

The formula is derived by multiplying both sides of the equation for the slope: $m = (y - y_1)/(x - x_1)$ by $(x - x_1)$. The point slope formula can be used if two points are given, because the slope can be found; then either point can be used for (x_1, y_1).

Example 10: Find the linear function that passes through the points $(1, 9)$ and $(3, 3)$.

Step 1: $m = \Delta y/\Delta x = -3$.
Step 2: Let the point be $(1, 9)$ for (x_1, y_1) (either point can be used).
Step 3: Substitute into the point slope formula:

$$y - y_1 = m(x - x_1)$$
$$y - 9 = -3(x - 1) = -3x + 12$$

Example 11: In the table below the independent variable X represents the quantity of an item produced by a firm over some time interval. The dependent variable C represents the firm's total cost of production (frequently the variable TC is used to indicate total cost). Find the linear total cost function that passes through the points given in the table.

Output (X)   *Cost (C)*

$\left.\begin{array}{c}1 \\ \\ 2\end{array}\right]\Delta x = 1$ $\left.\begin{array}{c}6 \\ \\ 10\end{array}\right]\Delta c = 4$

The point slope formula could be used, but the table gives us immediately the values of the slope of C and the C-axis intercept and thus $C = 4x + 2$.

Example 12:   In special cases for linear functions parallel to one of the axes, it is best to express the line directly from the graph. The points (3, 7) and (5, 7) are expressed by $y = 7$. The points (5, 1) and (5, 6) are expressed by $x = 5$.

It is important to realize that the slope of a linear function is constant; conversely, if the slope of a function is constant, then the function is linear. On the other hand, if the slope of a function is continually changing, then the function is not linear; conversely, if a function is not linear, then its slope is continually changing.

The idea that the slope of a nonlinear function is continually changing is fundamental to the study of calculus (Chapter 4); however, a simple example is given so that the problem can be somewhat appreciated on algebraic and geometric levels.

Example 13:   The graph of the curve $y = x^2$ can be sketched in the first quadrant by plotting the following points that satisfy the function: (0, 0), (1, 1), (2, 4), (3, 9), ... The value for $\Delta y/\Delta x$ can be calculated from point to point and the slope is continually changing (see Figure 1-12). The slopes indicated in Figure 1-12 do not represent the change of y with respect to x at a point on the curve. Rather, the figure gives the slope of a line, between two points, which can be regarded as the average slope of the function between the points. For example, the slope of the line from (0, 0) to (1, 1) is +1; this represents the average slope over the entire interval. If we assign one value of x in the interval from $x = 0$ to $x = 1$ that would be representative of the slope of +1, we are permitted to use the midpoint of the interval, which is $x = 1/2$. If we sketched a line tangent to the curve at $x = 1/2$, then the slope of this line *could* be taken as +1 (see Figure 1-13).

The conclusion cannot be made that for every nonlinear function the midpoint of the Δx interval represents the x value where $\Delta y/\Delta x$ is the average slope. Instead we are *temporarily* permitted to use this technique until the problem is studied in detail in Chapter 4.

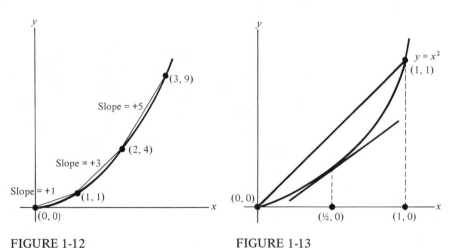

FIGURE 1-12   FIGURE 1-13

PROBLEMS 1-4

*1. Find both $\Delta y/\Delta x$ and $\Delta x/\Delta y$ for the lines in Problems 1 and 2 at the end of Section 1-3.

*2. Find the linear expressions determined by the following points:

*a. $(2, 3)$ and $(-5, -7)$	f. $(0, 5)$ and $(5, 0)$
*b. $(2, 4)$ and $(10, 4)$	g. $(1, 10)$ and $(-7, -10)$
*c. $(4, 1)$ and $(4, 7)$	h. $(0, 0)$ and $(6, 0)$
*d. $(-5, 7)$ and $(4, -2)$	i. $(0, 0)$ and $(0, 6)$
e. $(-5, -4)$ and $(1, 4)$	j. $(-3, 0)$ and $(7, 0)$

*3. For each of the following, set up tables for a few values of x and y. From the table find the slope of y. Use the definition of the slope; that is, divide changes in y by corresponding changes in x as obtained from the table:

*a. $y = 4x + 10$	c. $y = 5$
b. $y = 12 - 3x$	d. $x = 5$

*4. By definition:

$$\frac{\Delta y}{\Delta x} = \frac{f(x + \Delta x) - f(x)}{\Delta x}$$

Slope of linear functions can be found by using the definition:

$$\frac{f(x + \Delta x) - f(x)}{\Delta x}$$

and the process involves three steps:

Step 1: Evaluate $f(x + \Delta x)$.
Step 2: Subtract $f(x)$ from $f(x + \Delta x)$.
Step 3: Divide the result by Δx.

Find the slopes of the following linear functions; use this definition and represent the results graphically:

*a. $y = 8x$	c. $y = 12 - 3x$
*b. $y = 4x + 10$	d. $y = 5$

1-5 THE INTERSECTION OF LINEAR FUNCTIONS

Two linear functions intersect once and only once in the plane if their slopes are not the same. Assuming that the functions are explicit in the same variable, we set the two equations equal to each other and solve the equation to find the point of intersection. The resulting solution is substituted in either of the original equations, and the remaining coordinate is obtained.

Example 1:   Find the intersection of:

$$y = -3x + 12$$
$$y = 3x + 6$$

Step 1: $-3x + 12 = 3x + 6$ gives $x = 1$.
Step 2:   Substitution of $x = 1$ into either equation gives $y = 9$. Check $(1, 9)$ in both equations (see Figure 1-14).

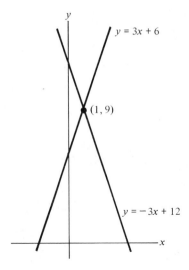

$y = 3x + 6$

$(1, 9)$

$y = -3x + 12$

FIGURE 1-14

Example 2:   Find the point of intersection of:

$$x = -y + 5$$
$$x = 2y - 10$$

Step 1: $-y + 5 = 2y - 10$ gives $y = 5$.
Step 2:   Substitution of $y = 5$ into either equation gives $x = 0$. Check $(0, 5)$ in both equations.

Example 3:   There is no point of intersection for:

$$y = 2x + 4$$
$$y = 2x + 6$$

These lines are parallel, because they have the same slope. Any algebraic attempt to find the point of intersection will fail, because $2x + 6 \neq 2x + 4$.

Example 4:   The expressions:

$$y = 2x + 3$$
$$2y = 4x + 6$$

represent the same linear function and the question of intersection is not relevant. Any algebraic attempt to find the point of intersection will fail.

Example 5:   Finding the point of intersection of two linear variables involves the elimination of one of the variables. The previous examples have done this by direct substitution; however, the basic assumption of algebra can be used on implicit functions to accomplish the same end. Find the point of intersection of:

$$2y + 6x = 24$$
$$y - 3x = 6$$

Step 1:   Multiply the first equation by $1/2$ to give $y + 3x = 12$.
Step 2:   Adding both equations gives $y = 9$.
Step 3:   Substituting $y = 9$ in each equation gives $x = 1$.

The point of intersection is $(1, 9)$. This is the same problem as found in Example 1.

PROBLEMS 1-5

*1. Sketch the graphs of the following sets of equations and indicate their point of intersection (if any).

*a.	$y = 2x + 8$	d.	$y = 4$	f.	$y = 2x + 8$	
	$y = 6x$		$y = 4x + 8$		$y = 2x + 4$	
*b.	$y = 8 - 3x$	e.	$x = 4$	g.	$y = 8 - 2x$	
	$y = 3x + 4$		$y = 4x + 8$		$y = 3x + 1$	
c.	$y = x + 1$					
	$2y = 2x + 2$					

*2. Sketch the graphs of the following sets of equations and indicate their point of intersection (if any).

*a. $-5x + 3y = 2$ c. $x + 2y = 4$ e. $2x + 3y = 7$

    $x + 7y = 4$ $x - 4y = 8$ $4x + 6y = -3$

*b. $2x + 3y = -4$ d. $x = 5$ f. $ax + by = c$

    $3x - 2y = 6$ $y = 7$ $dx + ey = f$

1-6 THE APPLICATION OF LINEAR FUNCTIONS TO DEMAND AND SUPPLY

Mathematical convention describes the independent variable (x) on the horizontal axis and the dependent variable (y) on the vertical axis. In economics this convention is broken occasionally, as in the case of demand and supply functions. This presents no problem as long as the substitution is understood. The agreement will be that quantity (demanded or supplied) will be depicted on the x axis, and price will be depicted on the y axis. Remember that if y represents price and x represents quantity, then for $y = mx + b$ (where y is price and x is quantity), m represents the slope of $y = f(x)$, which is $\Delta y/\Delta x$ (change in price divided by change in quantity); and $1/m$ represents the slope of $x = g(y)$, which is $\Delta x/\Delta y$ (change in quantity divided by change in price).

The reason for the reversal of variable roles with regard to demand and supply will be made evident when we consider revenue. The "demand" for a product must be considered from the viewpoints of both the consumer and the individual firm. The individual firm's viewpoint will be studied in Section 1-8.

Demand from the Consumer's Viewpoint

Demand is the schedule of amounts that consumers will purchase at different prices. The table below demonstrates a buyer's demand for an item. The specific commodity, time period, units for price, and units for quantity will be omitted:

Price (y)	Quantity demanded (x)
$20	0
15	1
10	2
5	3
0	4

The mathematical expression that represents the demand curve is given by $y = 20 - 5x$. The function can be expressed graphically (see Figure 1-15).

An important distinction exists between demand and quantity demanded. The consumer's *demand* for an item is represented by an entire schedule; *quantity demanded* is the dependent variable and is located on the horizontal axis. Movement

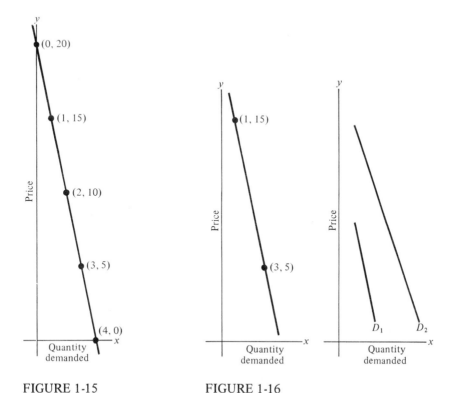

FIGURE 1-15   FIGURE 1-16

along the consumer's demand curve represents *changes in quantity demanded* at various price levels; a shift in the entire demand curve represents a *change in demand* (see Figure 1-16).

The left half of Figure 1-16 represents change in quantity demanded. As price decreases from $15 to $5, quantity demanded changes by +2 units. The right half of Figure 1-16 represents change in demand; D_1 and D_2 represent different demand schedules. The movement from D_1 to D_2 represents an increase in demand.

Total Market Demand

The idea of an individual buyer's demand curve for a product can be easily extended to all consumers in the market simply by summing all the individual demand curves. Let D_1, D_2, ..., D_n represent demand curves for a set of n individuals, which constitutes all buyers in the market. By summing $D_1 + D_2 + ... + D_n$, we obtain the *total market demand curve* (D); this can be geometrically expressed (Figure 1-17).

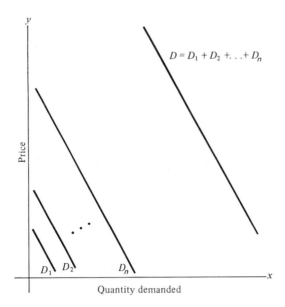

$$D = D_1 + D_2 + \ldots + D_n$$

FIGURE 1-17

The Law of Demand

The *law of demand* states that there is an inverse relationship between price (y) and quantity demanded (x). Stated another way, as price increases, quantity demanded decreases; as price decreases, quantity demanded increases. For example:

Price (y)	Quantity demanded (x)
$20	0
15	1
10	2
5	3
0	4

As price decreases, quantity demanded increases (and conversely). (See Figure 1-18.) In this downward-sloping demand curve the slope of $y = f(x)$ is -5, and the slope of $x = g(y)$ is $-1/5$.

From a geometrical point of view the demand curve can be pictured with various slopes (see Figure 1-19). If the demand curve appeared horizontal (D_1), then price would remain fixed and quantity demanded would vary. At the other end of the spectrum, if the demand curve appeared vertical (D_2), then quantity demanded would remain fixed and price would vary.

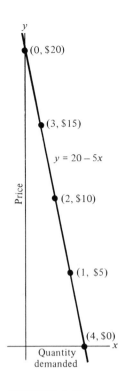

FIGURE 1-18

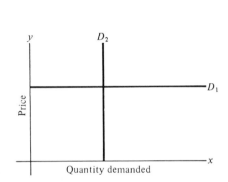

FIGURE 1-19

Law of Supply

A supply schedule demonstrates the different amounts of a product that sellers will offer for sale at different prices. The *law of supply* states that there is a direct relationship between price (y) and quantity supplied (x). This means that, as price increases, quantity supplied increases; and as price decreases, quantity supplied decreases. In the following analysis the specific commodity, time period, units for price, and units for quantity will be omitted. The following example demonstrates the law of supply for $y = 3x + 4$.

Price (y)	Quantity supplied (x)
$ 4	0
7	1
10	2
13	3

As price increases, quantity supplied increases (and conversely). (See Figure 1-20.)

Movement along a specific supply curve represents a *change in quantity supplied,* whereas a shift in the supply curve itself represents a *change in supply* (see Figure 1-21). The left half of Figure 1-21 represents change in quantity supplied. As price increases from $7 to $13, quantity supplied increases by 2 units. The right half of Figure 1-21 represents change in supply; S_1 and S_2 represent changes in supply. The movement from S_1 to S_2 represents an increase in supply.

From a geometrical point of view the supply curve can be pictured with various slopes (see Figure 1-22). If the supply curve appeared horizontal (S_1), then price would remain fixed and quantity supplied would vary. At the other end of the spectrum, if the supply curve appeared vertical (S_2), then quantity supplied would remain fixed and price would vary.

Market Equilibrium

Market equilibrium (ME) is defined as the point of intersection of demand and supply. It is the unique price that results in the same value for total quantity supplied and total quantity demanded. If price increased then quantity supplied would exceed quantity demanded (and conversely) (see Figure 1-23).

Example 1:   Find the point of market equilibrium for the following demand and supply curves (see Figure 1-24).

$y = 20 - 5x$ (represents demand)
$y = 3x + 4$ (represents supply)

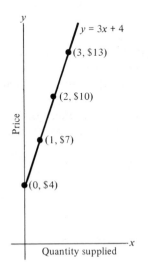

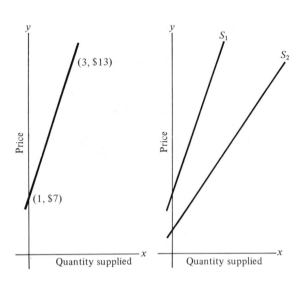

FIGURE 1-20   FIGURE 1-21

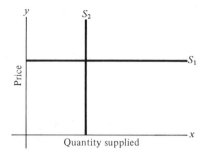

FIGURE 1-22

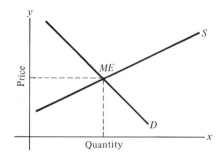

FIGURE 1-23

Solution. Set the two expressions equal to each other and solve for x:

$$20 - 5x = 3x + 4$$
$$x = 2$$
$$y = 10$$

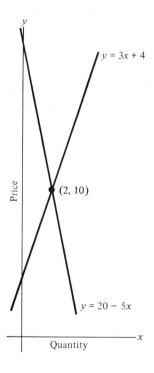

FIGURE 1-24

PROBLEMS 1-6

*1. Assume that $y = 100 - 20x$ represents the total market demand curve for a particular commodity. Set up a demand schedule. Plot the graph of the demand curve and indicate the intercepts. In this example y represents price and x represents quantity demanded.

*2. The quantity demanded for a certain item is 20, when the price of the item is $160. The quantity demanded for the same item is 50, when the price of the item is $100. Assume that demand is linear. Find the expression that represents demand. Express the answer in explicit form $y = mx + b$, where y represents price, and x represents quantity demanded.

3. Assume that $y = 3x + 15$ represents the total market supply curve for a particular commodity. Set up a supply schedule and plot the graph of the supply curve. In this example y represents price and x represents quantity supplied.

4. The quantity supplied for a certain item is 10, when the price is $27. The quantity supplied for the same item is 20, when the price is $47. Assume that supply is linear. Find the expression that represents supply. Express the answer in the explicit form $y = mx + b$, where y represents price, and x represents quantity supplied.

*5. For the following demand expressions find *both* the slope of $y = f(x)$ and the slope of $x = g(y)$:

*a. $y = 20 - 2x$ c. $y = 40 - 10x$ e. $x = 10$

*b. $y = 16 - 3x$ d. $y = 10$

*6. Find the point of market equilibrium (*ME*) for the following sets of supply and demand expressions and plot the graphs. In these examples y represents price, and x represents quantity.

*a. $y = 20 - 2x$ (demand)   c. $y = 20 - 2x$ (demand)

  $y = 2x + 4$ (supply) $y = 5$ (supply)

 b. $y + 4x = 30$ (demand)   d. $x = -2y + 8$ (demand)

  $2y - 3x = 7$ (supply) $x = 2y - 4$ (supply)

7. If supply is represented by $y = x + 1$ and market equilibrium occurs at the point (6, 7), find the demand expression of the form $y = mx + b$ (when m is negative and b is positive), if quantity demanded is 0 when the price is 19.

1-7   ELASTICITY OF DEMAND: THE CONSUMER'S VIEWPOINT

The elasticity of demand from the consumer's viewpoint is a measure of the consumer's response to a price change. Although elasticity applies to other concepts in economics, the consideration here will be limited to that of demand. Keep in mind that the variable x represents quantity demanded and that the variable y represents price.

What Is Elasticity of Demand?

If demand is represented by a linear function, then the elasticity of demand at some point (x, y) is:

$$E_d = \frac{\Delta x}{\Delta y} \cdot \frac{y}{x} = \frac{\text{relative change in quantity demanded}}{\text{relative change in price}}$$

In this definition $\Delta x/\Delta y$ represents the slope of $x = g(y)$ at the point (x, y). The fraction y/x represents a specific price divided by quantity demanded at that price. We assume that demand is linear, which means that $\Delta x/\Delta y$ is fixed for every point on a particular schedule.

The value of $\Delta x/\Delta y$ ranges from 0 to $-\infty$, and thus E_d will fall in the same range. By definition, if the elasticity of demand is between 0 and -1, demand is said to be *relatively inelastic*; this means that the consumer is unresponsive to price changes, and the relative change in quantity demanded is less than 100 percent. If the elasticity of demand is between -1 and $-\infty$, demand is said to be *relatively elastic*; this means that the consumer is sensitive to price changes, and the relative change in quantity demanded is greater than 100 percent. The elasticity-of-demand scale is given by:

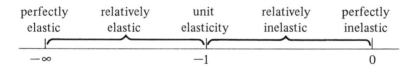

perfectly elastic	relatively elastic	unit elasticity	relatively inelastic	perfectly inelastic
$-\infty$		-1		0

Note: The negative notation on elasticity is sometimes dropped in economic writing, and E_d is represented by a number ranging from 0 to $+\infty$.

Example 1:   Assume that the total market demand for a product is represented by $y = 20 - 5x$. The slope of $y = f(x)$ is -5, and the slope of $x = g(y)$ is $-1/5$. For any point on $y = 20 - 5x$ the elasticity is:

$$E_d = \left(\frac{\Delta x}{\Delta y}\right)\left(\frac{y}{x}\right) = \left(\frac{-1}{5}\right)\left(\frac{y}{x}\right)$$

Find E_d at the following points: (0, 20), (1, 15), (2, 10), (3, 5), (4, 0). (See Figure 1-25.)

For $(x, y) = (0, 20), E_d = (-1/5)(20/0) = -\infty$ (perfectly elastic)
For $(x, y) = (1, 15), E_d = (-1/5)(15/1) = -3$ (relatively elastic)
For $(x, y) = (2, 10), E_d = (-1/5)(10/2) = -1$ (unit elasticity)

For $(x, y) = (3, 5)$, $E_d = (-1/5)(5/3) = -1/3$ (relatively inelastic)
For $(x, y) = (4, 0)$, $E_d = (-1/5)(0/4) = 0$ (perfectly inelastic)

Figure 1-25 illustrates that unit elasticity occurs at the midpoint of the line, that elasticity occurs above this point, and that inelasticity occurs below this point. *This conclusion is true only for linear functions.*

Example 2:   For the inverse relationship between price and quantity demanded, elasticity varies from perfectly elastic to perfectly inelastic (see Figure 1-26).

$y = mx + b$ (m is negative and b is positive)

Example 3:   If quantity demanded is constant and price varies, then demand is perfectly inelastic. In this example the slope of $y = f(x)$ is undefined, and the slope of $x = g(y)$ ($\Delta x/\Delta y$) is 0 (see Figure 1-27).

$$E_d = \left(\frac{\Delta x}{\Delta y}\right)\left(\frac{y}{x}\right) = 0 \text{ (perfectly inelastic)}$$

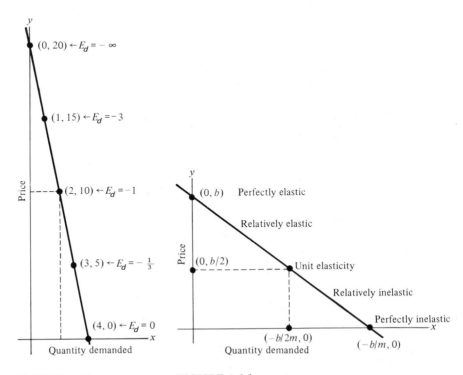

FIGURE 1-25   FIGURE 1-26

Example 4:   If price is constant and quantity demanded varies, then demand is perfectly elastic. In this example the slope of $y = f(x)$ is 0, and the slope of $x = g(y)$ is undefined, or infinite (see Figure 1-28).

$$E_d = \left(\frac{\Delta x}{\Delta y}\right)\left(\frac{y}{x}\right) = -\infty \text{ (perfectly elastic)}$$

We can obtain a deeper understanding of elasticity with respect to the total market demand curve (see Example 2) by relating the meaning of Examples 3 and 4 to the downward-sloping curve.

Point Elasticity

Using the formula to find the elasticity of demand often becomes a mechanical procedure, and the idea of elasticity as a measure of consumer response to a change in price is often lost. Therefore, the worded form of the definition will be considered:

$$E_d = \frac{\text{relative change in quantity demanded}}{\text{relative change in price}} = \frac{\dfrac{\Delta x}{x}}{\dfrac{\Delta y}{y}}$$

Example 5:   Use the definition above to find the elasticity of demand for $y = 20 - 5x$ at the point $(3, 5)$. To determine a relative change another point on the curve is needed, so $(2, 10)$ will be used:

Price (y)   *Quantity demanded (x)*

$$\left.\begin{matrix}10\\5\end{matrix}\right]\Delta y = 5 \qquad\qquad \left.\begin{matrix}2\\3\end{matrix}\right]\Delta x = 1$$

$$E_d = \frac{\dfrac{\Delta x}{x}}{\dfrac{\Delta y}{y}} = -\left(\frac{\dfrac{1}{3}}{\dfrac{5}{5}}\right) = \frac{-33\ 1/3\%}{100\%} = -\frac{1}{3}$$

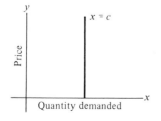

FIGURE 1-27

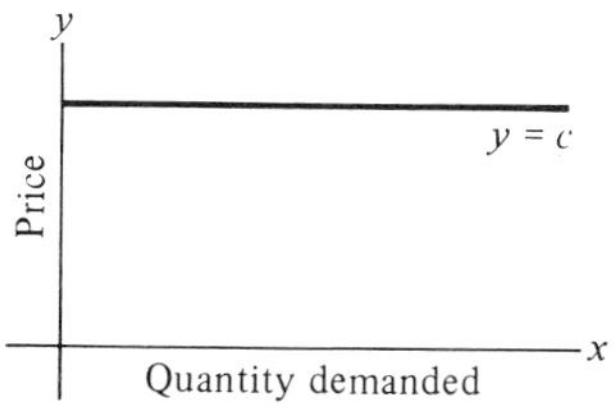

y = c (Figure 1-28)

Price — Quantity demanded

FIGURE 1-28

This example demonstrates the consumer's response to a change in price at the point (3, 5) on the demand curve: The relative change in quantity demanded decreases 33 1/3 percent, as the relative change in price increases 100 percent. E_d is relatively inelastic at this point, which means that consumers are relatively unresponsive to a change in price.

Arc Elasticity

In basic economics arc elasticity is frequently used to overcome a major problem with point elasticity. The economist generally works with a demand schedule, and demand is very likely not linear. In this case the slope of $x = g(y)$ at some particular point is not obtainable. The arc elasticity formula finds an "average" elasticity between two points (x_1, y_1) and (x_2, y_2). Instead of using a specific point we employ the midpoint of the "arc" determined by (x_1, y_1) and (x_2, y_2):

$$\left(\frac{x_1 + x_2}{2}, \frac{y_1 + y_2}{2} \right)$$

In the arc elasticity formula Δx represents the change in quantity demanded, and Δy represents the change in price between the two points (x_1, y_1) and (x_2, y_2). The formula for arc elasticity is:

$$E_d = \frac{\dfrac{\Delta x}{\dfrac{x_1 + x_2}{2}}}{\dfrac{\Delta y}{\dfrac{y_1 + y_2}{2}}}$$

Example 6:   From the demand schedule below determine the arc elasticity between the points (2, 8) and (3, 7).

Price (y)   Quantity (x)

Price (y)	Quantity (x)
9	1
8	2
7	3
6	4

$\Delta y = -1 \quad \Delta x = 1$

$$E_d = -\left(\frac{\dfrac{1}{2+3}}{\dfrac{2}{1}} \middle/ \dfrac{\dfrac{1}{8+7}}{2} \right) = -3$$

Which is relatively elastic. Note that demand is linear in this example, and point elasticity can be determined. The point elasticity at the midpoint of the arc from $(2, 8)$ to $(3, 7)$ is also -3, which demonstrates that are elasticity gives an "average" elasticity over the interval.

PROBLEMS 1-7

*1. Find the elasticity of demand for all integer points on the following demand curves, where x represents quantity and y represents price:

   *a. $y = 20 - 2x$ c. $y = 14 - 2x$

    b. $y = 16 - 2x$ d. $y = 5 - x$

*2. Find the elasticity of demand for the following demand expressions, where x represents quantity and y represents price:

   *a. $y = 17$ c. $x = 10$

    b. $y = 23$ d. $x = 85$

*3. Find the point at which $E_d = -1$ for the following demand expressions, where x represents quantity demanded and y represents price (the notation E_d represents the elasticity of demand):

   *a. $y = 40 - 2x$ d. $y = 17 - 5x$ g. $y = 80 - 4x$

    b. $y = 10 - 5x$ e. $y = 8 - x$

    c. $y = 10 - 3x$ f. $y = 9 - x$

4. Given the demand expression $y = 20 - 2x$, find the point (x, y) where:

   a. $E_d = -1$ b. $E_d = -2$ c. $E_d = -\left(\dfrac{1}{2}\right)$

1-8   REVENUE AND DEMAND FROM THE INDIVIDUAL FIRM'S VIEWPOINT

Total Revenue

A firm's *total revenue* function is:

$$\text{total revenue} = TR = R = yx$$

where x represents the number of items (quantity) sold, and y represents the price of each item. When the price (y) of a product is given, a firm's revenue can be expressed as a function of quantity sold:

$$R = f(\text{quantity sold}) = f(x)$$

We assume that quantity produced equals quantity sold. Moreover, the specific item manufactured, units for quantity, units for revenue, and the time period over which $R = f(x)$ is defined will generally be omitted.

Marginal Revenue

Marginal revenue is the change in revenue with respect to the corresponding change in quantity sold at some point (x, R). If $R = f(x)$ is linear, then marginal revenue is the slope of the revenue function; this means that MR is constant at every point on the graph of $R = f(x)$:

marginal revenue (MR) = slope of $R = f(x)$ at a point

$$= \frac{\text{change in revenue}}{\text{change in quantity sold}} = \frac{\Delta R}{\Delta x}$$

Average Total Revenue

Average total revenue (average revenue per unit) is total revenue divided by quantity sold:

$$\text{average total revenue } (ATR) = \frac{R}{x} = \frac{yx}{x} = y = \text{price}$$

Example 1:   If the market price for a product is fixed at $y = \$3$, then a firm's total revenue function is $R = yx = 3x$. Marginal revenue is the slope of revenue and measures the change in revenue; therefore, $MR = \Delta R/\Delta x = \$3$. Average total revenue is total revenue divided by quantity sold, which is $ATR = 3x/3 = \$3 = y = \text{price}$ (see Figure 1-29).

Demand from the firm's point of view is important, because it reflects the seller's revenue per unit and sales. To the individual firm demand is defined as a schedule that shows the various quantities that could be sold at the price given in that market.

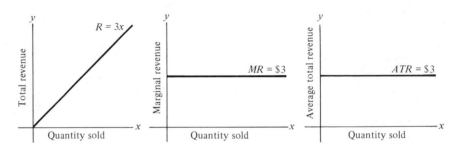

FIGURE 1-29

We assume that a firm's *production* or *output* is synonymous with *quantity demanded* or *quantity sold* (or simply quantity); these variables will frequently be used interchangeably on the horizontal axis. The two significant markets to be considered from the seller's viewpoint are purely competitive markets and imperfectly competitive markets. These markets will be given mathematical definitions instead of economics definitions (which involve a listing of various market characteristics).

Demand and Revenue to a Purely Competitive Seller

Demand to a purely competitive seller is a schedule that reflects a fixed price regardless of quantity sold (demanded). The purely competitive seller offers a standardized product and, because the firm produces only a small fraction of total output, sees its sales having no effect on market price. It can sell any amount at the existing market price:

$$y = c$$

where c is fixed (see Figure 1-30).

If price is fixed, then the purely competitive firm's revenue function is:

$$R = yx = cx$$

where c is constant (see Figure 1-31).

Marginal revenue to a purely competitive seller is the slope of revenue (see Figure 1-32):

$$MR = \text{slope of revenue} = c = \text{price}$$

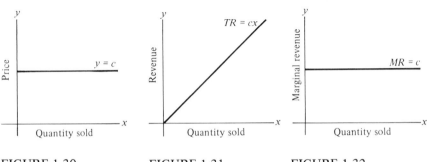

FIGURE 1-30   FIGURE 1-31   FIGURE 1-32

Average total revenue to a purely competitive seller is total revenue divided by quantity sold (see Figure 1-33).

$$ATR = \frac{cx}{x} = c = MR = \text{price}$$

Example 2:   Assume that the price of a product in a purely competitive market is given by $y = \$3$. Then the demand schedule for the purely competitive firm is:

Product price (y) (ATR)	Quantity sold (x)
$3	0
3	1
3	2
3	3

The demand curve for the purely competitive firm is horizontal (see Figure 1-34).

Total revenue, average total revenue, and marginal revenue can be seen by extending the demand schedule (change in revenue is constant). (See Figure 1-35.)

Price (y) (ATR)	Quantity sold (x)	Revenue (R = xy)	$MR = \dfrac{\Delta R}{\Delta x}$	$ATR = \dfrac{R}{x}$
$3	0	$ 0		
3	1	3	$\dfrac{\Delta R}{\Delta x} = \dfrac{3}{1} = \$3$	$\dfrac{R}{x} = \dfrac{3}{1} = \$3$
3	2	6		$\dfrac{R}{x} = \dfrac{6}{2} = \$3$
3	3	9		$\dfrac{R}{x} = \dfrac{9}{3} = \$3$
3	4	12	$\dfrac{\Delta R}{\Delta x} = \dfrac{6}{2} = \$3$	
3	5	15		

Demand and Revenue to an Imperfectly Competitive Seller

Demand to an imperfectly competitive seller is a schedule that reflects an inverse relationship between product price (y) and quantity sold (x). The imperfectly competitive seller has a larger share of the market and realizes that its actions will affect

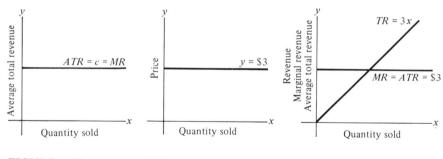

FIGURE 1-33   FIGURE 1-34   FIGURE 1-35

market price, and thus the firm must accept a lower price to obtain a larger volume of sales. Demand is expressed by $y = mx + b$ (where m is negative and b is positive). (See Figure 1-36.)

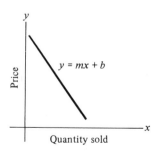

FIGURE 1-36

If price is given by $y = mx + b$ (where m is negative and b is positive), then the imperfectly competitive seller's revenue function is:

$$R = yx = (mx + b)x = mx^2 + bx$$

In this case revenue is no longer linear. Revenue functions of this nature will be studied in detail later; however, a reasonable analysis of revenue can be obtained from the demand and revenue schedule.

Example 3:   Assume that the demand curve for an imperfectly competitive firm is represented by $y = 16 - 4x$, where y represents price and x represents quantity sold (see Figure 1-37). The firm's demand schedule is:

Price (y) (ATR)	Quantity sold (x)
$16	0
12	1
8	2
4	3
0	4

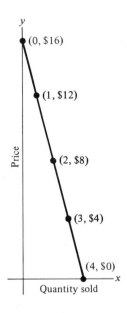

FIGURE 1-37

The firm's total revenue (R) can be determined from the revenue schedule:

Price (y) (ATR)	Quantity (x)	Revenue (yx)
$16	0	$ 0
12	1	12
8	2	16
4	3	12
0	4	0

By plotting integer points for quantity sold (x) and revenue (yx) we obtain the graph of revenue. For this example price is given by $y = 16 - 4x$, and thus revenue is expressed as:

$$R = xy = x(16 - 4x) = 16x - 4x^2$$

The revenue expression is not linear (see Figure 1-38).

By connecting the points on the revenue function we obtain a revenue curve in the shape of an inverted parabola. (This curve will be studied in Chapter 2.)
    The average total revenue (see Figure 1-39) of the firm is:

$$ATR = \frac{R}{x} = \frac{yx}{x} = y = mx + b = \text{price} = 16 - 4x$$

Earlier we noted that if $y = f(x)$ is a linear function, then its slope is constant, and, conversely, if the slope of $y = f(x)$ is constant, then the function is linear. On the other hand, if $y = f(x)$ is nonlinear, then its slope is continually changing, and, conversely, if the slope of a function is continually changing, then the function is nonlinear. The concept of the slope of a linear function is not immediately transferable to the concept of the slope of a curve; at this point the slope of a curve must be "approached." We can, however, obtain an appreciation for the slope of a curve from the definition of the slope of a line. The revenue function in the previous example, $R = 16x - 4x^2$, is nonlinear, and thus its slope (MR) is not constant $(MR$ is continually changing). This can be seen from the revenue schedule by using the definition:

$$MR = \frac{\Delta R}{\Delta x}$$

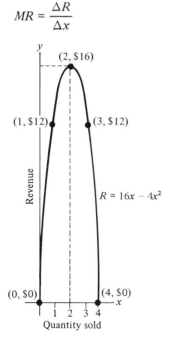

FIGURE 1-38

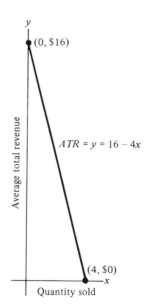

FIGURE 1-39

Price (x) (ATR)	Quantity sold (x)	Revenue (R = xy)	Marginal revenue $MR = \dfrac{\Delta R}{\Delta x}$
$16	0	$ 0	
12	1	12	$ 12
8	2	16	+4
4	3	12	−4
0	4	0	−12

We can obtain *MR* by plotting the midpoints of Δx against ΔR. We do this because $\Delta R/\Delta x$ represents the average change in revenue, and the midpoint of Δx is a more representative level of quantity to associate with ΔR. The two-point formula gives us the expressions for *MR*: $MR = 16 - 8x$ (we note that the slope of *MR* is twice that of *ATR*). (See Figure 1-40.)

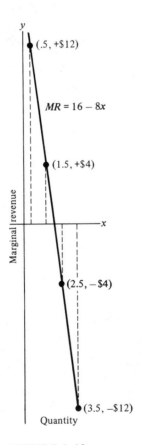

y

(.5, +$12)

$MR = 16 - 8x$

(1.5, +$4)

x

(2.5, −$4)

(3.5, −$12)

Marginal revenue

Quantity

FIGURE 1-40

The preceding discussion leads to some significant conclusions: If an imperfectly competitive firm's demand function is linear, then its revenue function is an inverted parabola, and MR is linear when the slope of MR is twice that of ATR (see Figures 1-41 and 1-42).

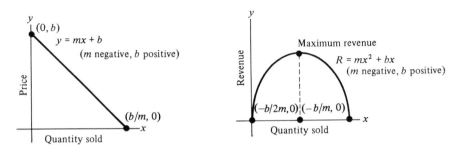

FIGURE 1-41

Moreover, if MR is positive, then TR increases as x increases. If MR is negative, then TR decreases as x increases. If $MR = 0$, then TR is neither increasing nor decreasing (reaches a maximum). Note also that the value of x that maximizes revenue is the midpoint of the x-axis intercept of ATR (see Figure 1-42).

Earlier we learned that in economics convention places the independent variable, price (y), on the vertical axis and the dependent variable, quantity (x), on the horizontal axis. [The mathematical convention would be to place the independent variable

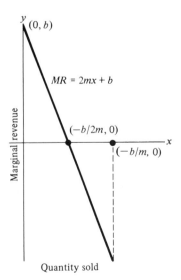

FIGURE 1-42

(price) on the horizontal axis and the dependent variable (quantity) on the vertical axis.] By breaking away from the mathematical convention, we are permitted to superimpose the graphs of demand, revenue, and marginal revenue on the same rectangular coordinate system and view the relationships among a firm's demand, revenue, and marginal revenue functions (see Figure 1-43). We can also generalize the relationships between y, R, and MR (see Figure 1-44). *Note*: Do not assume that maximum revenue ($16) is necessarily the same value as the y-axis intercept for demand ($16). A general expression for the R value of maximum revenue will be seen in Problems 1-8.

If demand for the imperfectly competitive firm is not linear, then the above analysis changes somewhat and will be considered in detail in Chapter 4.

PROBLEMS 1-8

*1. The following functions represent demand to a purely competitive firm. For each function set up a schedule, indicating price, quantity sold, revenue, marginal revenue, and average total revenue. (Notice that price and average total revenue are equal.) Sketch the graphs of average total revenue, marginal revenue, and total revenue on the same axis:

*a. $y = \$5$ b. $y = \$10$ c. $y = \$100$

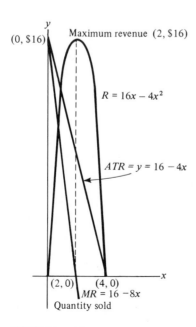

FIGURE 1-43

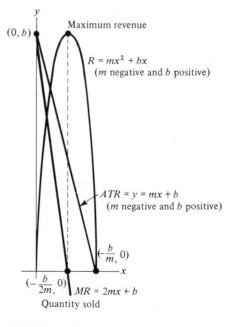

FIGURE 1-44

*2. The following functions represent demand to an imperfectly competitive firm. For each function set up a schedule, indicating price, quantity sold, revenue, marginal revenue, and average total revenue. (Notice that price and average total revenue are the same.) Sketch the graphs of average total revenue, revenue, and marginal revenue on the same axis and indicate the point of maximum total revenue (note that the slope of marginal revenue is twice that of demand):

*a. $y = 20 - 2x$ b. $y = 100 - 25x$ c. $y = 30 - 5x$

3. An evergeen nursery sells balsam fir transplants according to the following schedule:

Quantity	50-249	250-499	500+
	each	each	each
5-year transplants	$ .48	$ .30	$ .19
4-year transplants	.38	.24	.15

   a. Represent the schedule of the 5-year transplants graphically by placing quantity on the horizontal axis. This represents marginal revenue.

   b. Represent the schedule for the 4-year transplants graphically by placing quantity on the horizontal axis. This represents MR.

   c. Sketch graphs, indicating the company's revenue for x evergreens, where x varies from 50 to 750 for both 4-year and 5-year transplants.

   d. What is the firm's revenue if it sells 249 5-year transplants? What is the firm's revenue if it sells 250 5-year transplants?

   e. How much would 249 5-year transplants cost? How much would 250 5-year transplants cost? How much would 156 5-year transplants cost?

1-9   ELASTICITY OF DEMAND: THE INDIVIDUAL FIRM'S VIEWPOINT

The formula for the point elasticity of demand was given in Section 1-7, and the meaning of elasticity was related to the consumer. From the viewpoint of the individual firm the elasticity of demand takes on a different meaning:

$$E_d = \frac{\text{relative change in quantity sold}}{\text{relative change in price}} = \left(\frac{\Delta x}{\Delta y}\right)\left(\frac{y}{x}\right)$$

Quantity sold is directly related to revenue, and thus E_d is a measure of the firm's change in revenue with respect to price. This important fact will be studied in the following analysis.

    The value of $\Delta x/\Delta y$ changes from 0 to $-\infty$, and thus E_d varies from 0 to $-\infty$. By definition, if the elasticity of demand is between 0 and -1, then demand is relatively inelastic. This means that the individual firm's revenue is decreasing. If the elasticity of demand is between -1 and $-\infty$, then demand is relatively elastic. This means that the firm's revenue is increasing. If $E_d = -1$ (unit elasticity), then the firm's revenue reaches a maximum. The elasticity scale is given by

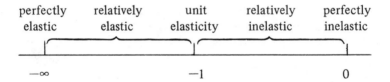

The elasticity of demand from the individual firm's viewpoint can best be understood by evaluating E_d for the market models established in Section 1-8.

Elasticity to a Purely Competitive Firm

Assume that the fixed price is given by $y = \$3$, which means that revenue is: $R = yx = 3x$. The elasticity of demand is perfectly elastic and is:

$$E_d = \frac{\Delta x}{\Delta y} \frac{y}{x} = -\infty$$

Because E_d is perfectly elastic, then as x increases, revenue always increases (see Figure 1-45).

Elasticity to an Imperfectly Competitive Firm

Assume that the demand expression is $y = 16 - 4x$ and that revenue is: $R = yx = 16x - 4x^2$. When E_d is relatively elastic, revenue increases as quantity sold increases; when E_d is unit elasticity, revenue reaches a maximum; and when E_d is relatively inelastic, revenue decreases as quantity increases (see Figures 1-46 and 1-47).

PROBLEMS 1-9

*1. Find the elasticity of demand for a purely competitive firm whose demand equation is given by $y = \$10$. What is the significance of E_d in this situation with regard to the firm's total revenue function?

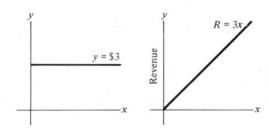

FIGURE 1-45

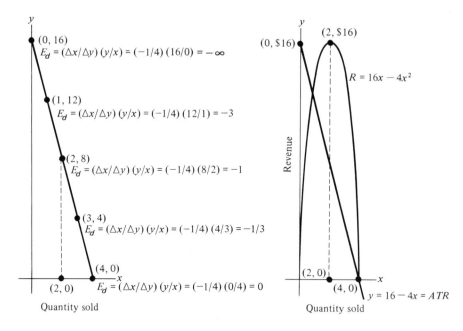

FIGURE 1-46   FIGURE 1-47

*2. Find the elasticity of demand for an imperfectly competitive firm whose demand equation is given by $y = 20 - 2x$. Evaluate E_d for all integer values of x and y. Also indicate the significance of E_d with regard to the firm's total revenue function for all integer points that lie on the graph of $y = 20 - 2x$.

3. If demand to an imperfectly competitive firm is given by $y = 30 - 5x$, then find the point on the demand curve where $E_d = -1$. What is the significance of this point with respect to the firm's total revenue function?

*4. If demand to an imperfectly competitive firm is linear passing through the points $(0, a)$ and $(a, 0)$, then prove that the elasticity of demand is -1 at the point where demand intersects the guideline $y = x$ (see Figure 1-48):

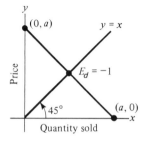

FIGURE 1-48

5. If demand to an imperfectly competitive firm is expressed by $y = mx + b$ (where m is negative and b is positive), then prove that the point of unit elasticity is co-ordinates determined by the midpoint of the x- and y-axis intercepts (see Figure 1-49):

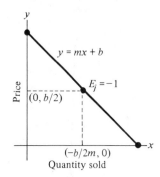

FIGURE 1-49

6. If demand to an imperfectly competitive firm is given by $y = mx + b$ (where m is negative and b is positive), then find a general expression that represents the coordinates for maximum revenue.

1.10   DEMAND AND ELASTICITY OF DEMAND FROM TWO VIEW-POINTS

Demand and the elasticity of demand may differ considerably, depending on the viewpoint adopted. From the standpoint of the individual firm a demand curve may appear as perfectly elastic (see Figure 1-50).

The overall market demand curve may be downward sloping with varying elasticity. A value of $E_d = -1/3$ indicates relative inelasticity (see Figure 1-51).

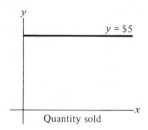

FIGURE 1-50

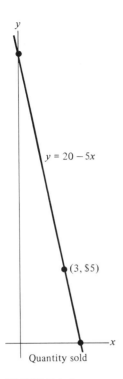

$y = 20 - 5x$

(3, $5)

Quantity sold

FIGURE 1-51

1.11   COST FUNCTIONS

Time is an important factor in determining a firm's total cost of production. A seller must analyze its short-range production problems as well as plan for long-term production objectives. With respect to a firm's cost, the *short run* is a time interval in which certain costs, such as rent, are fixed. The *long run* is a time interval, sufficiently lengthy that all costs become variable. A firm's short-run cost function will be essentially the subject matter of this text, and the long-run analysis will be considered in the problems of later chapters.

Total Cost

The total cost of production function relates a firm's total cost (C) to output (x) such that $C = f(x)$. The independent variable x (output) is on the horizontal axis, and the dependent variable C (total cost) is on the vertical axis. We assume that $C = f(x)$ is linear; however, we will see in Chapter 3 that $C = f(x)$ is generally represented by a curve. The total cost function in the short run can be expressed by:

$$\text{total cost} = \text{variable cost} + \text{fixed cost}$$
$$TC = VC + FC$$

The specific item, the time period, units for time, units for quantity produced, and units for total cost will not generally be given.

Marginal Cost

Marginal cost is the change in total cost with respect to the change in output at some point (x, C). If total cost is linear, then marginal cost is the slope of the cost function, which means that marginal cost is constant at every point on the graph of $C = f(x)$. If total cost is explicitly represented by $C = mx + b$, then:

$$\text{marginal cost} \quad = \quad MC = m = \frac{\Delta C}{\Delta x}$$

MC represents the change in cost at some level of production.

Average Total Cost, Average Fixed Cost, Average Variable Cost

If the total cost function is given by the explicit form:

$$C = mx + b$$

then fixed cost $(FC) = b$ (the y-axis intercept); variable cost $(VC) = mx$; average total cost $(ATC) = C/x$; average fixed cost $(AFC) = FC/x$; and average variable cost $(AVC) = VC/x = m = MC$.

C and VC are parallel, and the distance between the lines is FC (see Figure 1-52). The sum of FC and VC gives C (see Figure 1-53). Marginal cost, MC, is the slope of TC and will always be horizontal if total cost is linear. When we recognize that MC is horizontal, then the cost function becomes a linear function whose slope equals MC (see Figure 1-54).

Example 1:   Sketch the graph of $TC = 2x + 100$. On the same axes sketch the graphs of VC, FC, and MC (see Figure 1-55).

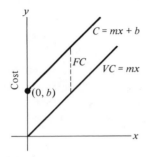

FIGURE 1-52

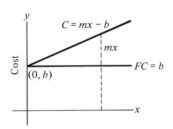

FIGURE 1-53

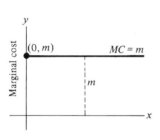

FIGURE 1-54

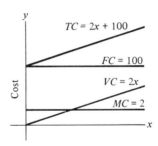

FIGURE 1-55

Example 2: Sketch the graph of ATC for $C = 2x + 100$ (see Figure 1-56). The graph of ATC is not linear and does not have intercepts, so the graph is obtained by plotting points:

$$ATC = \frac{TC}{x} = \frac{2x + 100}{x}$$

The following table is used to find values of ATC:

X	TC	ATC
0	100	infinitely large
1	102	102
2	104	52
.	.	.
.	.	.
.	.	.
10	120	12
.	.	.
.	.	.
.	.	.
1000	2100	2.10

From the table and Figure 1-56 we see that ATC approaches: $MC = 2$. ATC will equal MC only at $+\infty$. The straight line that the curve approaches in this manner is an *asymptote*. When we recognize that when ATC behaves in this manner, then the cost function is linear with a slope of MC.

Example 3. Sketch the graph of AFC when $C = 2x + 100$. The graph of AFC is not linear and does not have intercepts, so points must be plotted:

$$AFC = \frac{FC}{X} = \frac{100}{X}$$

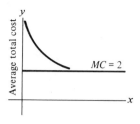

FIGURE 1-56

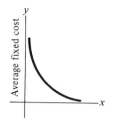

FIGURE 1-57

X	FC	AFC
0	100	infinitely large
1	100	100
2	100	50
·	·	·
·	·	·
·	·	·
1000	100	0.1

AFC = 100/x approaches the x axis as a horizontal asymptote (see Figure 1-57).

Example 4:   Marginal cost is the slope of the cost function. If *TC* is given explicitly in terms of *x*, then marginal cost is the coefficient of *x*. Economically speaking, *MC* is the change in cost with respect to the change in output. Frequently a table is used to determine marginal cost in economics. The following table determines *MC* for *C* = 2*x* + 100:

x	C	MC
1	102	
		2
2	104	
		2
3	106	
		2
4	108	

Cost changes by +2 with every unit change of output:

$$MC = \frac{\Delta C}{\Delta X} = \frac{2}{1} = 2$$

PROBLEMS 1-11

*1. Sketch the graphs of total cost, marginal cost, fixed cost, and variable cost on the same axis for:

    *a. $C = 4x + 800$ b. $C = 6x + 900$ c. $C = 10x + 500$

*2. Sketch the graphs of average fixed cost and average total cost for:

    *a. $C = 4x + 800$ b. $C = 6x + 900$ c. $C = 10x + 500$

3. From the following cost schedule determine the total cost function, marginal cost, and fixed cost:

X	C
10	$ 60
20	110
30	160

4. Given that average total cost $= 7 + 15/x$, find the total cost function.

5. Given that marginal cost $= \$17$ and fixed cost $= \$300$, find the total cost function.

6. If we assume that cost is linear, how can we find a company's cost of production function? Is our assumption good?

*7. For a purely competitive firm should marginal revenue be greater than marginal cost, or should MC be greater than MR?

8. If the government placed a tax of amount t per unit on a commodity produced by a manufacturer then the firm would realize an increase in the total cost of production of tx, where x represents quantity produced.

    a. If total cost before taxation is given by $C = mx + b$ (where m and b are positive), then determine the total cost function after taxation and represent both cost functions on the same axis.

    b. Given that $C = 20x + 200$ (before taxation) and the tax imposed is 0.5 per unit quantity. Sketch graphs of total cost and average total cost for both before and after taxation.

    c. Given that $C = 20x + 200$ (before taxation) and the tax imposed is 0.5 per unit. The firm's revenue function is $R = 30.5x$. Superimpose the graphs of cost and revenue, indicating the break-even points before and after taxation.

1.12   BREAK-EVEN ANALYSIS AND PROFIT FUNCTIONS

Break-even analysis involves superimposing the graphs of revenue and cost on the same axis and finding their point of intersection. We will restrict our analysis to linear functions. Thus, purely competitive firms with linear cost functions will be the singular consideration. We assume that MR is greater than MC. This simply means that the slope of revenue is greater than the slope of cost. Therefore, although revenue begins at $(0, 0)$, it will intersect the total cost function.

The Break-Even Point

The singular point of intersection is the *break-even point* (*BE*) and is obtained by finding where:

$TR = TC$ or where $R = C$

If *TR* and *TC* are given explicitly, then the equation is solved for x. This value is substituted into either *TR* or *TC* to find the revenue or cost at this level of output (see Figure 1-58). If output (x) is to the left of the *BE* point (shaded area), cost exceeds revenue (negative profits, or loss); if production is to the right of the *BE* point (shaded area), revenue exceeds cost (positive profits).

Example 1:   Sketch the graph of $R = 4x$ and $C = 2x + 100$ on the same axis indicating the *BE* point (see Figure 1-59).

Example 2:   Given that $R = 4x$ and $C = 2x + 100$, sketch the graph of *MC* and *MR* on the same axis (see Figure 1-60).

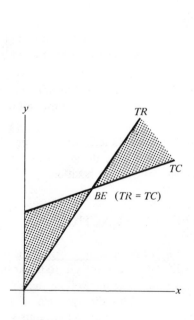

FIGURE 1-58

FIGURE 1-59

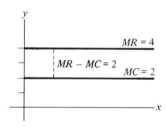

FIGURE 1-60

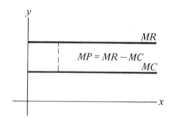

FIGURE 1-61

Total Profit

The difference between revenue and cost represents *total profit:*

total profit = total revenue − total cost
$$P = R - C$$

Marginal Profit

Marginal profit is the change in profit with respect to the change in output at some point (x, P). If $P = f(x)$ is linear, then marginal profit is the slope of $P = f(x)$, which means that marginal profit is constant:

$$\text{marginal profit} = MP = \frac{\Delta P}{\Delta x} = MR - MC$$

Marginal profit is the slope of profit and is determined by subtracting marginal revenue from marginal cost (see Figure 1-61).

If cost and revenue are linear, then the graph of profit is linear and can be determined by the intercept technique. Letting $X = 0$ results in the P-axis intercept, which is fixed cost (FC). Letting $P = 0$ results in the x-axis intercept, which is the break-even point (BE). (See Figure 1-62.) Positive profits are the shaded area to the right of BE; negative profits are the shaded area to the left of BE.

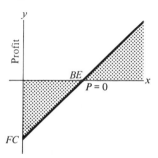

FIGURE 1-62

Example 3:   Given that $TR = 4x$ and $TC = 2x + 100$, find the profit function and sketch the graph of profit, indicating FC and the BE point. Use the intercept technique. (See Figure 1-63). Positive profits are the shaded area to the right of BE; negative profits are the shaded area to the left of BE.

Step 1: $P = R - C.$
Step 2: $P = (4x) - (2x + 100).$
Step 3: $P = 2x - 100.$
Step 4:   When $x = 0$, $FC = -100$, and when $P = 0$, $BE = 50$.

The Contribution Margin

The *contribution margin* can be used to find the break-even point. The contribution margin is the difference between MR and MC (which is marginal profit). The contribution margin can be used in a formula to find the break-even point of production (X_{BE}):

$$X_{BE} = \frac{FC}{MR - MC} = \frac{FC}{MP}$$

The proof of this formula will be left as an exercise. As a particular example, find the break-even point for $R = 4x$ and $C = 2x + 100$.

Example 4:   In this example $MR = 4$ and $MC = 2$ and $MR = MR - MC = 2$. By the above formula:

$$X_{BE} = \frac{FC}{MP} = \frac{100}{2} = 50$$

At this point $C = R$ and $P = 0$ (see Figure 1-64).

PROBLEMS 1-12

*1. Superimpose the graphs of cost and revenue, and indicate the break-even points for the following functions. Also sketch the graphs of marginal revenue and marginal cost:

*a. $C = 4x + 12$ c. $C = 14x + 100$ e. $C = 2x + 100$
      $R = 24x$ $R = 15x$ $R = 2.5x$
b. $C = 5x + 17$ d. $C = .5x + 7$
      $R = 6x$ $R = 5x$

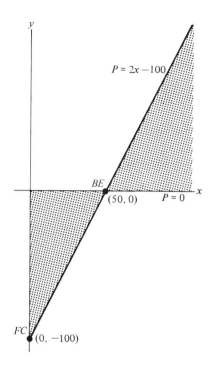

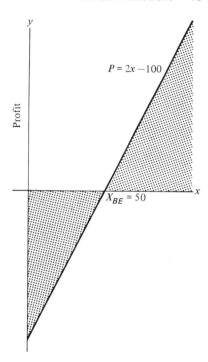

FIGURE 1-63   FIGURE 1-64

2. If a firm's marginal revenue is $10, what is its total revenue function? If the firm's marginal cost is $5 and fixed cost is $20, what is its total cost function? Sketch the graphs of cost and revenue on the same system, and indicate the firm's break-even point.

3. If a firm's marginal revenue is $8, its marginal cost is $4, and the break-even point is at $x = 10$, then find fixed cost. Sketch the graphs of cost and revenue on the same system.

*4. Sketch the graphs of total profit for the following cost and revenue functions. Indicate fixed cost and the break-even point as well as positive and negative profit areas:

*a. $C = 4x + 12$ c. $C = 14x + 100$
     $R = 24x$ $R = 15x$
*b. $C = 5x + 17$ d. $C = 4x + 12$
     $R = 6x$ $R = 10x$

*5. For the following cost and revenue functions sketch the graphs of marginal profit where marginal profit is the difference between marginal revenue and marginal cost:

    *a. $C = 4x + 12$ *b. $C = 5x + 17$ c. $C = 14x + 100$

       $R = 24x$ $R = 6x$ $R = 15x$

6. If a firm's marginal profit is \$10, its marginal cost is \$10, and fixed cost is \$100, find the firm's:

    a. revenue function   b. cost function   c. profit function

*7. Use the contribution margin formula to find the break-even points for the following cost and revenue functions. The formula is $X_{BE} = FC/(MR - MC)$:

    *a. $C = 4x + 12$ c. $C = 14x + 100$

       $R = 24x$ $R = 15x$

    *b. $C = 5x + 17$ d. $C = 4x + 12$

       $R = 6x$ $R = 10x$

8. Prove that the x value for the break-even point for the profit function is obtained by the formula: $X_{BE} = FC/(MR - MC) = FC/MP$. In this formula $MR - MC$ represents the contribution margin.

9. A firm manufactures two calculators, a standard-use calculator and a special-use calculator. The following table indicates projections for the coming year:

	Standard-use calculator		Special-use calculator		
	Units	Amount	Units	Amount	Totals
Sales	10,000	\$80,000	6,000	\$60,000	\$140,000
Costs:					
Fixed		2,000		3,300	5,300
Variable		60,000		42,000	102,000
Total Costs		62,000		45,300	107,300
Income before taxes		18,000		14,700	32,700

    a. Find the break-even output (in units) for the standard-use calculator (assume that the facilities are not jointly used). What is the break-even volume in terms of dollars? Sketch the graphs of total cost and total revenue on the same axis and indicate the break-even point.

    b. Find the break-even point (in units) for the special-use calculator (assume that the facilities are not jointly used). What is the break-even volume in terms of dollars? Sketch the graphs of total cost and total revenue on the same axis and indicate the break-even point.

    c. The contribution margin is defined as marginal profit. What is the contribution margin for the standard-use calculator? What is the contribution margin for the special-use calculator? What is the composite contribution margin?

1-13   THE CONSUMPTION FUNCTION AND THE MULTIPLIER

Microeconomics studies specific aspects of the economy, such as an individual firm's demand, revenue, and profit functions. On the other hand, macroeconomics studies general aspects of the economy, such as the relationship between total national income and total national consumption. The consumption function is included in the study of macroeconomics. The function states that personal consumption expenditure (C) is a function of disposable personal income (I). In the expression $C = f(I)$ the independent variable I is on the horizontal axis, and the dependent variable C is on the vertical axis. We assume that $C = f(I)$ is linear and that:

$C + S = I$ (consumption + savings = disposable income)

The Marginal Propensity to Consume

The *marginal propensity to consume* (MPC) is the rate of change of consumption with respect to income at some point (I, C). When consumption is linear, the MPC is constant at every point and is the slope of $C = f(I)$. The following equation represents the change in consumption at some level of income:

$$MPC = \frac{\Delta C}{\Delta I}$$

The Marginal Propensity to Save

The *marginal propensity to save* (MPS) is the rate of change of savings with respect to income at some point (I, S). When the savings function is linear, the MPS is constant at every point and is the slope of $S = f(I)$. The following equation represents the change in savings at some level of income:

$$MPS = \frac{\Delta S}{\Delta I}$$

The Average Propensities to Consume and to Save

The *average propensity to consume* (APC) = C/I. The *average propensity to save* (APS) = S/I. The slope of the consumption function is between 0 and 1. Stated another way, consumption is between 0 and 100 percent of disposable income:

$0 < MPC < 1$

At any level of income the percentage consumed and the percentage saved is 100 percent:

$MPC + MPS = 1 = 100\%$

The Consumer's Break-Even Point

The *consumer's break-even point* (*CBEP*) is the point at which consumption equals disposable income. *CBEP* is also the level of income (*I*) at which savings is 0. Solving $S = 0$ or $C = I$ gives *CBEP*.

Note: In economic writing, the variable *DI* (disposable income) is frequently used instead of *I*, and income is conventionally labeled *Y* on the horizontal axis.

The linear consumption function may be expressed as $C = mI + b$. *CBEP* is found by solving $mI + b = I$ (see Figure 1-65). The shaded area to the left of *CBEP* represents negative savings; the shaded area to the right of the *CBEP* represents positive savings.

The savings function may be expressed as $S = (1 - m)I - b$. The savings function is found by using $S = I - C$ (see Figure 1-66). The shaded area to the left of *CBEP* represents negative savings; the shaded area to the right of *CBEP* represents positive savings.

The marginal propensities to consume and to save may be expressed graphically (see Figure 1-67). Remember that $MPC + MPS = 1$.

Example 1:   Given that $C = .75I + 6$, sketch the graph of consumption and the guideline indicating the *CBEP*. The *CBEP* is found by solving $.75I + 6 = I$ or $I = 24$ (see Figure 1-68). The shaded area to the left of *CBEP* represents negative savings; the shaded area to the right of *CBEP* represents positive savings.

Example 2:   Given that $C = .75I + 6$, sketch the graph of savings by using the intercept technique and pointing out the *CBEP*. The savings function is found by using $S = I - C$ where $S = I - (.75I + 6)$ and $S = .25I - 6$. By the intercept technique, let $I = 0$ and obtain $S = -6$, and let $S = 0$ and obtain $I = 24$ (see

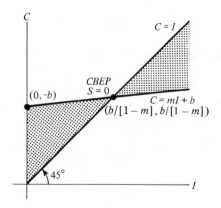

FIGURE 1-65

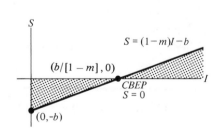

FIGURE 1-66

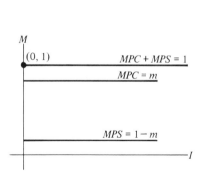

FIGURE 1-67

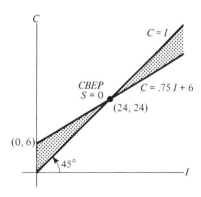

FIGURE 1-68

Figure 1-69). The shaded area to the left of *CBEP* represents negative savings; the shaded area to the right of *CBEP* represents positive savings.

Example 3:   Given that $C = .75I + 6$, sketch the graphs of marginal propensities to consume and to save. The slope of consumption is .75 and the slope of savings is .25 (see Figure 1-70).

The Multiplier: An Infinite Geometric Progression

The *multiplier effect* in the economy refers to the "multiplied" impact of any change in spending—investment, consumption, or government spending. Assume, for instance, that investment spending changes by some amount. This amount is income to the recipients who spend a portion of the newly received income and save a portion; that is, they have a marginal propensity to consume (*MPC*) and a marginal propensity to save (*MPS*). The amount that they spend is received as income by a second set of recipients who in turn spend a fraction and save a fraction. These successive rounds of respending continue; the process ceases only when the initial spending increase is matched by a saving "leakage" of the same amount.

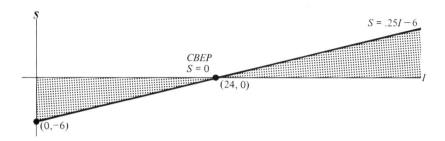

FIGURE 1-69

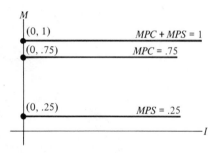

FIGURE 1-70

The following table assumes that $MPC = 75\%$ and new spending is $10. The successive rounds of respending in this example are assumed to go on theoretically indefinitely.

Assumed increase in new spending	Change in income
Initial round	$10.00
Second round	7.50
Third round	5.62
.	.
.	.
.	.
Total	$40.00

The table shows that the change in income forms an infinite geometric progression:

$$S = \$10 + \$10(.75) + \$10(.75^2) + \$10(.75^3) + \ldots$$

In the Algebra Review section the sum of an infinite geometric progression with first term a and common ratio r between 0 and 1 is given by:

$$S = \frac{a}{1 - r}$$

Using this formula (with $r = .75$) to find the sum of the change in income, we obtain:

$$S = \frac{\$10}{1 - .75} = \$40$$

This shows that the $10 of new investment generates new income of $40; the multiplier in this situation is 4.

The formula to determine the multiplier is derived immediately from $S = a/(1 - r)$, in which new investment spending is based on $a = \$1$, and the common ratio r is the marginal propensity to consume (MPC). By replacing S in the infinite geometric progression formula by the letter M, we can define the multiplier as:

$$M = \frac{1}{1 - MPC} = \frac{1}{MPS}$$

PROBLEMS 1-13

*1. Sketch the graphs of consumption and the guideline indicating the consumer's break-even point. Also sketch the graphs of savings indicating the consumer's break-even point:

   *a. $C = .60I + 20$ b. $C = .75I + 16$ c. $C = .80I + 10$

*2. Sketch the graphs of the marginal propensity to consume and the marginal propensity to save for:

   *a. $C = .60I + 20$ b. $C = .75I + 16$ c. $C = .80I + 10$

3. Given that $MPS = .35$ and fixed consumption is 12, find the consumption function, the savings function, and the consumer's break-even point.

*4. Find the multiplier if:

   *a. $MPC = 60\%$ c. $MPC = 82\%$

    b. $MPS = 20\%$ d. $MPS = 13\%$

5. Find the consumption function given that consumption is 10 when income is 0 and that the consumer's break-even point occurs at an income of 20.

1-14   DETERMINANTS: SOLVING SYSTEMS OF EQUATIONS

Solving a system of simultaneous equations can be accomplished with the use of determinants. A 2×2 *determinant* (two rows and two columns) is expressed as:

$$\begin{vmatrix} a & b \\ c & d \end{vmatrix} = ad - bc$$

Example 1:   Evaluate the following 2×2 determinants:

$$\begin{vmatrix} 4 & 4 \\ 5 & 8 \end{vmatrix} = 32 - 20 = 12$$

$$\begin{vmatrix} 4 & -4 \\ 5 & 8 \end{vmatrix} = 32 + 20 = 52$$

$$\begin{vmatrix} 1 & 5 \\ 1 & 5 \end{vmatrix} = 5 - 5 = 0$$

Two distinct nonparallel straight lines of the form:

$ax + by = c$
$dx + ey = f$

intersect once and only once in the plane. The point of intersection (x, y) can be found by using determinants in this manner:

$$x = \frac{\begin{vmatrix} c & b \\ f & e \end{vmatrix}}{\begin{vmatrix} a & b \\ d & e \end{vmatrix}} = \frac{ce - bf}{ae - bd}$$

$$y = \frac{\begin{vmatrix} a & c \\ d & f \end{vmatrix}}{\begin{vmatrix} a & b \\ d & e \end{vmatrix}} = \frac{af - cd}{ae - bd}$$

Note that the denominators in the above terms are the same.

The system is based on using the coefficients of the variables and the constants in the determinant in a specific order. In the following terms, same variables are arranged in columns, and constants are isolated:

$ax + by = c$
$dx + ey = f$

The steps to solve the simultaneous equations are:

Step 1:   The denominators for both x and y are the same and are obtained by removing the coefficients of the variables in columns and writing them in the determinant (while moving from *left to right*).

Step 2:   The numerator for x is obtained by placing the column of constants (do not change the signs of the constants) and the column of coefficients for y in the determinant (while moving from left to right):

Step 3:   The numerator for y is obtained by placing the column of coefficients of x and the column of constants in the determinant (while moving from left to right).

The proof that this procedure solves the system of two equations in two unknowns will be left as an exercise. The system can be expanded to n equations in n unknowns; we will consider this problem later.

Example 2:   Sketch the graphs of the following (see Figure 1-71) and find the point of intersection using determinants for:

$$2x + y = 20$$
$$-3x + y = 5$$

$$x = \frac{\begin{vmatrix} 20 & 1 \\ 5 & 1 \end{vmatrix}}{\begin{vmatrix} 2 & 1 \\ -3 & 1 \end{vmatrix}} = 3; \qquad y = \frac{\begin{vmatrix} 2 & 20 \\ -3 & 5 \end{vmatrix}}{\begin{vmatrix} 2 & 1 \\ -3 & 1 \end{vmatrix}} = 14$$

Solving Systems of Three Equations in Three Unknowns

A 3 X 3 determinant is defined as:

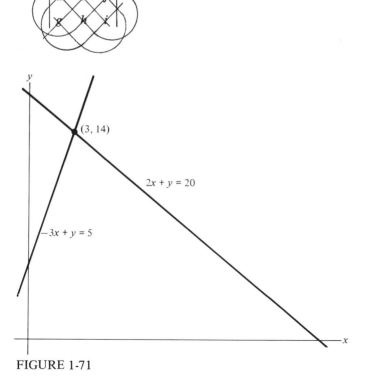

$$= aei + bfg + chd - ceg - fha - ibd$$

2x + y = 20

(3, 14)

−3x + y = 5

FIGURE 1-71

In this expansion all possible diagonals with three elements are formed; the "downhill" diagonals are taken with their sign; whereas the "uphill" diagonals have a change in sign.

Example 3:

$$\begin{vmatrix} -1 & -2 & -3 \\ 4 & 2 & 2 \\ 3 & 2 & 1 \end{vmatrix} = -2 - 12 - 24 + 18 + 4 + 8 = -8$$

The system of three equations in three unknowns can be solved in a similar manner as the system of two equations in two unknowns:

$$a_1 x + b_1 y + c_1 z = d_1$$
$$a_2 x + b_2 y + c_2 z = d_2$$
$$a_3 x + b_3 y + c_3 z = d_3$$

The (x, y, z) that satisfies all three equations simultaneously is obtained by:

$$x = \frac{\begin{vmatrix} d_1 & b_1 & c_1 \\ d_2 & b_2 & c_2 \\ d_3 & b_3 & c_3 \end{vmatrix}}{\begin{vmatrix} a_1 & b_1 & c_1 \\ a_2 & b_2 & c_2 \\ a_3 & b_3 & c_3 \end{vmatrix}} \; ; \; y = \frac{\begin{vmatrix} a_1 & d_1 & c_1 \\ a_2 & d_2 & c_2 \\ a_3 & d_3 & c_3 \end{vmatrix}}{\begin{vmatrix} a_1 & b_1 & c_1 \\ a_2 & b_2 & c_2 \\ a_3 & b_3 & c_3 \end{vmatrix}} \; ; \; z = \frac{\begin{vmatrix} a_1 & b_1 & d_1 \\ a_2 & b_2 & d_2 \\ a_3 & b_3 & d_3 \end{vmatrix}}{\begin{vmatrix} a_1 & b_1 & c_1 \\ a_2 & b_2 & c_2 \\ a_3 & b_3 & c_3 \end{vmatrix}}$$

Example 4:   Solve the system for x, y, and z:

$$x + y + z = 6$$
$$x + 2y + 2z = 9$$
$$x + y + 3z = 8$$

$$x = \frac{\begin{vmatrix} 6 & 1 & 1 \\ 9 & 2 & 2 \\ 8 & 1 & 3 \end{vmatrix}}{\begin{vmatrix} 1 & 1 & 1 \\ 1 & 2 & 2 \\ 1 & 1 & 3 \end{vmatrix}} = \frac{6}{2} = 3$$

$$y = \frac{\begin{vmatrix} 1 & 6 & 1 \\ 1 & 9 & 2 \\ 1 & 8 & 3 \end{vmatrix}}{2} = \frac{4}{2} = 2$$

$$z = \frac{\begin{vmatrix} 1 & 1 & 6 \\ 1 & 2 & 9 \\ 1 & 1 & 8 \end{vmatrix}}{2} = \frac{2}{2} = 1$$

The values $x = 3$, $y = 2$, and $z = 1$ satisfy all three equations simultaneously.

Evaluating Determinants by the Cofactor Method

Determinants of order $n \times n$ are often evaluated by the use of cofactors. The following definition gives the value of a 3×3 determinant, but the procedure can be used for evaluating an $n \times n$ determinant. Double subscripts are used to indicate the row-column position of the elements (the first subscript represents the row, and the second subscript represents the column).

$$\begin{vmatrix} a_{11} & a_{12} & a_{13} \\ a_{21} & a_{22} & a_{23} \\ a_{31} & a_{32} & a_{33} \end{vmatrix} = a_{11} \begin{vmatrix} a_{22} & a_{23} \\ a_{32} & a_{33} \end{vmatrix} - a_{12} \begin{vmatrix} a_{21} & a_{23} \\ a_{31} & a_{33} \end{vmatrix} + a_{13} \begin{vmatrix} a_{21} & a_{22} \\ a_{31} & a_{32} \end{vmatrix}$$

The 2×2 determinants are called *minors*, and the minors with signs are called *cofactors*. If the sum of the subscripts of the cofactor is even, the sign of the minor is positive. If the sum of the subscripts of the cofactor is odd, the sign of the minor is negative. The elements of the minor are obtained by striking out the elements of the ith row and jth column of a_{ij}. The determinant can be evaluated along any row or any column.

Example 5:   Evaluate the following 3×3 determinant by expanding along the first row and using cofactors:

$$\begin{vmatrix} -1 & -2 & -3 \\ 4 & 2 & 2 \\ 3 & 2 & 1 \end{vmatrix} = -1 \begin{vmatrix} 2 & 2 \\ 2 & 1 \end{vmatrix} + 2 \begin{vmatrix} 4 & 2 \\ 3 & 1 \end{vmatrix} -3 \begin{vmatrix} 4 & 2 \\ 3 & 2 \end{vmatrix} = -8$$

Example 6:   Evaluate the following 3×3 determinant by expanding along the second column using cofactors:

$$\begin{vmatrix} -1 & -2 & -3 \\ 4 & 2 & 2 \\ 3 & 2 & 1 \end{vmatrix} = 2 \begin{vmatrix} 4 & 2 \\ 3 & 1 \end{vmatrix} + 2 \begin{vmatrix} -1 & -3 \\ 3 & 1 \end{vmatrix} -2 \begin{vmatrix} -1 & -3 \\ 4 & 2 \end{vmatrix} = -8$$

PROBLEMS 1-14

*1. Use determinants to solve the following systems:

*a. $2x + y = 4$ f. $3x + 5y = 2$ *j. $x + y + 2z = -3$
    $3x - y = 18$ $6x + 10y = 2$ $3x + 2y - 4z = 1$

b. $2x + y = 4$ g. $2x + 4y = 8$ $-x + 2y - 4z = -3$
    $3x - y = 6$ $x + 2y = 7$ k. $x + y + z = 12$

c. $-5x + 3y = 3$ h. $-5x + 8y = -2$ $2x + y - z = 2$
    $x + 7y = 4$ $-x - y = -1$ $-x - y + 2z = 6$

d. $2x + 3y = -4$ i. $5x = 10$ l. $x + y + z = 4$
    $3x + 2y = 3$ $2x + 4y = 12$ $3x - 5y - 6z = -2$

e. $2x + 4y = 8$ $2x + 2y + 2z = 8$
    $x + 2y = 4$

*2. Evaluate the following determinants by using cofactors; expand along the first row:

*a. $\begin{vmatrix} 1 & 2 & 3 \\ 3 & 4 & 5 \\ 3 & 2 & 5 \end{vmatrix}$ c. $\begin{vmatrix} 3 & -2 & 6 \\ 2 & 3 & -1 \\ -1 & 3 & -4 \end{vmatrix}$

b. $\begin{vmatrix} 2 & 3 & -1 \\ -2 & 2 & 3 \\ 4 & -5 & 2 \end{vmatrix}$ d. $\begin{vmatrix} 1 & 1 & 1 \\ 3 & -5 & -6 \\ 2 & 2 & 2 \end{vmatrix}$

3. Evaluate the determinants in Problem 2 by using cofactors; expand along the third column:

4. Prove that the solutions to:

$$ax + by = c$$
$$dx + ey = f$$

are given by:

$$x = \frac{\begin{vmatrix} c & b \\ f & e \end{vmatrix}}{\begin{vmatrix} a & b \\ d & e \end{vmatrix}}; \quad y = \frac{\begin{vmatrix} a & c \\ d & f \end{vmatrix}}{\begin{vmatrix} a & b \\ d & e \end{vmatrix}}$$

Use the algebraic method of elimination to solve for x and y, and express the solution in determinant form. This method of solving systems of equations is known as *Cramer's Rule*, after mathematician Gabriel Cramer. In order that a solution to the system exist, the denominator *ae-bd* cannot be 0. A denominator *ae-bd* of 0 would imply that the lines are parallel or are the same lines.

*5. Prove that if two columns (or rows) of a determinant are the same, then the value of the determinant is 0. Use a 2 × 2 determinant for the proof.

*6. Prove that if two columns (or rows) of a determinant are interchanged, then the value of the determinant changes signs and the numerical value is the same. Use a 2 × 2 determinant for the proof.

7. What would be the result of multiplying all elements of a column (or row) of a determinant by the same number? Use a 2 × 2 determinant.

8. What would be the result of adding one column (or row) to another column (or row) for a 2 × 2 determinant?

9. What is the advantage of the determinant method for solving systems of equations over the straight algebraic approach of elimination?

10. Use determinants to find:

a. The point of market equilibrium for:

$y = m_1 x + b_1$ (representing demand)
$y = m_2 x + b_2$ (representing supply)

b. The break-even point for:

$C = m_1 x + FC$ (representing cost)
$R = m_2 x$ (representing revenue)

1-15   LINEAR PROGRAMMING: THE GRAPHIC TECHNIQUE

This section introduces the concept of linear programming and considers selected business examples. The graphical approach in solving linear programming problems is used. A more sophisticated technique for solving linear programming problems is given by the *simplex method*, which will be discussed in Chapter 5. The simplex method uses ordinary algebraic techniques and tables to solve linear programming problems and was especially developed for problems that involve three or more variables and in which the graphic method becomes abstract.

Linear programming is an extremely useful tool that is used in the quantitative aspects of business management. The application of linear programming centers around a firm's problem of most effectively utilizing resources such as labor, capital, time, materials, and so on in order to maximize profits, to minimize cost, or to determine production scheduling and planning. Linear programming is concerned with techniques that are used to analyze linear functions that are subjected to certain

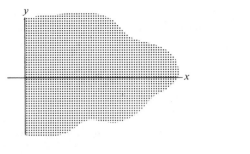

FIGURE 1-72

FIGURE 1-73

restrictions or *restraints*. The linear function that is subjected to maximization or minimization is the *objective function*.

Linear programming involves solving systems of linear inequalities and/or equalities. Before we describe a specific problem, we present a few examples of linear inequalities.

Example 1:　$x > 0$ is the shaded area to the right of the y axis (see Figure 1-72).

Example 2:　$x > 0$ and $y > 0$ is the area in the first quadrant (see Figure 1-73).

Example 3:　$2x + 4y = 8$ represents points on the line (see Figure 1-74).

Example 4:　$2x + 4y < 8$ represents points under the line $2x + 4y = 8$ (see Figure 1-75). (Verify this by convenient point substitution: $x = 0, y = 0$.)

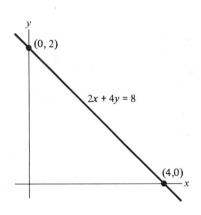

FIGURE 1-74

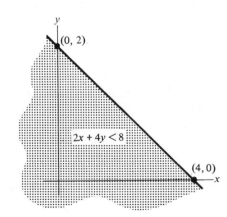

FIGURE 1-75

Example 5:   Two equations may be represented graphically (see Figure 1-76):

$$5x + y < 10$$
$$2x + 4y < 8$$
$$x > 0; y > 0$$

Production Scheduling

Production scheduling can best be explained by example: A company produces two types of pocket calculators. The standard-use calculator requires 1 hour per case in department A and 3 hours per case in department B. The special-use calculator requires 2 hours per case in department A and 4 hours per case in department B. Department A has a maximum of 8 hours available a day for production, whereas department B has a maximum of 20 hours a day available. A production chart is used to demonstrate the restraints:

	Department A *(8 hours available)*	*Department B* *(20 hours available)*
Standard-use	1 hour	3 hours
Special-use	2 hours	4 hours

Let x indicate the number of cases of standard-use calculators to be produced and let y indicate the number of cases of special-use calculators to be produced. The set of inequalities that describes the problem is:

$$1x + 2y \leqslant 8$$
$$3x + 4y \leqslant 20$$
$$x \geqslant 0; y \geqslant 0$$

Note that production cannot be negative.

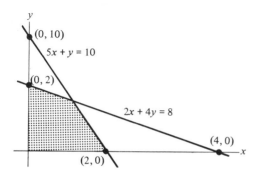

FIGURE 1-76

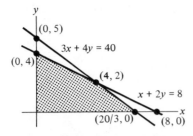

FIGURE 1-77

A graphical interpretation of these restraints indicates the feasible amount of production scheduling (Figure 1-77, shaded area). Any point within the shaded area would satisfy the restraints of the problem.

Profit Maximization

In the previous example, if the profit is $50 on each case of standard-use calculators and $80 on each case of special-use calculators, determine the optimum number of standard- and special-use calculators to be scheduled for production in order to *maximize profits*. Let x be the optimum number of cases of standard-use calculators to be produced and y be the optimum number of cases of special-use calculators to be produced. The objective function to be maximized is:

$$\text{profit} = P = \$50x + \$80y$$

At this point the maximum profit, P, is not known but can be seen by superimposing the objective function in the restraint area (see Figure 1-78). For hypothetical profits P_1, P_2, P_3, P_4, and P_5 we see that the objective function will be maximized by P_4, which occurs at the intersection (4, 2) of the two lines. The slope of the profit function is between the slopes of the restraints.

Minimizing Cost

A firm that produces latex paints has a contract that requires that a minimum of 60 units of the chemical aquaphobe and 80 units of the chemical chromodine go into each drum of paint. The firm can buy the chemicals in a prepared mix from two different companies. Company X has a mix of 2 units of aquaphobe and 4 units of chromodine that costs $6, and company Y has a mix of 1 unit of aquaphobe and 1 unit of chromodine that costs $2. How many mixes from company X and company Y should the firm purchase to honor contract requirements and yet *minimize cost*?
    The production chart summarizes the problem:

	Aquaphobe	Chromodine	Cost/mix
Company X	2 units	4 units	$6
Company Y	1 unit	1 unit	$2
Required units	60 units	80 units	

The restraints can be expressed as:

$$2x + y \geqslant 60$$
$$4x + y \geqslant 80$$

The objective function is to minimize cost (see Figure 1-79).

$$C = 6x + 2y$$

The point of intersection of the restraint functions is at $(10, 40)$, and the shaded area in the figure below represents the restraint area. The slope of the objective function is -3, which is between the slopes of the restraint functions of -2 and -4. Cost can be visualized as being minimized by letting C_1, C_2, and C_3 come down to its lowest point, C_4, in the restraint area. The lowest point is at $(10, 40)$. Thus, the objective function is minimized at $x = 10$ and $y = 40$, which means that 10 mixes from company X and 40 mixes from company Y minimize cost, and minimum cost is:

$$C = \$6(10) + \$2(40) = \$140$$

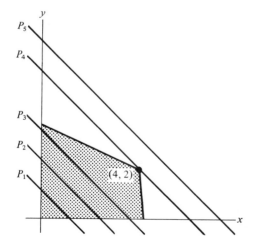

FIGURE 1-78

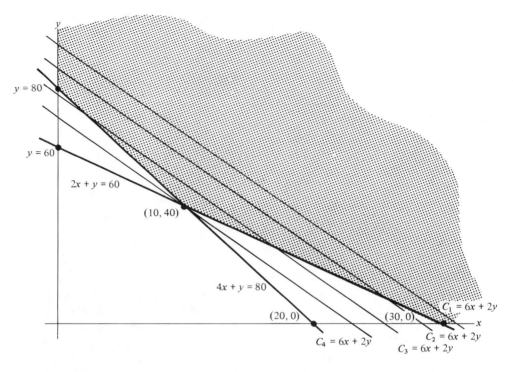

FIGURE 1-79

PROBLEMS 1-15

*1. The following production chart is for a firm that produces both standard-use and special-use calculators; the firm uses two departments in the assembling process. Profit for each case of standard-use calculators is $60, and profit for each case of special-use calculators is $30. Find the numbers of cases of standard-use calculators (x) and special-use calculators (y) that are necessary to schedule for production in order to maximize the profit function.

	Department A	Department B
Standard-use	1 hour/case	5 hours/case
Special-use	1 hour/case	1 hour/case
Available hours	12 hours	20 hours

*2. Repeat Problem 1 when the profit for each case of standard-use calculators is $30, and the profit for each case of special-use calculators is $60.

*3. Repeat Problem 1 when the profit for each case of standard-use calculators is $80, and the profit for each case of special-use calculators is $10.

4. The following production chart is for a firm that produces standard-use and special-use calculators; the firm uses three departments in the assembling process. Profit for each case of standard-use calculators is $100, and profit for each case of special-use calculators is $100. Find the number of cases of standard-use calculators (x) and special-use calculators (y) that is necessary to schedule for production in order to maximize the profit function.

	Department A	Department B	Department C
Standard-use	1 hour/case	5 hours/case	5 hours/case
Special-use	1 hour/case	1 hour/case	1 hour/case
Available hours	12 hours	20 hours	10 hours

5. Minimize $C = 14x + 4y$ subject to the restraints:

$$4x + y \geqslant 80$$
$$12x + y \geqslant 160$$

6. Minimize $C = 20x + 20y$ subject to the restraints:

$$3x + 3y \geqslant 90$$
$$7x + 3y \geqslant 40$$

1-16   THE BEST-FITTING LINE: LINEAR REGRESSION

If a set of data consisting of N points (x, y) has "good linear correlation," it is obvious from the scatter diagram (see Figure 1-80) that a straight line exists that best fits the data. The concept of "good linear correlation" will be accepted intuitively for now and will be revisited later.

For the set of N points (x, y) the slope m and y-axis intercept b for $y = mx + b$ are given by the following expressions in which the sigma (Σ) notation is used (see Appendix A):

$$b = \frac{\Sigma Y \Sigma X^2 - \Sigma X \Sigma XY}{N \Sigma X^2 - (\Sigma X)^2}$$

$$m = \frac{N \Sigma XY - \Sigma X \Sigma Y}{N \Sigma X^2 - (\Sigma X)^2}$$

Example 1:   Find the line that best fits the following set of data: $(0, 1)$, $(1, 3)$, $(2, 5)$. These points fall exactly on the line $y = 2x + 1$; this example will serve as a particular proof of the procedure for determining the best-fitting line. In this example $N = 3$ (points).

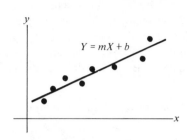

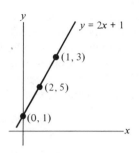

FIGURE 1-80   FIGURE 1-81

X	Y	X^2	XY
0	1	0	0
1	3	1	3
2	5	4	10
$\Sigma = $ 3	9	5	13

$$b = \frac{(9)(5) - (3)(13)}{(3)(5) - (9)} = 1$$

$$m = \frac{(3)(13) - (3)(9)}{(3)(5) - (9)} = 2$$

The best-fitting line is $y = 2x + 1$ (see Figure 1-81).

Example 2:   Find the line that best fits the following points: $(0, 1)$, $(1, 4)$, $(2, 5)$, $(3, 5)$, $(4, 9)$. $N = 5$.

X	Y	X^2	XY
0	1	0	0
1	4	1	4
2	5	4	10
3	5	9	15
4	9	16	36
$\Sigma = $ 10	24	30	65

$$b = \frac{(24)(3) - (10)(24)}{(5)(30) - 100} = \frac{70}{50} = 1.4$$

$$m = \frac{(5)(65) - (10)(24)}{50} = \frac{85}{50} = 1.7$$

The best-fitting line is $y = 1.7x + 1.4$ (see Figure 1-82).

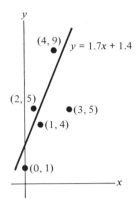

FIGURE 1-82

Uses of the Best-Fitting Line

The best-fitting line is often referred to as the least-square line, because it is obtained by finding the line where the distance squared from each point to the line is smallest. For historical reasons the least-square line is called the regression line. This linear regression has two major uses in mathematical economics.

1. *Determining linear functions.* To accept certain linear economic functions as exactly linear would be naive. Most likely these functions fall along a straight line and must be fit to a straight line. If economic variables form a scatter diagram with good linear correlation, then the best-fitting line is a means of obtaining linear functions that represent demand, supply, revenue, cost, profit, consumption, and savings. Moreover, if marginal functions can be best fit, then the linear expressions of these functions can be found. We can obtain a demand expression from the regression line (see Figure 1-83).

2. *Forecasting.* If economic functions can be best fit for the variables x and y, then $y = mx + b$ can be used to forecast values of y for new values of x. A good example of this is the consumption function. If we have observations for x (income)

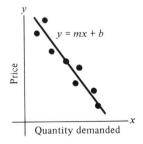

FIGURE 1-83

and *y* (consumption), then the line that best fits the data would be the consumption function $C = mx + b$. For any new x we can forecast consumption. Moreover, the slope of consumption represents the marginal propensity to consume (see Figure 1-84).

Example 3:   The demand for a commodity over a time interval is indicated by the following table. Assume that the data have "good linear correlation." Find the line that best represents demand.

Price (y)	Quantity (x)
6	1
5	3
4	4
3	5
1	6

Solution.   The following table gives the necessary sums to find the slope (*m*) and *y*-axis intercept (*b*) for $y = mx + b$.

x	y	x^2	xy
1	6	1	6
3	5	9	15
4	4	16	16
5	3	25	15
6	1	36	6
$\Sigma =$ 19	19	87	58

$$b = \frac{(19)(87) - (19)(58)}{(5)(87) - (19)^2} = 7.4$$

The best-fitting line that represents demand is: $y = 7.4 - .96x$ (see Figure 1-85).

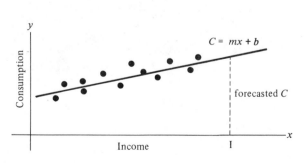

FIGURE 1-84

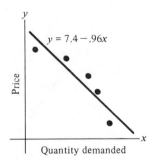

FIGURE 1-85

The line that best fits the data is such that the sum of the perpendicular distances from the points to the line is as small as possible. The following table gives these distances:

x	Best-fitting values (y_1)	Original data (y_2)	$d = \|y_1 - y_2\|$
1	6.4	6	.4
2	4.5	5	.5
3	3.6	4	.4
4	2.6	3	.4
5	1.6	1	.6
			$\Sigma = 2.3$

Any other line that represented the data would have $d = \|y_1 - y_2\|$ greater than 2.3 (see Figure 1-86).

Example 4:   The following table represents data relating net disposable income (I) to consumption (C). Assume that the data have "good linear correlation." Find the line that best fits $C = f(I)$, and forecast the value for consumption if net disposable income is 6 $(I = 6)$.

Income (I)	Consumption (C)
1	11
2	12
3	12
4	13
5	14

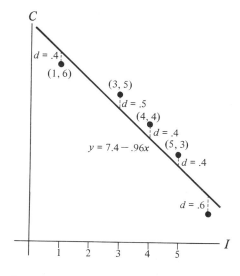

FIGURE 1-86

Solution.   The following table gives the necessary sum to find the slope (m) and the y-axis intercept for $C = mI + b$.

I	C	I^2	IC
1	11	1	11
2	12	4	24
3	12	9	36
4	13	16	52
5	14	25	70
Σ = 15	62	55	193

$$b = \frac{(62)(55) - (15)(193)}{(5)(55) - 225} = 10.3$$

$$m = \frac{(5)(193) - (15)(62)}{50} = .7$$

$m = .7$ represents the marginal propensity to consume. The best-fitting line that represents consumption is: $C = .7I + 10.3$ (see Figure 1-87). The forecasted value for a "new" income of $I = 6$ is:

$$C = (.7)(6) + 10.3 = 15.5$$

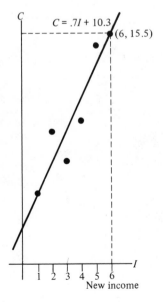

FIGURE 1-87

The following table demonstrates that $C = .7I + 10.3$ is a "good fit" for the data.

I	Best-fitting values (C_1)	Original data (C_2)	$d = |C_1 - C_2|$
1	11	11	0
2	11.7	12	.3
3	12.4	12	.4
4	13.1	13	.1
5	13.8	14	.2
			$\Sigma = 1.0$

Any other line that represented this data would have $d = |C_1 - C_2|$ greater than 1.0 (see Figure 1-88).

The Correlation Coefficient

Until now we have assumed that "good linear correlation" exists between two variables. In practice we should involve a method to determine if linear correlation does indeed exist before we find the regression line. The measure that gives the amount of linear agreement for a set of N points (x, y) is the *correlation coefficient:*

$$r = \frac{N\Sigma XY - \Sigma X\Sigma Y}{\sqrt{[N\Sigma X^2 - (\Sigma X)^2][N\Sigma Y^2 - (\Sigma Y)^2]}}$$

The value of the correlation coefficient is between +1 and −1 inclusively; (1) if r is close to 1, there is strong positive linear correlation; (2) if r is close to −1, there is strong negative linear correlation; (3) if r is close to 0 there is little or no linear correlation.

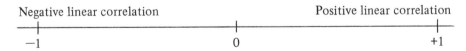

Negative linear correlation   Positive linear correlation

−1   0   +1

little or no linear correlation

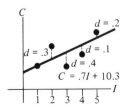

FIGURE 1-88

"Close to +1" or "close to −1" is generally accepted and interpreted by the following table, which depends on the number N of sets of points (x, y):

N	r	N	r
5	.87	14	.53
6	.81	15	.51
7	.75	20	.44
8	.70	30	.36
9	.66	40	.31
10	.63	50	.27
11	.60	60	.25
12	.57	80	.22
13	.55	100	.19

Example 5:   Determine the nature of the correlation for the following points: $(0, 1)$, $(1, 4), (2, 5), (3, 5), (4, 9)$. $N = 5$.

X	Y	X²	Y²	XY
0	1	0	1	0
1	4	1	16	4
2	5	4	25	10
3	5	9	25	15
4	9	16	81	36
$\Sigma = 10$	24	30	148	65

$$r = \frac{(5)(65) - (10)(24)}{\sqrt{[(5)(30) - 100] [(5)(148) - 576]}} = \frac{85}{\sqrt{8200}} = .93$$

For $N = 5$ the table shows that:

The formula gives $r = .93$, which indicates strong positive linear correlation for the set of data. Because of the linear correlation the best-fitting line can be determined.

PROBLEMS 1-16

*1. Find the correlation coefficient for the following sets of data and determine if linear correlation exists. If linear correlation exists, find the best-fitting line:

*a. X   Y

0	0
1	2
2	4
3	6
4	8

b. X   Y

0	5
1	4
2	3
3	2
4	1
5	0

c. X   Y

1	1
2	5
3	1
4	2
5	7

*d. X   Y

0	2
1	3
2	6
3	6
4	6

e. X   Y

0	10
1	8
2	6
3	4
4	2
5	0
6	-2
7	-4

2. The demand for a commodity over a time interval is indicated by the following table. Find the correlation coefficient and interpret the result:

Price (y)	Quantity demanded (x)
6	1
5	3
4	4
3	5
1	6

3. The following table represents data relating net disposable income (I) to consumption (C). Find the correlation coefficient and interpret the result:

Income (I)	Consumption (C)
1	11
2	12
3	12
4	13
5	14

4. The following table represents a number of single-unit houses in a certain area as recorded by a planning office from the period extending from January 1, 1976, to January 1, 1980 (assume 1980 to be the present year).

Year (x)		Number of houses ($\times$ 10,000) (y)
1976	1	2.
1977	2	2.09
1978	3	2.21
1979	4	2.29
1980	5	2.41

    a. Assume that linear correlation does exist. Determine the equation for the re-
gression line and plot the graph on the same axis as the scatter diagram. Indicate the distance from the points of the scatter diagram to the best-fitting line
to demonstrate that the best-fitting line comes "close" to the points in the
scatter diagram. To simplify the arithmetic let the years 1976 through 1980 be
$-, 1, 2, 3$, and 4, respectively.

    b. Using the best-fitting line, forecast the number of single-dwelling houses for
the next three years (1981, 1982, 1983), which would be represented by 5, 6,
and 7, respectively.

5. The following table relates consumption to net disposable income. Assume that
linear correlation does exist. Find the regression line and forecast consumption
for an income of $I = 50$. Sketch the graph of $C = f(I)$ and the scatter diagram on
the same axis.

Income (I)	Consumption (C)
0	9
10	15
20	20
30	25
40	31

SECOND DEGREE FUNCTIONS

2

2-1 CURVE SKETCHING THE SECOND-DEGREE FUNCTION

The second-degree, or quadratic, function has the general explicit form:

$$y = ax^2 + bx + c$$

The second-degree function forms a symmetrical U-shaped curve called a *parabola*. The parabola is the simplest of all curves and plays an important role in business and economics. The model second-degree function is $y = x^2$. This particular expression represents the simplest of all mathematical curves and will be used as a basis for understanding the general explicit form (see Figure 2-1). The graph of $y = x^2$ is obtained by plotting a few convenient points:

$$f(-1) = 1 \qquad\qquad f(1) = 1$$
$$f(-2) = 4 \qquad\qquad f(2) = 4$$
$$f(-3) = 9 \qquad f(0) = 0 \qquad f(3) = 9$$
$$\cdot \qquad\qquad\qquad\qquad \cdot$$
$$\cdot \qquad\qquad\qquad\qquad \cdot$$
$$\cdot \qquad\qquad\qquad\qquad \cdot$$

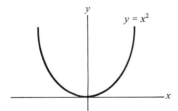

FIGURE 2-1

    The same general parabola will result with any positive coefficient. In this case the parabola is said to be *concave up*; the low point is called the *vertex*. The function

$y = -x^2$ means to square x and negate the result. This means that y is never positive. Therefore, the model with any negative coefficient would be *concave down*, and the vertex would be the high point.

Vertical Adjustment of the Model in the Plane

For $y = cx^2 + v$, where c and v are constants, there results a vertical adjustment of the model by v units. The proof that adding a constant generates a vertical adjustment should be geometrically intuitive (see Figure 2-2).

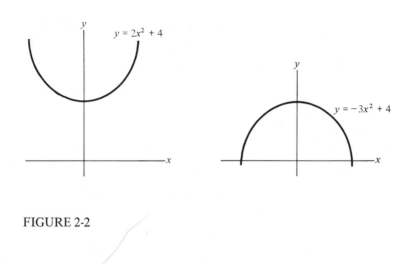

FIGURE 2-2

Horizontal Adjustment of the Model in the Plane

For $y = (x - h)^2$ there results a horizontal adjustment of the model in the plane by h units (see Figure 2-3).

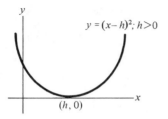

FIGURE 2-3

PROBLEMS 2-1

*1. Plot the graphs of the following functions:

    *a. $y = 4x^2$ c. $y = .5x^2$

    b. $y = -4x^2$ d. $y = -.5x^2$

*2. Plot the graphs of the following functions:

    *a. $y = 3x^2 + 4$ c. $y = -3x^2 + 4$

    b. $y = 3x^2 - 4$ d. $y = -3x^2 - 4$

*3. Plot the graphs of the following functions:

    *a. $y = (x - 7)^2$ c. $y = -(x - 7)^2$

    b. $y = (x + 7)^2$ d. $y = -(x + 7)^2$

*4. Plot the graphs of the following functions:

    *a. $y = (x - 5)^2 + 2$ b. $y = (x + 5)^2 - 2$ c. $y = (x - 5)^2 - 2$

2-2   THE ZEROS OF THE SECOND-DEGREE FUNCTION

The general procedure for plotting the graph of the second-degree function is to use the intercept technique. The parabola $y = ax^2 + bx + c$ crosses the y axis at c, so there is no problem finding the y-axis intercept. The x-axis intercept(s) are found by letting $y = 0$ and solving the equation:

$$ax^2 + bx + c = 0$$

It is possible that a parabola of the form $y = ax^2 + bx + c$ never crosses the x axis. In this situation the equation $ax^2 + bx + c = 0$ has no solution. We will use the intercept technique for a few specific examples, and then results will be generalized.

Example 1:   Plot the graph of $y = x^2 + 2x - 3$. Use the intercept technique (see Figure 2-4).

Step 1. $x = 0, y = 3$.

Step 2. $y = 0, x^2 + 2x - 3 = (x + 3)(x - 1) = 0$, and $x = -3, x = 1$.

Step 3.   By inspection of the x axis intercepts the x value for the vertex is $x = -1$ and the y value is $f(-1) = -4$.

Step 4.   The parabola is concave up; and the vertex is $(-1, -4)$.

Example 2:   Plot the graph of $y = -x^2 + 6x - 8$. Use the intercept technique (see Figure 2-5).

Step 1. $x = 0, y = -8$, and $y = 0, x = 2, 4$.

Step 2.   The parabola is concave down and the vertex is $(3, 1)$:

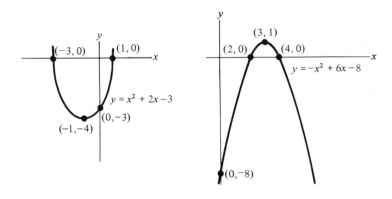

FIGURE 2-4   FIGURE 2-5

Example 3:   The zeros of some parabolic functions, such as the following, cannot be obtained by direct factoring:

$$y = x^2 + 8x + 2$$

Since the x-axis intercepts cannot be found at this point, this situation brings out the problem of finding the zeros of:

$$ax^2 + bx + c = 0$$

in the case where the expression is not factorable.

The Quadratic Formula

In the case in which $ax^2 + bx + c = 0$ is not factorable, the *quadratic formula* is used to find the zeros. The formula will be derived below using the method of completing the square.
Solve:

$$ax^2 + bx + c = 0$$

Step 1.   Divide both sides by a in order to isolate the constant term:

$$x^2 + \frac{bx}{a} = \frac{-c}{a}$$

Step 2.   Add $b^2/4a^2$ (obtained by taking 1/2 the coefficient of x and squaring it) to both sides to make a perfect square:

$$x^2 + \frac{bx}{a} + \frac{b^2}{4a^2} = \frac{b^2}{4a^2} + \frac{-c}{a}$$

Step 3.   Reduce:

$$\left(x + \frac{b}{2a}\right)^2 = \frac{b^2 - 4ac}{4a^2}$$

Step 4.   Take the square root of both sides:

$$x + \frac{b}{2a} = \pm \sqrt{\frac{b^2 - 4ac}{4a^2}}$$

Step 5.   Solve for x:

$$x = \frac{-b}{2a} \pm \frac{\sqrt{b^2 - 4ac}}{2a}$$

Step 6.   Write the result over the common denominator in order to obtain the zeros of the quadratic equation:

$$x = \frac{-b \pm \sqrt{b^2 - 4ac}}{2a}$$

The quadratic formula should be viewed in two ways. First, it gives the solutions (or zeros) to the equation $ax^2 + bx + c = 0$. Second, the quadratic formula can be looked at from a geometrical point of view; it gives the x-axis intercepts, provided they exist. The following conclusions about the formula can be made (see Figure 2-6): (1) If $b^2 - 4ac$ (called the discriminant) is negative, there are no x-axis intercepts (or zeros); (2) if $b^2 - 4ac$ is positive, there are two unique x-axis intercepts (if $b^2 - 4ac = 0$, then there is a single solution at $x = -b/2a$); (3) the vertex (x, y) of the parabola is:

$$x = \frac{-b}{2a} \quad \text{and} \quad y = f\frac{-b}{2a}$$

This is seen in the formula by visualizing $-b/2a$ as the x axis focal point in locating the zeros.

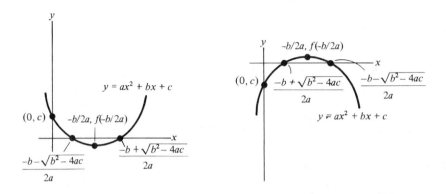

FIGURE 2-6

The quadratic formula contains all the information concerning the zeros and the vertex:

$$x = \frac{-b \pm \sqrt{b^2 - 4ac}}{2a}$$

Example 4: Plot the graph of the following parabola, indicating the intercept(s) and the vertex (see Figure 2-7).

$$y = x^2 + 4x + 2$$

Step 1. The y-axis intercept is 2, and y is concave up.
Step 2. The x-axis intercepts are:

$$x = \frac{-4 \pm \sqrt{16 - 4(1)(2)}}{2}$$

$$x = \frac{-4 \pm \sqrt{8}}{2}$$

$$x = \frac{-4 + \sqrt{8}}{2} = -.6$$

$$x = \frac{-4 - \sqrt{8}}{2} = -3.4$$

Step 3.   The vertex is $(-2, -2)$:

$$x = \frac{-4}{2} = -2; \quad y = f(-2) = -2$$

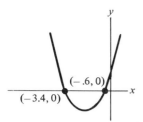

FIGURE 2-7

Example 5:   Plot the graph of $y = x^2 + 8x + 17$, indicating the intercept(s) and the vertex.

Step 1.   The y-axis intercept is 17, and y is concave up.
Step 2.   The x-axis intercepts are:

$$x = \frac{-8 \pm \sqrt{64 - 68}}{2}$$

$$x = \frac{-8 \pm \sqrt{-4}}{2}$$

$\sqrt{-4}$ is imaginary; hence there are no x-axis intercepts.

Step 3.   The vertex is $(-4, 1)$.

$$x = \frac{-8}{2} = -4; \quad y = f(-4) = 1$$

Example 6:   Plot the graph of $y = -x^2 + 4x + 2$, indicating intercept(s) and the vertex (see Figure 2-8).

Step 1.   The y-axis intercept is 2, and y is concave down.
Step 2.   The x-axis intercepts are

$$x = \frac{-4 \pm \sqrt{24}}{-2}$$

$$x = \frac{-4 + \sqrt{24}}{-2} = -.44$$

$$x = \frac{-4 - \sqrt{24}}{-2} = 4.4$$

Step 3.   The vertex is $(2, 6)$:

$$x = \frac{-4}{-2} = 2; \qquad y = f(2) = 6$$

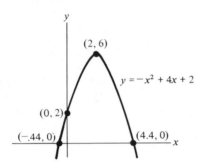

FIGURE 2-8

PROBLEMS 2-2

*1. Factor the following if possible. If the equations factor, find the zeros:

*a. $x^2 - 10x + 16$	f. $x^2 + 16$	j. $2x^2 + 5x + 2$
*b. $x^2 + 10x + 16$	g. $x^2 + 10x + 7$	k. $6x^2 + 9x + 2$
*c. $x^2 + 6x - 16$	h. $16 - 6x - x^2$	l. $5x^2 + 17x - 12$
d. $x^2 - 6x - 16$	i. $16 + 6x - x^2$	m. $2x^2 + 3x + 1$
e. $x^2 - 16$		

*2. Use the quadratic formula to solve the following equations:

*a. $2x^2 + 8x + 3 = 0$	d. $-2x^2 + 8x + 3 = 0$	g. $2x^2 + 4x - 3 = 0$
*b. $2x^2 + 8x - 3 = 0$	e. $-2x^2 - 8x - 3 = 0$	h. $-2x^2 + 4x + 3 = 0$
c. $2x^2 - 8x - 3 = 0$	f. $2x^2 + 4x + 3 = 0$	i. $-2x^2 - 4x + 3 = 0$

*3. Sketch the graphs of the following quadratic functions; indicate vertices and intercept(s):

*a. $y = x^2 - 10x + 16$ g. $y = x^2 + 4x + 4$ l. $y = -2x^2 + 8x + 3$

*b. $y = x^2 + 10x + 16$ h. $y = x^2 - 4x + 4$ m. $y = 2x^2 + 4x - 3$

c. $y = x^2 + 6x - 16$ i. $y = x^2 + 4x + 2$ n. $y = -2x^2 + 4x + 3$

d. $y = -x^2 + 10x - 6$ j. $y = x^2 - 4x + 2$ o. $y = -2x^2 - 4x + 3$

e. $y = -x^2 - 6x + 16$ k. $y = 2x^2 + 8x + 3$ p. $y = -2x^2 + 4x - 3$

f. $y = 6x^2 + 9x + 2$

*4. Give examples of quadratic functions in which:

*a. The function has x-axis intercepts of 5 and 7 and is concave up

b. The function has x-axis intercepts of 5 and 7 and is concave down

c. The function has x-axis intercepts of 5 and -7 and is concave up

d. The function has x-axis intercepts of -5 and -7 and is concave down

e. The function has a double zero at 6

f. The function has a double zero at -6

g. The function is concave up with vertex at $(2, 2)$

*5. Given that the following three points lie on the parabola $y = ax^2 + bx + c$, find a, b, and c by solving simultaneous equations: $(2, 3), (3, 10), (4, 21)$.

2-3   REVERSAL OF VARIABLE ROLES

A general graphical interpretation of the quadratic function $y = ax^2 + bx + c$ was given earlier. If the roles of x and y are interchanged and x and y remain on the standard axes, then the resulting expression:

$$x = ay^2 + by + c$$

can be expressed graphically by rotating the previously seen form, $y = ax^2 + bx + c$, 90 degrees in the plane (see Figure 2-9). When a is positive, the parabola opens to the right.

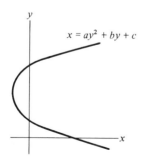

FIGURE 2-9

The quadratic formula gives the y-axis intercepts and the y value for the vertex:

$$y = \frac{-b \pm \sqrt{b^2 - 4ac}}{2a}$$

The circled term is the y value for the vertex.

Example 1:   Plot the graph of $x = y^2 - 6y + 8$; indicate the intercept(s) and the vertex (see Figure 2-10). This second-degree function is factorable, so the quadratic formula is not needed.

Step 1.   When $y = 0, x = 8$.
Step 2.   When $x = 0$:

$$y^2 - 6y + 8 = 0$$
$$(y - 2)(y - 4) = 0$$
$$y = 2$$
$$y = 4$$

Step 3.   The graph is concave to the right and the y value for the vertex is 3. By substitution, the x value for the vertex is -1.

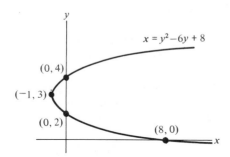

FIGURE 2-10

PROBLEMS 2-3

*1. Sketch the graphs of the following; indicating intercept(s) and vertices:
    *a. $x = y^2 - 10y + 16$ d. $x = 2y^2 + 8y + 3$
    b. $x = y^2 + 10y + 16$ e. $x = 2y^2 + 4y + 3$
    c. $x = 16 - 6y - y^2$

2. Find the point(s) of intersection for $x = y^2 - 4$ and $x = 8 - y$. Sketch the graphs of both expressions on the same axis. Which expression could represent demand? Which expression could represent supply?

2.4   APPLICATIONS OF SECOND-DEGREE FUNCTIONS TO DEMAND AND SUPPLY

Finding the point of market equilibrium for demand and supply in the case of second-degree functions is the same as in the linear one. If the functions are given explicitly, then the expression for demand is set equal to the expression for supply.

Example 1:   Sketch the graphs of D and S on the same axes, and find the point of ME for:

$$y = -x^2 + 10 \quad \text{(represents } D\text{)}$$
$$y = x^2 + 2x + 4 \quad \text{(represents } S\text{)}$$

The graph of D is the basic mode and the graph of S does not have x-axis intercepts. The vertex for S is at $(-1, 3)$. The point of intersection of S with D is found by solving:

$$x^2 + 2x + 4 = -x^2 + 10$$
$$x^2 + x - 3 = 0$$

where

$$x = \frac{-1 \pm \sqrt{1 - 4(1)(-3)}}{2}$$

Only the positive x is meaningful, so

$$x = \frac{-1 + \sqrt{13}}{2} = 1.3$$

is the x value for ME; $y = f(1.3) = 8.3$ (see Figure 2-11).

PROBLEMS 2-4

*1. Sketch the graphs of demand and supply; indicate the point of market equilibrium:

    *a. $y = x^2 + 3x + 2$ and $y = 9 - x^2$

    *b. $y = 9 - x^2$ and $y = 7x + 1$

    c. $y = 10 - x^2$ and $y = x^2 + 1$

    d. $y = x^2 + 6x + 8$ and $y = 40 - x^2$

    e. $x = 16 - y^2$ and $y = x + 2$

    f. $y = -x^2 - 2x + 10$ and $y = x^2 + 2x + 1$

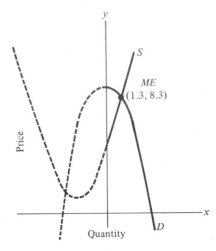

FIGURE 2-11

2. Devise examples of supply and demand functions (both second-degree functions) in which the point of market equilibrium is at $x = 10$.

2-5   APPLICATION OF SECOND-DEGREE FUNCTIONS TO REVENUE

In Chapter 1 we pointed out that a firm's revenue function is linear in the case of a purely competitive seller and a parabola in the case of an imperfectly competitive seller (provided that the demand expression is linear). We now turn to a detailed study of revenue characterized by an *imperfectly competitive market*. An imperfectly competitive firm's demand curve appears in the form $y = mx + b$ (where m is negative, and b is positive). (See Figure 2-12.) Then by definition $R = yx$, and thus:

$$R = xy = x(m + b)$$

where m is negative and b is positive, or

$$R = mx^2 + bx$$

The firm's revenue function is a parabola, concave down, with x-axis intercepts $(0, 0)$ and $(-b/m, 0)$. The vertex is $-b/2m, f(-b/2m)$. As expected, R increases at a decreasing rate until *maximum revenue* is reached and then decreases at a decreasing rate (see Figure 2-13).

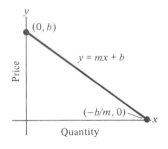

FIGURE 2-12

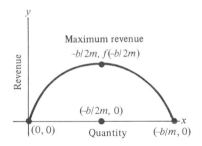

FIGURE 2-13

The elasticity of demand can be examined with respect to an imperfectly competitive firm's revenue function by superimposing the graphs of demand and revenue to show that the elasticity of demand is −1 when revenue reaches its maximum point. To the left of the point −$b/2m$ demand is relatively elastic; to the right of this point demand is relatively inelastic (see Figure 2-14).

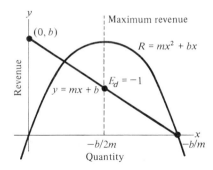

FIGURE 2-14

A note of importance: By placing price on the vertical axis and quantity on the horizontal axis, revenue and demand can be depicted on the same axes. Therefore, for the sake of variable consistency economists have conventionally placed the independent variable, price, on the vertical axis.

Example 1: Demand to a firm is given by $y = 20 - x$. Sketch the graph of y, indicating various elasticities along the line (see Figure 2-15). Sketch the graph of R, when demand is $y = 20 - x$ (see Figure 2-16).

$R = x(20 - x)$
$R = 20x - x^2$

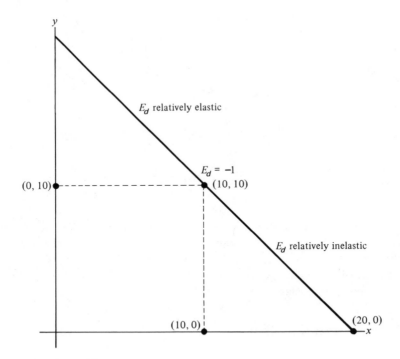

FIGURE 2-15

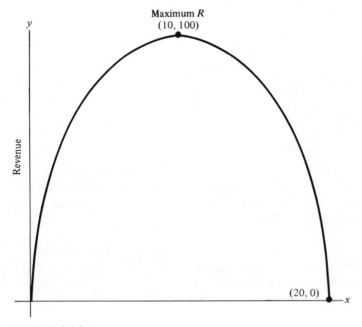

FIGURE 2-16

Superimpose the graphs of demand and revenue above on the same axes (see Figure 2-17). When E_d is relatively elastic, revenue increases as x increases. Maximum revenue is reached when $E_d = -1$. When E_d is relatively inelastic, revenue decreases as x increases.

In Chapter 1 we saw that if demand (ATR) to an imperfectly competitive firm is given by $y = mx + b$ (where m is negative and b is positive) then marginal revenue is expressed by $MR = 2mx + b$ (see Figure 2-18).

The graph of MR tells us that R increases at a decreasing rate from $x = 0$ to $x = -b/2m$, and R decreases at a decreasing rate from $x = (-b/2m)$ to $x = -b/m$. When $x = -b/2m$ $MR = 0$, $E_d = -1$, and R reaches a maximum. These important conclusions can be supported by an example.

Example 2:   If demand to an imperfectly competitive firm is given by $y = 10 - x$, set up a schedule to demonstrate that the expression for marginal revenue is $MR = 10 - 2x$ and that the firm's total revenue function increases at a decreasing rate from $x = 0$ to $x = 5$, reaches a maximum at $x = 5$, and decreases at a decreasing rate from $x = 5$ to $x = 10$.

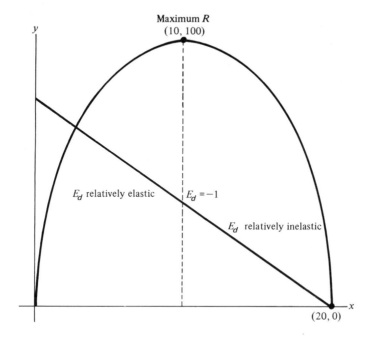

FIGURE 2-17

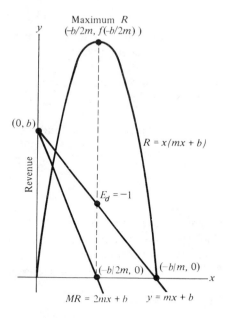

FIGURE 2-18

Solution.   In the following table the slope of *MR* is −2, and by interpolation the *y*-axis intercept is 10. The expression for marginal revenue is $MR = 10 - 2x$ (see Figure 2-19).

$\dfrac{ATR}{y = 10 - x}$	X	R	$MR = \dfrac{\Delta R}{\Delta X}$
10	0	0	
9	1	9	9
8	2	16	7
7	3	21	5
6	4	24	3
5	5	25	1
4	6	24	−1
3	7	21	−3
2	8	16	−5
1	9	9	−7
0	10	0	−9

When *MR* is positive yet decreasing, *R* increases at a decreasing rate. Maximum *R* occurs at $x = 5$, and $MR = 0$ for $x = 5$. When *MR* is negative yet decreasing, *R* decreases at a decreasing rate.

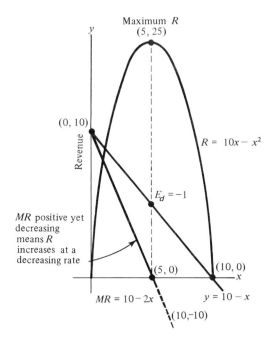

Maximum R
$(5, 25)$

$(0, 10)$

$R = 10x - x^2$

$E_d = -1$

MR positive yet
decreasing
means R
increases at a
decreasing rate

$(5, 0)$

$(10, 0)$

$MR = 10 - 2x$

$y = 10 - x$

$(10, -10)$

FIGURE 2-19

PROBLEMS 2-5

*1. Demand to a purely competitive firm is given by $y = 5$. Sketch the graphs of y, total revenue, and marginal revenue. What is the graph of average total revenue? What is the elasticity of demand for the firm?

2. Demand to an imperfectly competitive firm is given by $y = 40 - 2x$. Sketch the graphs of y, total revenue, and marginal revenue. What is the graph of average total revenue? At what point is the elasticity of demand equal to -1? At what point is marginal revenue equal to 0?

3. The following functions represent demand to imperfectly competitive firms. Superimpose the graphs of demand and total revenue indicating elasticities in general. Indicate the point of maximum revenue. If marginal revenue is positive, what do we know about the total revenue function? If the elasticity of demand is relatively elastic, what do we know about the revenue function?

   a. $y = 50 - 5x$
   b. $y = 50 - 2x$

4. Assume that the total revenue function is a parabola. Reconstruct the demand expression (see Figure 2-20):

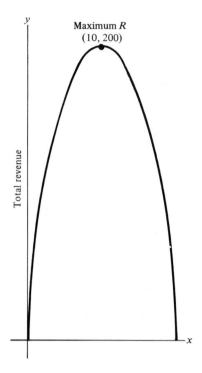

FIGURE 2-20

5. Assume that demand to an imperfectly competitive firm is given by $y = mx + b$ (where m is negative and b positive).

   a. If E_d is relatively elastic, what is the effect on TR when ATR increases?

   b. If E_d is relatively inelastic, what is the effect on TR when ATR increases?

   c. If MR is negative, what do we know about E_d?

   d. If MR is positive, what is the effect on TR when ATR decreases?

6. Demand to an imperfectly competitive firm is given by $y = 8 - x$. Set up a schedule to find MR, and demonstrate (using MR) that, as x increases, TR increases at a decreasing rate, TR reaches a maximum, and then TR decreases at a decreasing rate.

ALGEBRAIC AND EXPONENTIAL FUNCTIONS

3

3-1 ALGEBRAIC FUNCTIONS

The graphs of first-degree and second-degree functions were initially obtained by plotting points to establish a "model." This approach is often used initially, and when basic "models" have been established, generalizations can be made.

The intercept technique is perhaps the most important algebraic curve-sketching method, but this technique has meaning only if the intercepts exist or are easy to obtain. In this section we will establish some basic "models" for curve sketching expressions of the form:

$$y = x^n$$

where n is an integer or fraction.

In all the following examples the coefficient of x will be ± 1. Keep in mind that the same general picture will result for any coefficient.

Example 1: $y = x^2$ (or any positive even-integer exponent: $y = x^4$, $y = x^6$, ...). In the following seven figures a solid line denotes a positive coefficient, and a dotted line denotes a negative coefficient (see Figure 3-1). The functions $y = x^2$, $y = x^4$, $y = x^6$, ... do not appear exactly the same when superimposed on each other in the plane. In fact, they have only three points in common: $(0, 0)$, $(1, 1)$, $(-1, 1)$. However, they all appear U-shaped, and a general appreciation of the graphs is what we seek at this point.

Example 2: $y = x^3$ or any positive odd-integer exponent: $y = x^5$, $y = x^7$, ... (See Figure 3-2.)

Example 3: $y = x^{-1}$ or any negative odd-integer exponent: $y = x^{-3}$, $y = x^{-5}$, ... (See Figure 3-3.)

Example 4: $y = x^{-2}$ or any negative even-integer exponent: $y = x^{-4}$, $y = x^{-6}$, ... (See Figure 3-4.)

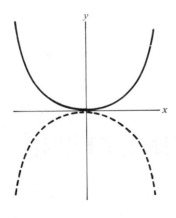

FIGURE 3-1   FIGURE 3-2

Example 5: $y = x^{1/2} = \sqrt{x}$ or any positive fraction less than 1: $y = x^{1/3}$, ... (See Figure 3-5.)

Example 6: $y = x^{3/2}$ or any positive fractional exponent greater than 1: $y = x^{4/3}$, ... (See Figure 3-6.)

Example 7: $y = x^{-1/2}$ or any negative fractional exponent: $y = x^{-3/2}$, ... (See Figure 3-7.)

Many important interrelationships can be brought out with respect to the seven models. The graph of $y = x^n$ for any positive number greater than 1 appears concave up in the first quadrant. The graphs of $y = x^n$, where n is a positive fraction less than 1, appear concave down in the first quadrant. The graphs of $y = x^n$, where n is negative, demonstrate a reciprocal action between x and y (if x increases, then y decreases, and conversely). If a negative coefficient appears in any of the models, the sense of the graph is merely reversed.

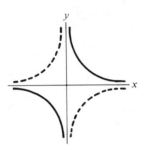

FIGURE 3-3   FIGURE 3-4

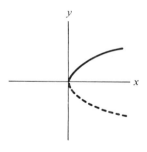

FIGURE 3-5

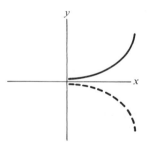

FIGURE 3-6

Vertical and Horizontal Adjustments of $y = x^n$

Vertical and horizontal adjustments of the models in the plane can be made by using:

$$y = (x - h)^n + v$$

where h is the horizontal adjustment and v the vertical adjustment.

Example 8: $y = 20x^{-1} + 2$
    (See Figure 3-8.)

Example 9: $y = (x - 4)^4$
    (See Figure 3-9.)

Example 10: $y = -(x - 4)^4 + 4$
    (See Figure 3-10.)

Example 11: $y = \sqrt{x} + 2$
    (See Figure 3-11.)

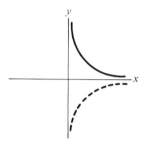

FIGURE 3-7

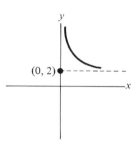

FIGURE 3-8

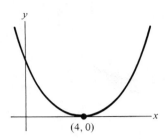

FIGURE 3-9

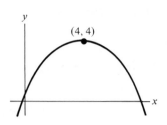

FIGURE 3-10

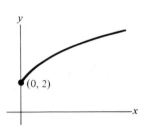

FIGURE 3-11

PROBLEMS 3-1

*1. Plot the graphs of the following by using basic models:

*a. $y = 2x^3 + 7$ f. $y = 7x^{-1} + 3$ k. $y = 2x^{5/3}$

*b. $y = -3x^5 + 4$ g. $y = -5x^{-2} + 2$ l. $y = 2(x - 3)^2$

c. $y = 4x^5 + 5$ h. $y = 6x^{-5} - 3$ m. $y = -3(x + 5)^3$

d. $y = -x^4 - 32$ i. $y = 3\sqrt{x} + 4$ n. $y = 3(x - 2)^{-2}$

e. $y = x^{-1} - 5$ j. $y = -5\sqrt{x} - 3$ o. $y = (x - 2)^{1/2}$

*2. The following model functions have a horizontal translation of 2 units to the right. For $y = f(x)$ make the substitution $z = x - 2$; this results in a transformation (change) of $y = f(x)$ to $y = f(z)$. Sketch *both* the graphs of $y = f(x)$ in the (x, y) plane and the graphs of $y = f(z)$ in the (z, y) plane. After you sketch the graphs, can you see and benefit in the transformation?

*a. $y = (x - 2)^2$ c. $y = \dfrac{1}{(x - 2)^2}$ e. $y = (x - 2)^{1/2}$

b. $y = (x - 2)^3$ d. $y = \dfrac{1}{(x - 2)}$

3-2 APPLICATIONS OF BASIC ALGEBRAIC MODELS

For the linear cost function expressed by $TC = mx + b$ (where both m and b are positive), average total cost (ATC) is defined as:

$$ATC = \frac{TC}{x} = \frac{mx + b}{x} = m + \frac{b}{x}$$

where m and b are positive (see Figure 3-12). The average fixed cost (AFC) is defined as:

$$AFC = \frac{FC}{x} = \frac{b}{x}$$

where b is positive (see Figure 3-13).

Example 1: Assume that $TC = C = 4x + 100$ (see Figure 3-14). Then:

$$ATC = \frac{4x + 100}{x} = 4 + \frac{100}{x}$$

$$ATC = \frac{100}{x}$$

We need only view the several basic algebraic model functions to realize that there are countless uses of these models in basic business and economics. For example, the idea of *concavity* is essential when we describe the behavior of the consumption function, if we assume that consumption is not represented by a linear function. In this situation the consumption function must be *concave down* in order to insure that the marginal propensity to consume does not exceed 100 percent.

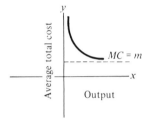

FIGURE 3-12

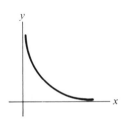

FIGURE 3-13

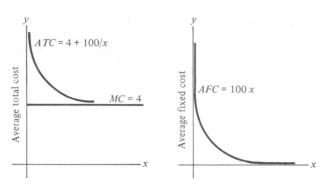

FIGURE 3-14

Example 2:   Given that consumption is represented by $C = \sqrt{I} + 2$, sketch the graphs of C and $C = I$ (the guideline) on the same axis (see Figure 3-15). Find the consumer's break-even point (*CBEP*) by solving $C = I$:

Solution.

$$\sqrt{I} + 2 = I$$
$$\sqrt{I} = I - 2$$
$$I = I^2 - 4I + 4$$
$$0 = I^2 - 5I + 4$$
$$(I - 1)(I - 4) = 0$$

where $I = 1$ and $I = 4$.

At this point it is important to realize that the expression $I^2 - 5I + 4$ is not the same as the original problem: $\sqrt{I} + 2 = I$. In other words, by squaring both sides of the equation, we could have introduced extraneous (extra) zeros. Therefore, the values $I = 1$ and $I = 4$ must be checked in the original equation to be solved. Solve $\sqrt{I} + 2 = 1$. Check with $I = 1$:

$$\sqrt{1} + 2 \neq 1$$

1 is extraneous. Check with $I = 4$:

$$\sqrt{4} + 2 = 4$$

The solution is 4.

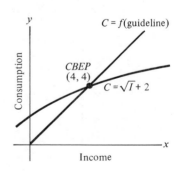

FIGURE 3-15

The model $C = \sqrt{I} + 2$ is used for consumption, because $\sqrt{I}$ "dampens" the consumption function. This means that as income increases, consumption increases but does so at a decreasing rate. This ensures that the marginal propensity to consume will not exceed 100 percent. Although the marginal propensity to consume and the marginal propensity to save cannot be found at a point, the delta definition gives us a change in consumption and savings over an interval:

I	$C = \sqrt{I} + 2$	$MPC = \dfrac{\Delta C}{\Delta I}$	$MPS = 1 - MPC$
1	3		
2	3.41	41%	59%
3	3.73	32%	68%
4	4	27%	73%
5	4.24	24%	76%
.			
.			
.			

MPC is less than 100 percent, and consumption increases at a decreasing rate. As MPC decreases, MPS increases.

PROBLEMS 3-2

*1. For the following total cost functions, sketch the graphs of total cost, average total cost, and average fixed cost:

   *a. $TC = 5x + 88$ b. $TC = 10x + 188$

*2. Find the point of market equilibrium for supply and demand. Sketch the graphs, and indicate the ME point.

$$y = 2x^{1/2} + 4$$
$$y = -4x^{1/2} + 16$$

3. If the consumption function is represented by a curve, then, in order to ensure that the marginal propensity to consume is less than 100 percent, the function must be concave down and yet still increase as income increases. Stated another way, consumption increases as income increases, but it does so at a decreasing rate. For the consumption function $C = 2\sqrt{I} + 10$:

   a. Sketch the graphs of consumption and the guideline, and indicate the consumer's break-even point.

   b. Show that consumption increases as income increases but that it does so at a decreasing rate. This means that $\Delta C/\Delta I$ is positive but that $\Delta C/\Delta I$ decreases as I increases. To demonstrate this, set up a consumption schedule for convenient values of I. Include an additional column for $\Delta C/\Delta I$ to represent the marginal propensity to consume.

4. National income analysis explains that there is an inverse relationship between the money market (M) and the interest rate (i). This relationship is described by the *liquidity preference function*: $M = f(i)$. The interest rate (i) that results in a boundless quantity of money demanded (M) is called the *liquidity trap*. Although the interest rate (i) is the independent variable, it is conventionally placed on the vertical axis, and money (M) is placed on the horizontal axis. Sketch the graph of the following liquidity preference function and indicate the liquidity trap:

$$M = f(i) = \frac{8}{i - .04}$$

where i represents the interest rate, and M represents the quantity demanded (money).

5. Sketch the graph of $y = 1/(1 + x^2)$, and use it as a model to draw the graphs of:

   a. $y = \dfrac{4}{1 + x^2}$ b. $y = \dfrac{-1}{1 + x^2}$

6. Sketch the graph of $x^2 + y^2 = 16$, using the intercept technique. What is this figure? What application might the graph have? In general, how would the graph of $x^2 + y^2 = a^2$ appear (in this equation a is positive)?

7. Sketch the graph of $(x - 4)^2 + (y - 5)^2 = 1$ by using translations.

8. Sketch the graphs of the following figures by using the intercept technique. What application might the graphs have?

   a. $\dfrac{x^2}{9} + \dfrac{y^2}{16} = 1$ b. $\dfrac{x^2}{16} + \dfrac{y^2}{9} = 1$

3-3   POLYNOMIALS

This section develops the theory of curve sketching polynomials. Polynomials are algebraic functions in which all the exponents of the variable x consist of positive integer numbers. The *Fundamental Theorem of Algebra* states that, if $y = f(x)$ is an nth-degree polynomial, the maximum number of zeros (x-axis intercepts) is n. The theorem is seen inductively from the following illustrations:

Polynomial	Expression	Maximum number of factors	Maximum number of zeros
First degree	$y = mx + b$	1	1
Second degree	$y = ax^2 + bx + c$	2	2
Third degree	$y = ax^3 + bx^2 + cx + d$	3	3
Fourth degree	$y = ax^4 + bx^3 + cx^2 + dx + e$	4	4
.		.	.
.		.	.
.		.	.
nth degree		n	n

The basic models furnish information concerning the behavior of polynomials with positive or negative leading coefficients (see Figure 3-16). For example, $y = x^3$ begins below the x axis and ends above the x axis (as x increases). Conversely, $y = -x^3$ begins above the x-axis and ends up below the x-axis. This is true for the general case of the third-degree function. The leading coefficient determines the extreme behavior of the function. The Fundamental Theorem states that a third-degree function crosses the x axis at most three times. However, it is possible that the third-degree function crosses the x axis only once or perhaps crosses once and is tangent at some other point. A point of tangency is a result of a double root. In summary:

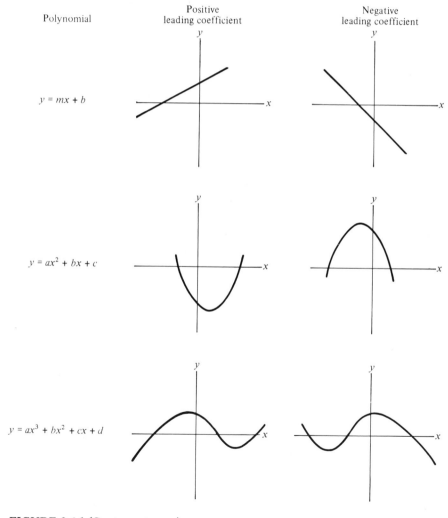

FIGURE 3-16 (Cont. next page)

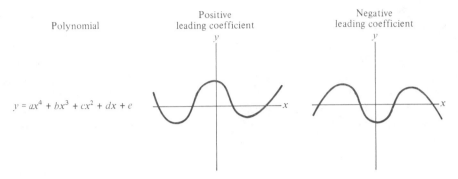

Polynomial

Positive
leading coefficient

Negative
leading coefficient

$y = ax^4 + bx^3 + cx^2 + dx + e$

FIGURE 3-16

Example 1:   Plot the graph of $y = x^3 - 6x^2 + 8x$ by using the intercept technique.

Solution.

$$x^3 - 6x^2 + 8x = x(x^2 - 6x + 8) = 0$$
$$x(x - 2)(x - 4) = 0$$

which means that the x-axis intercepts are $x = 0, +2, +4$. The leading coefficient is positive, so the graph begins below the x axis and ends above the axis (see Figure 3-17).

A note of importance: We cannot conclude that the maximum and minimum points fall at the midpoints of the intercepts. Finding these points will be solved with calculus. At this time maximum and minimum points can be approximated by plotting points only.

Example 2:   Plot the graph of $y = 4x - x^3$ by using the intercept technique.

Solution.

$$4x - x^3 = x(x^2 - 4) = x(x - 2)(x + 2) = 0$$

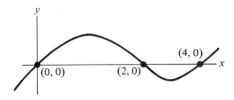

FIGURE 3-17

which means that the x-axis intercepts are $x = 0, +2, -2$. The leading coefficient is negative, so the graph begins above the x axis and ends below the axis (see Figure 3-18).

Example 3:   Plot the graph of $y = x^3 + 2x^2 - x - 2$ by using the intercept technique.

Solution.

$$x^3 + 2x^2 - x - 2 = (x - 1)(x + 1)(x + 2) = 0$$

which means that the x-axis intercepts are $x = 1, -1, -2$. The leading coefficient is positive, so the graph begins below the x axis and ends above the x axis (see Figure 3-19).

Example 4:   Plot the graph of $y = x^3 + 4x^2 - 10x - 4$ by using the intercept technique.

Solution.

$$x^3 + 4x^2 - 10x + 4 = (x - 2)(x^2 + 6x + 2) = 0$$

The leading coefficient is positive, so the graph begins below the x axis and ends above the axis (see Figure 3-20). There is only one rational root; the quadratic formula must be used to find the other two roots.

$$x^3 + 4x^2 - 10x + 4 = (x - 2)(x^2 + 6x + 2) = 0$$

$x = 2$ is the rational root. $x^2 + 6x + 2$ is not factorable, so the quadratic equation gives the zeros:

$$x = \frac{-6 \pm \sqrt{28}}{2}$$

and $x = -.35, -5.65$.

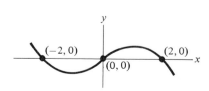

FIGURE 3-18

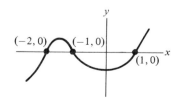

FIGURE 3-19

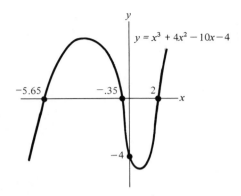

FIGURE 3-20

This example demonstrates that if one root of the third-degree function can be found, then the other two roots are assured by the quadratic equation. If one root of the cubic equation is found and the discriminant in the quadratic formula is negative, then the third-degree function crosses the x axis only once. For example, $y = x^3 + 3x^2 + 4x + 2$ factors to $y = (x + 1)(x^2 + 2x + 2)$, and there is only one real root at $x = -1$.

PROBLEMS 3-3

1. Plot the graphs of the following polynomials by using the intercept technique.

   a. $y = x^2 - x^3$
   b. $y = x - x^3$
   c. $y = 8x - 2x^3$
   d. $y = 2x^3 - x^2$
   e. $y = x^5 - x^3$
   f. $y = 2x - 4x^3$
   g. $y = x^3 + x^2$

*2. Plot the graphs of the following by using the intercept technique:

   *a. $y = x^3 - 8x^2 + 15x$
   b. $y = -15x + 8x^2 - x^3$
   c. $y = x^3 + 8x^2 + 15x$
   d. $y = x^3 + 2x^2 + 4x$

*3. Plot the graphs of the following by using the intercept technique:

   *a. $y = x^3 - 2x^2 - 4x + 8$
   b. $y = -8 + 4x + 2x^2 - x^3$
   c. $y = x^3 + x^2 - x - 10$
   d. $x^3 - 6x^2 + 11x - 6$
   e. $y = -x^3 - x^2 + x + 10$

4. Sketch the graph of the following total cost function by using the intercept technique: $TC = x^3 - x^2 + 2x + 4$.

5. Sketch the graph of the following total profit function by using the intercept technique, and approximate the point of maximum profit: $TP = -x^3 + 4x^2 + 7x - 10$.

6. Given that $TR = 4x$ and $TC = 5 + 3x - 5x^2 + x^3$:

   a. Superimpose the graphs of total revenue and total cost, indicating the break-even points. From the graph approximate maximum profit.

   b. Sketch the graph of total profit, indicating the break-even points and approximate profit.

3-4   THE ORIGIN OF TOTAL COST FUNCTIONS:
THE PRODUCTION FUNCTION

The Production Function

The *production function* expresses a firm's total product (output) as a function of its units of input. Labor and capital are units commonly used to represent input variables; however, in this section we will generalize and accept the input variable to be simply U:

$$\text{total product} = f(\text{units of input})$$
$$X = f(U)$$

The independent variable U is placed on the horizontal axis, and the dependent variable X is placed on the vertical axis. The production function demonstrates that, as units of input increase, total product increases, first at an increasing rate (concave up; increasing returns) and then at a decreasing rate (concave down; decreasing returns). (See Figure 3-21.) The point at which concavity changes is called the *point of inflection*. (Techniques to find this point will be given in Chapter 4.) The total product curve eventually turns down (negative returns).

The third-degree polynomial is the mathematical expression best suited to represent the production function, because it is the simplest algebraic expression whose concavity can be controlled from one sense to another. The point of inflection and the point of maximum total product can only be approximated at this time.

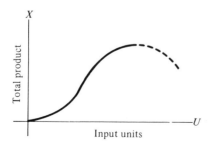

FIGURE 3-21

Example 1:   Plot the graph of the following total product function:

$$X = 9U^2 - U^3$$

Solution.   The horizontal axis intercepts are found by solving:

$$9U^2 - U^3 = 0$$

which gives $U = 0$ and $U = 9$ as the zeros. The table below gives the maximum total product. The integer value for the point of inflection is found by analyzing the slope of the total product function by using the delta function:

$$\frac{\Delta X}{\Delta U}$$

The term *marginal product* is used to indicate the value of $\Delta X/\Delta U$. Between 0 and 5 units of input, total product is increasing. Maximum total product occurs at 6 units of input. Between 7 and 9 units of input, total product is decreasing. The point of inflection for $X = f(U)$ occurs at $U = 3$ because from $U = 0$ to $U = 3$, $X = f(U)$ is increasing at an increasing rate (concave up) and from $U = 3$ on, $X = f(U)$ is increasing at a decreasing rate (concave down). (See Figure 3-22.)

Units of input (U)	Total product (P)	Marginal product $MP = \dfrac{\Delta X}{\Delta U}$
0	0	
1	8	8
2	28	20
3	54	26
4	80	26
5	100	20
6	108	8
7	98	
8	64	
9	0	

Total Cost Curves

The production function gives total output in terms of units of input, or $X = f(U)$, where U is on the horizontal axis and X is on the vertical axis (see Figure 3-23). We assume that units of input (U) can be expressed in terms of total product (X) for a specified domain and range and that the expression will be a third-degree polynomial.

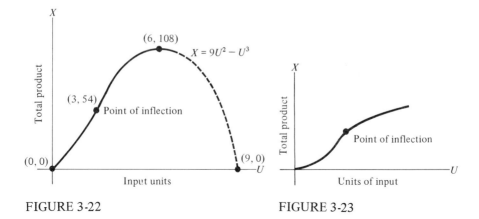

FIGURE 3-22   FIGURE 3-23

If we place units of input (U) on the vertical axis and total product (X) on the horizontal axis, we obtain an equivalent figure with axes reversed, given by:

$$U = g(X) = dx^3 + ex^2 + fx$$

If we assume that $U = g(X) = dx^3 + ex^2 + fx$ expresses units of input in terms of output for an appropriate domain and range, then the total cost of production function can be expressed by:

$$TC = P_u g(X) + FC$$

where

    TC = total cost
    P_u = price per unit for input units
    $g(X) = dx^3 + ex^2 + fx$ (units of input in terms of output)
    FC = fixed cost

If P_u (price per unit for input units) is fixed, then the total cost function could be expressed as a third-degree polynomial (see Figure 3-25):

$$TC = P_u(dx^3 + ex^2 + fx) + FC = rx^3 + sx^3 + tx + FC$$

This analysis must be made on an intuitive basis, because we are departing from the theory and the applied problem of relating the production function to the total cost function. Here we intend merely to demonstrate that total cost functions appear first concave down and then concave up because of their relationship to the production function. From a mathematical point of view the simplest polynomial that behaves in this manner is the third-degree function. We will use this function customarily to represent total cost over a specified domain and range.

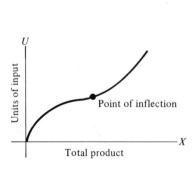

FIGURE 3-24

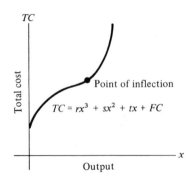

FIGURE 3-25

PROBLEMS 3-4

*1. Plot the graph of the production function $X = f(U) = 12U^2 - U^3$, where X represents a firm's total product and is on the vertical axis and U represents input units and is on the horizontal axis. Approximate maximum total product.

2. Plot the graph of $X = f(L) = 6L^2 - L^3$, where X represents a firm's total product and is on the vertical axis and L represents quantity of labor and is on the horizontal axis. Approximate maximum total product.

3. Plot the graph of $X = f(K) = 24K^2 - 2K^3$, where X represents a firm's total product and is on the vertical axis and K represents quantity of capital and is on the horizontal axis. Approximate maximum total product.

3-5   COST AND PROFIT FUNCTIONS

Third-degree functions are classically used in business and economics to determine total cost functions. In this section third-degree cost functions are especially designed to increase as x increases as it goes from concave down to concave up. We cannot infer that every increasing third-degree polynomial in the first quadrant behaves in this manner. (Techniques to control concavity will be studied in Chapter 4.)

In order for total cost to increase, the leading coefficient must be positive (see Figure 3-26, left). This means that total profit is a third-degree polynomial with a negative leading coefficient, because $P = R - C$.

The x value for maximum total profit is located *approximately* at the midpoint of the BE points and *not exactly* at the midpoint (see Figure 3-26, right), because TP is not symmetrical.

When revenue is represented by a purely competitive firm, total revenue is expressed as a straight line with a positive slope, and the greatest distance between TR and TC represents maximum profit (see Figure 3-27).

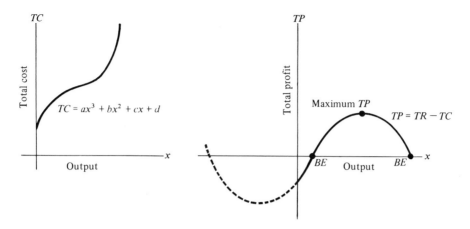

FIGURE 3-26

The x value for maximum total profit occurs at *approximately* the midpoint of the x break-even values. (The exact value of x that will result in maximum profit will be determined, using techniques of calculus, in Chapter 4.)

When revenue is represented by an imperfectly competitive firm, total revenue is expressed as a concave-down parabola and the greatest distance between TR and TC represents maximum profit (see Figure 3-28).

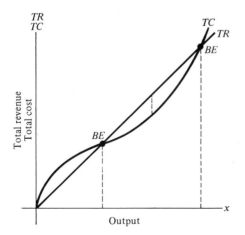

FIGURE 3-27

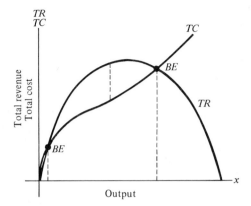

FIGURE 3-28

The x value for maximum total profit occurs approximately at the midpoint of the x break-even values.

Example 1:   Given that $TC = C = x^3 - 3x^2 + 6x + 3$ and $TR = R = 7x$, sketch the graphs of the total cost function, profit function, and the revenue and cost functions.

Solution.   The graph of TC does not factor, but the function is increasing for positive x values, because $f(0) = 3, f(1) = 7, f(2) = 11, f(3) = 21, \ldots$ The leading coefficient is positive. The graph of TC is assumed to go from concave down to concave up (see Figure 3-29).

By definition $P = R - C$, and thus the profit function is:

$$P = -x^3 + 3x^2 + x - 3$$

The profit function factors, and the zeros are $x = -1$, $x = 1$, and $x = 3$. The leading coefficient is negative, so the graph begins above the x axis and ends below the x axis (see Figure 3-30). The approximation for maximum profit occurs at $(2, 3)$.

As previously pointed out, the x value for the maximum point of profit does not generally fall at the midpoint of the x axis intercepts. This point must be approximated, because the third-degree function does not have symmetry in the general case.

The points of intersection of the revenue and cost functions are found by solving:

$$R = C$$
$$7x = x^3 - 3x^2 + 6x + 3$$
$$0 = x^3 - 3x^2 - x + 3$$
$$0 = (x + 1)(x - 1)(x - 3)$$

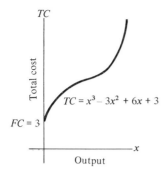

$TC = x^3 - 3x^2 + 6x + 3$

$FC = 3$

FIGURE 3-29

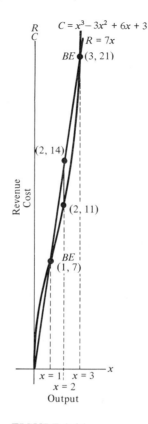

$C = x^3 - 3x^2 + 6x + 3$

$R = 7x$

$BE \; (3, 21)$

$(2, 14)$

$(2, 11)$

$BE \; (1, 7)$

$x = 1 \quad x = 3$

$x = 2$

Output

FIGURE 3-31

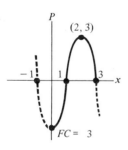

P

$(2, 3)$

$FC = 3$

FIGURE 3-30

and the *BE* points are $x = 1$ and $x = 3$ (see Figure 3-31). Maximum total profit is 3, and the approximation for maximum total profit is 2.

Example 2:   A firm's total cost function is given by:

$$TC = x^3 - 10x^2 + 100x + 10$$

Set up a schedule to demonstrate that *TC* increases first at a decreasing rate and then at an increasing rate. Although marginal cost cannot be found at a point, the delta definition can give us the change in cost over an interval and demonstrate the concavity of the cost function.

X	TC	$MC = \dfrac{\Delta C}{\Delta X}$
0	10	
1	101	91
2	178	77
3	247	69
4	314	67
5	385	71
6	466	81
7	563	97

TC increases at a decreasing rate in the interval (0, 3), because *MC* is positive and decreasing, until the point of inflection (at approximately $x = 3.5$). After that, *TC* increases at an increasing rate, because *MC* is positive and increasing (see Figure 3-32).

Example 3:   Use the delta definition of marginal cost to set up a schedule and determine the generally graphical appearance of marginal cost for a typical cost function given by:

$$C = x^3 - 10x^2 + 100x + 10$$

X	TC	$MC = \dfrac{\Delta C}{\Delta X}$
0	10	
1	101	91
2	178	77
3	247	69
4	314	67
5	385	71
6	466	81

Plotting the values for *MC* for corresponding *x* values we obtain a concave-up U-shaped curve (assumed to be a parabola) with its vertex in the first quadrant (see Figure 3-33).

In Example 2 we saw that the *x* value for the vertex of *MC* represents the *x* value for the point of inflection in *TC*. In Chapter 4 we will confirm that *MC* is indeed a concave-up parabola with its vertex in the first quadrant, if total cost is a typical third-degree function going from concave down to concave up while increasing. We will also demonstrate more concretely that the *x* coordinate for the vertex of *MC* represents the *x* coordinate for the point of inflection in total cost.

At this point we can make certain inductive conclusions regarding the relationship of *ATC* and *MC* to total cost. In Chapter 1 we demonstrated that, if total cost is represented by a first-degree polynomial, then marginal cost could be expressed by a

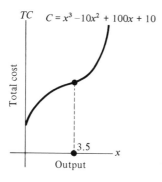

FIGURE 3-32

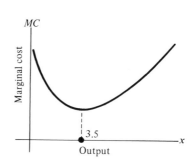

FIGURE 3-33

function of degree *one less* than total cost. We also pointed out that *ATC* would meet *MC* at minimum *ATC*, which means that *ATC* would have the same value as *MC* at infinity (see Figure 3-34).

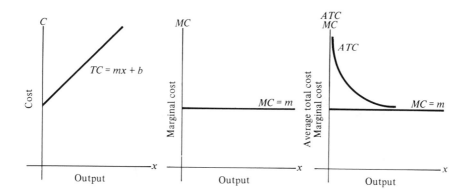

FIGURE 3-34

In Chapter 2 we demonstrated that, if total cost is represented by a second-degree polynomial, then marginal cost is represented by a first-degree polynomial (*MC* is a polynomial of degree *one less* than *TC*). We also showed that *MC* would intersect *ATC* at minimum *ATC* (see Figure 3-35).

These conclusions are also consistent for third-degree total cost functions. That is, if *TC* is represented by a third-degree polynomial that moves from concave down to concave up, then *MC* will be a second-degree polynomial with its vertex in the first quadrant and will be concave up. Moreover, *MC* will intersect *ATC* at minimum *ATC* (see Figure 3-36).

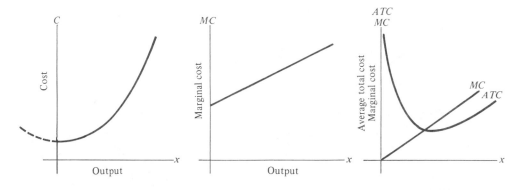

FIGURE 3-35

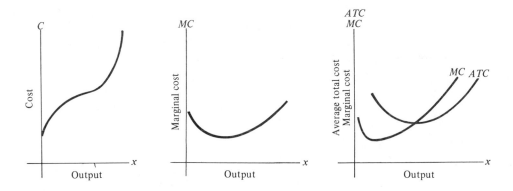

FIGURE 3-36

The above conclusions will be proved with rigor in Chapter 4.

PROBLEMS 3-5

*1. Sketch the graph of total cost for $TC = x^3 - 4x^2 + 3x + 10$.

*2. If total cost is given by $TC = x^3 - 4x^2 + 3x + 10$ and total revenue is given by $TR = 10x$, sketch the graph of total profit and approximate maximum total profit.

3. Given an example of a third-degree polynomial that represents total profit with break-even points at $x = 2$ and $x = 10$, sketch the graph of the example and approximate maximum total profit.

4. If total cost is represented by a third-degree polynomial, can you infer as to what the graph of marginal cost would be? Use the oversimplified total cost function $TC = x^3 + 2$ to substantiate your answer by setting up a table with values of X, TC, and MC. From this table sketch the graph of marginal cost.

3-6   EXPONENTIAL AND LOGARITHMIC FUNCTIONS

By definition an exponential function is one in which the variable is an exponent. The basic "model" to develop the art of curve sketching exponential functions will be:

$$y = 2^x$$

The graph is obtained by plotting a few convenient points: $f(0) = 1, f(1) = 2, f(2) = 4,$ $f(3) = 8, f(-1) = 1/2, f(-2) = 1/4 \ldots$ (see Figure 3-37).

FIGURE 3-37

The curve on the graph demonstrates exponential "growth." Exponential functions are known for their ability to increase or to decrease extremely fast. These functions can "outgrow" their algebraic counterparts with ease. As an example compare the algebraic function $y = x^2$ and $y = 2^x$:

x	$y = x^2$	$y = 2^x$
0	0	1
1	1	2
2	4	4
3	9	8
4	16	16
5	25	32
6	36	64
7	49	128
·	·	·
·	·	○
·	·	·
10	100	1024
·	·	·
·	·	·
·	·	·

A summary of "model" exponential functions follows; their graphs can be verified by plotting points and by letting x approach $\pm$ infinity (see Figures 3-38 through 3-43). (Dotted lines on the graphs indicate negative coefficients.)

Example 1:

$$y = b^x; \; b > 1$$

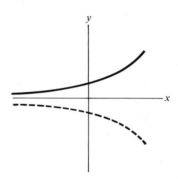

FIGURE 3-38

Example 2:

$$y = b^{-x}; \; b > 1$$

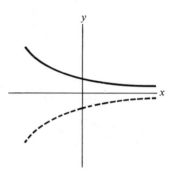

FIGURE 3-39

Example 3:

$$y = b^{x^2}; \; b > 1$$

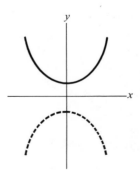

FIGURE 3-40

Example 4:

$$y = b^{-x^2} \; ; \; b > 1$$

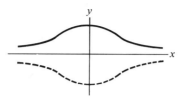

FIGURE 3-41

This is the "bell"-shaped curve or the "normal" curve.

Example 5:

$$y = b^x \; ; \; 0 < b < 1$$

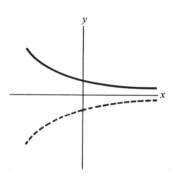

FIGURE 3-42

Example 6:

$$y = b^{-x} \; ; \; 0 < b < 1$$

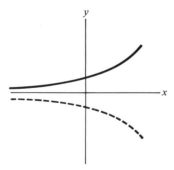

FIGURE 3-43

The coefficients of the preceding models were assumed to be +1. In the case of an arbitrary coefficient, K, the basic representation of the model will not change, but the y-axis intercept will be K instead of ±1 (see Figure 3-44). As in the algebraic case, vertical and horizontal translations of these models can be made.

Example 7:   Plot the graph of $y = 5e^x$, where $e = 2.71828 \ldots$ (see Figure 3-44).

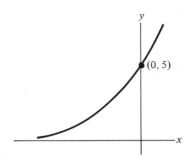

FIGURE 3-44

Logarithmic Functions

A logarithm is an exponent, and by convention:

$$(y = \log_b x) \text{ means } (x = b^y)$$

The "model" for the logarithm function will be $y = \log_{10} x$. In exponential form this function becomes: $x = 10^y$. The graph of $y = \log_{10} x$ or $x = 10^y$ can be obtained by plotting points from the following table (see Figure 3-45).

x	y
.	.
.	.
.	.
1/100	−2
1/10	−1
1	0
10	1
100	2
.	.
.	.
.	.

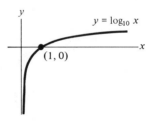

FIGURE 3-45

PROBLEMS 3-6

*1. Plot the graphs of the following exponential functions:

*a. $y = 3^x$ *c. $y = 3^{-x}$ e. $y = 3x^2$

*b. $y = (5)(3^x)$ d. $y = -3^x$ f. $y = 3^{-x^2}$

g. $y = \left(\dfrac{1}{3}\right)^x$

i. $y = -\left(\dfrac{1}{3}\right)^x$

k. $y = -10^{-x} + 5$

h. $y = \left(\dfrac{1}{3}\right)^{-x}$

j. $y = (\sqrt{2\pi})e^{-x^2}$

l. $y = \dfrac{10}{1 + 2^{-x}}$

*2. Given the following model functions $y = f(x)$ with horizontal translation con-
sisting of 2 units, make the substitution $z = x - 2$. This results in a transformation from $y = f(x)$ to $y = f(z)$. Sketch the graph of $y = f(x)$ in the (x, y) plane and
the graph of $y = f(z)$ in the (z, y) plane:

*a. $y = 2^{(x-2)^2}$

b. $y = e^{(x-2)^2}$, where $e = 2.71828 \ldots$

c. $y = e^{-(x-2)^2}$

d. $y = 6e^{-(x-2)^2}$

BASIC CALCULUS

4-1 DIFFERENTIAL CALCULUS

As we learned earlier, the single most important mathematical concept in business and economics is the slope of a linear function. In Chapter 1 the slope of a linear function was defined, and we noted that the words "slope" and "marginal" are synonymous. In Chapters 2 and 3 the concept of "slope" was virtually avoided, because the ideas of the slope of a line and the slope of a curve were not immediately interchangeable. If $y = f(x)$ is nonlinear, the slope is continually changing. The property that makes a function a curve is the fact that the slope is continually changing.

The study of *calculus* deals with slopes. Calculus is frequently categorized as differential calculus and integral calculus. Several sections in this chapter are devoted to differential calculus. Once a basic understanding of differential calculus has been obtained, we turn to integral calculus.

Differential calculus can be thought of as that branch of mathematics that is concerned with finding slopes of curves. The expression for the slope of a function is the *derivative of the function*. Stated another way, differential calculus is concerned with the problem of finding the slope of a straight line that is tangent to a curve at some point.

This problem can be stated pictorially (see Figure 4-1). The slope of the tangent line at (x, y) is the derivative of $y = f(x)$ at that point.

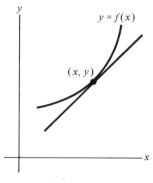

FIGURE 4-1

Definition of the Derivative of a Function

The slope of the tangent line at a point (x, y) for $y = f(x)$ is called the *derivative* of the function at the point (x, y). The derivative of a function is the single most important concept in mathematical economics, and the derivative of y with respect to x is:

$$\frac{dy}{dx} = y' = \lim_{\Delta x \to 0} \frac{f(x + \Delta x) - f(x)}{\Delta x} = \lim_{\Delta x \to 0} \frac{\Delta y}{\Delta x}$$

Observe that the definition of the derivative of $y = f(x)$ is essentially the same as the definition of the slope of a linear function, with the difference that $\Delta x \to 0$. By letting $\Delta x \to 0$ we find the slope at some particular point on $y = f(x)$. If $y = f(x)$ is linear, the slope is fixed, and there is no need to let $\Delta x \to 0$. However, for nonlinear functions the slope is changing, so letting $\Delta x \to 0$ is essential in finding the change in y with respect to the change in x for points on $y = f(x)$. The definition of the derivative of y with respect to x is:

$$\frac{dy}{dx} = y' = \text{slope of the tangent line at a point}$$

$$\frac{dy}{dx} = y' = \text{change of } y \text{ with respect to } x \text{ at a point}$$

It is also helpful to consider that the derivative of $y = f(x)$ gives us the "instantaneous" change of y with respect to x at some point (x, y) on the graph of $y = f(x)$, whereas $\Delta y/\Delta x$ gives the average change in y with respect to x over the interval in question. Both notations, dy/dx and y', are conventionally used to indicate the derivative of y with respect to x. The notation dy is the differential of y, and dx is the differential of x. Thus, the term "differential calculus" is used to refer to the branch of calculus concerned with derivatives of functions. A geometrical interpretation of the derivative of $y = f(x)$ follows. Figure 4-2 demonstrates the slope of a straight line between two points on the curve (the secant line), and Figure 4-3 demonstrates the derivative of $y = f(x)$ at a point. The slope of a line:

$$L_1 = \frac{\Delta y}{\Delta x} = \frac{f(x + \Delta x) - f(x)}{\Delta x}$$

represents the average change in y with respect to x over the interval.

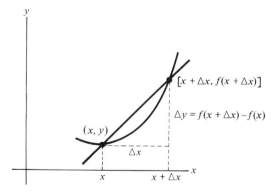

FIGURE 4-2

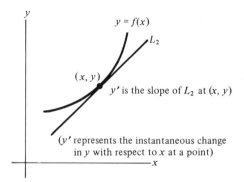

FIGURE 4-3

Finding Derivatives

The definition of the derivative can be applied directly to find the derivatives of functions. After a few examples we realize, however, there is a simple formula that can be used to find y' for algebraic functions.

Example 1:   Given that $y = 2x + 5$, find y' by using the definition of y'.

Solution.

$$y' = \lim_{\Delta x \to 0} \frac{f(x + \Delta x) - f(x)}{\Delta x}$$

$$y' = \lim_{\Delta x \to 0} \frac{[2(x + \Delta x) + 5] - (2x + 5)}{\Delta x}$$

We cannot let $\Delta x \to 0$ at this point, because division by 0 is undefined. Therefore, y' must be reduced, and the limit should be taken after the expression has completely been reduced.

$$y' = \lim_{\Delta x \to 0} 2 = 2$$

Conclusion.   Given that $y = 2x + 5$, then $y' = dy/dx = 2$. That is, for any point (x, y) on $y = f(x)$, the slope of the tangent line is 2.

Example 2:   Given that $y = x^2$, find y' by using the definition of y'.

Solution.

$$y' = \lim_{\Delta x \to 0} \frac{f(x + \Delta x) - f(x)}{\Delta x}$$

$$y' = \lim_{\Delta x \to 0} \frac{(x + \Delta x)^2 - x^2}{\Delta x}$$

y' must be reduced before we take the limit:

$$y = \lim_{\Delta x \to 0} \frac{x^2 + 2x\Delta x + \Delta x^2 - x^2}{\Delta x} = \frac{2x\Delta x + \Delta x^2}{\Delta x} = 2x + \Delta x$$

When we take the limit $\Delta x \to 0$, $y' = 2x$.

Conclusion.   Given that $y = x^2$, then $y' = 2x$. Notice that the derivative appears as a formula awaiting a value for x to determine the value of y', which represents the slope of the tangent line at a point. The derivative must appear as a formula with a variable, because the slope of $y = x^2$ is continually changing. A few examples give a geometrical appreciation of $y' = 2x$ as the derivative of $y = x^2$.

Example 3:   Find the slope of the tangent line for $y = x^2$ at $x = 1$. The derivative is $y' = 2x$ and at $x = 1$, $y' = 2$. Line L has slope of $+2$ (see Figure 4-4).

Example 4:   Find the slope of the tangent line for $y = x^2$ at $x = 2$. The derivative is $y' = 2x$ and for $x = 2$, $y' = 4$. Line L has slope of $+4$ (see Figure 4-5).

Example 5:   Find the slope of the tangent line for $y = x^2$ at $x = -1$. The derivative is $y' = 2x$ and at $x = -1$, $y' = -2$. Line L has slope of -2 (see Figure 4-6).

Example 6:   Find the slope of the tangent line for $y = x^2$ at $x = -2$. The derivative is $y' = 2x$ and at $x = -2$, $y' = -4$. Line L has slope of -4 (see Figure 4-7).

Example 7:   Find the slope of the tangent line for $y = x^2$ at $x = 0$. The derivative is $y' = 2x$ and at $x = 0$, $y' = 0$. Line L has slope of 0 (see Figure 4-8).

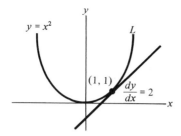

FIGURE 4-4

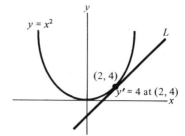

FIGURE 4-5

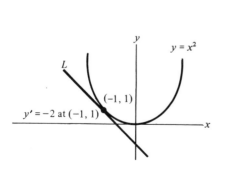

FIGURE 4-6

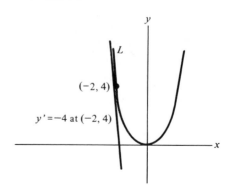

FIGURE 4-7

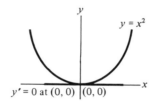

FIGURE 4-8

Example 8:   Given that $y = x^3$, find y' by using the definition of y'.

Solution.

$$y' = \lim_{\Delta x \to 0} \frac{(x + \Delta x)^3 - x^3}{\Delta x} = \frac{x^3 + 3x^2 \Delta x + 3x \Delta x^2 + \Delta x^3 - x^3}{\Delta x}$$

After dividing Δx into the numerator, take the limit:

$$y' = 3x^2$$

Conclusion.   The derivative of $y = x^3$ is $y' = 3x^2$. For example, when $x = 1, y' = 3$; when $x = -1$, $y' = 3$; when $x = 0$, $y' = 0$. These results can be given geometrical meaning (see Figure 4-9).

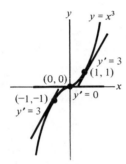

FIGURE 4-9

PROBLEMS 4-1

*1. Use the definition of the derivative:

$$y' = \lim_{\Delta x \to 0} \frac{f(x + \Delta x) - f(x)}{\Delta x}$$

to find the derivatives of the following functions:

*a. $y = c$ d. $y = 2x^2$

b. $y = mx + b$ e. $y = 2x^3$

c. $y = 3x - 4$ f. $y = x^4$

2. Give a geometrical interpretation of dy/dx for $y = 2x^2$ at $x = -2, x = -1, x = 0$, $x = 1, x = 2$.

4-2   THE DERIVATIVE OF $y = cx^n$

The examples in Section 4-1 showed that, for $y = x^2$, $y' = 2x$ and for $y = x^3$, $y' = 3x^2$. These examples inductively demonstrate the mechanical procedure for finding the derivative of a function of the form $y = x^n$. The exponent comes down and is multiplied by the function, and the exponent is reduced by 1 to form the derivative. This procedure holds for any exponent and any coefficient. This is known as the *power rule*.

The Power Rule

Given that $y = cx^n$:

$$\frac{dy}{dx} = y' = ncx^{n-1}$$

Proof.   The power rule will be proved for the case in which the coefficient of x is 1, and the exponent is a positive integer:

$$y' = \lim_{\Delta x \to 0} \frac{f(x + \Delta x) - f(x)}{\Delta x}$$

For $y = x^n$:

$$y' = \lim_{\Delta x \to 0} \frac{(x + \Delta x)^n - x^n}{\Delta x}$$

Using the binomial theorem for $(x + \Delta x)^n$:

$$y' = \lim_{\Delta x \to 0} \frac{x^n + nx^{n-1}\Delta x + \dfrac{n(n-1)x^{n-2}\Delta x^2}{2} + \ldots + \Delta x^n - x^n}{\Delta x}$$

The first and last terms cancel, and Δx divides into each term in the numerator. On taking the limit, we obtain:

$$y' = nx^{n-1}$$

Corollaries to the Power Rule

1. The derivative gives the slope of $y = f(x)$, so for the linear function $y = mx + b$, $y' = m$.

2. For $y = b$ (when b is constant), $y' = 0$.

3. For $x = b$ (when b is constant), y' is undefined.

4. The derivative of a sum is the sum of the derivatives: If $y = f(x) + g(x)$, then $y' = f'(x) + g'(x)$.

5. The derivative of a difference is the difference of the derivatives. If $y = f(x) - g(x)$, then $y' = f'(x) - g'(x)$.

The following examples demonstrate the power rule and its corollaries.

Example 1:   Find y' for the following (solution follows each problem):

a. $y = 3x - 5$ $y' = 3$

b. $y = 5$ $y' = 0$

c. $x = 0$ $y' = $ undefined

d. $y = 3x^5$ $y' = 15x^4$

e. $y = x^4 + 3x^3 - 5x^2 - 6x + 9$ $y' = 4x^3 + 9x^2 - 10x - 6$

f. $y = x^{-3}$ $y' = -3x^{-4}$

g. $y = x^{1/2}$ $y' = .5x^{-1/2}$

h. $y = \dfrac{x^3}{3} + \dfrac{x^2}{5} + 8$ $y' = x^2 + (2/5)x$

i. $y = -5x^{-4}$ $y' = 20x^{-5}$

j. $y = (-2/3)x^{-3/2}$ $y' = x^{-5/2}$

Example 2:   When $y = f(x)$ is not in the proper form $(y = cx^n)$ for differentiation, algebraic reductions must be made. Find y' for the following (solution follows each problem):

a. $y = \dfrac{x^4 + x^3}{x} = x^3 + x^2$ $y' = 3x^2 + 2x$

b. $y = \sqrt{x} = x^{1/2}$ $y' = .5x^{-1/2}$

c. $y = \dfrac{1}{x^2} = x^{-2}$ $y' = -2x^{-3}$

d. $3y = 6x^2$; $y = 2x^2$ $y' = 4x$

Example 3:   In order to find the derivative of $y = f(x)$ by using the power rule, we must give y explicitly and in the proper form $(y = cx^n)$. If y cannot be written in proper form, the derivative cannot be found by using the power rule. For example, $y = (x^3 - 3x^2 - 4x + 5)^{20}$, then y' can be found at this point only by expanding the function. The derivative of $y = \sqrt{x^2 - 5x + 6}$ is not obtainable by using the power rule. $y^2 = x$ is not explicit in y; however, it can be understood as $y = -\sqrt{x}$ or $y = \sqrt{x}$; y' can be found in each case.

Example 4:   Given that $y = 20x - x^2$, find the slope of the tangent line at the following points:

a. Point is (2, 36). For $y = 20x - x^2$, $y' = 20 - 2x$; at $x = 2$, $y' = 16$.

b. Point is (10, 100). For $y = 20x - x^2$, $y' = 20 - 2x$; at $x = 10$, $y' = 0$ (see Figure 4-10).

c. Point is (15, 75). For $y = 20x - x^2$, $y' = 20 - 2x$; at $x = 15$, $y' = -10$ (see Figure 4-11).

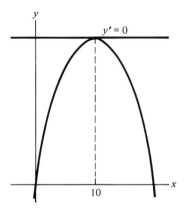

FIGURE 4-10

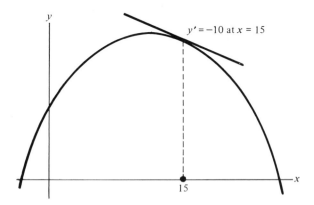

FIGURE 4-11

Example 5:   If a more representative variable is desired for $y = f(x)$, the substitution can be made and included in the derivative notation. For example, cost $= C =$ $2x^2 + 4x + 6$, $dC/dx = 4x + 4$; C' represents MC (x represents output); revenue $=$ $R = 20x - x^2$, $dR/dx = 20 - 2x$; R' represents MR (x represents output); consumption $= C = \sqrt{I} + 2$, $dC/dI = .5I^{-1/2}$; C' represents MPC (I represents income); profit $= P = -x^2 + 4x - 2$, $dP/dx = -2x + 4$; P' represents MP; total product $= X = 9U^2 - U^3$, $dx/dU = 18U - 3U^2$; X' represents the marginal productivity of U (U represents units of input).

PROBLEMS 4-2

*1. Find y' by using the power rule (and its corollaries):

*a. $y = mx + b$

*b. $y = 8 - 9x$

*c. $y = -4x^2 + 8x - 7$

*d. $y = 12x - x^2$

e. $y = 20x - 2x^2$

f. $y = ax^2 + bx + c$

g. $y = ax^3 + bx^2 + cx + d$

h. $y = -3x^3 + 6$

i. $y = \dfrac{x^3}{3} + \dfrac{x^2}{2} + .0034x - 7$

j. $y = .004x^4 - 6.43x + 7.65$

k. $y = \sqrt[3]{2x}$

l. $y = \dfrac{7}{x^5}$

m. $y = \dfrac{x^3 - 8}{x - 2}$

n. $y = (x^2 + 2)^2$

*2. Find dx/dy (the reciprocal of dy/dx) for the following:

*a. $y = 12 - 3x$ b. $y = 3x^2 - 5$ c. $y = 5x^3 - 3x^2 + 8x - 9$

*3. Find dz/dw for the following:

*a. $z = 3w + 5$

*b. $z = 4w^2 - 8w + 5$

c. $z = 3x^2 w$ ($x =$ constant)

d. $z = 3x^2 y^5 w^7$ ($x, y =$ constant)

e. $w = 8z^2 + 5$

*4. Using $f(x) = 6x$ and $g(x) = 4x$, give a particular proof that the derivative of a sum (or difference) is equal to the sum (or difference) of the derivatives; that is:

$$\frac{d}{dx}\left[f(x) \pm g(x) \right] = f'(x) \pm g'(x)$$

5. Using $f(x) = 8x$ and $g(x) = 4x$, give a particular proof that:

a. the derivative of the product *does not* equal the product of the derivatives; that is:

$$\frac{d}{dx}\left[f(x) \cdot g(x) \right] \neq f'(x) \cdot g'(x)$$

b. the derivative of a quotient *does not* equal the quotient of the derivatives; that is:

$$\frac{d}{dx}\left[\frac{f(x)}{g(x)}\right] \neq \frac{f'(x)}{g'(x)}$$

*6. Find the slopes of the tangent lines for the following functions at these values of x: $x = 0, x = 1, x = 2, x = -1, x = -2$. Interpret the results graphically:

*a. $y = 2x^2 + 4$ b. $y = x^3$ c. $y = \dfrac{1}{x}$

7. Find the slopes of the tangent lines for the following functions for these values of x: $x = 0, x = 1, x = 16$. Interpret the results graphically:

a. $y = \sqrt{x}$ b. $y = \sqrt[4]{x}$

8. Given that $y = 12x - 3x^2$, find the slope of the tangent lines for the following values of x: $x = 0, x = 1, x = 2, x = 3, x = 4$. Interpret the results graphically.

9. Given that $y = ax^2 + bx + c$, find the slope of the tangent line at $x = -b/2a$.

10. Find the slope of the tangent line for $y = 27 - x^3$ at the following values of x: $x = 0, x = 1, x = 2, x = 3$. Interpret the results graphically.

11. Find the slopes of the tangent lines for the following values of x: $x = 0, x = 1$, $x = 2, x = 10$ given that $y = x^3 + 2x^2 + 4x + 10$.

12. Assume that total cost is represented by $C = x^3 - 2x^2 + 8x + b$.

a. Find dC/dx at $x = 1, x = 2$, and $x = 10$. Interpret the results graphically.

b. Sketch the graph of dC/dx. What does the graph represent?

13. Assume that total revenue is given by $R = 100x - x^2$.

a. Find dR/dx for $x = 1, x = 10, x = 25, x = 40$. Interpret these results graphically.

b. Sketch the graph of dR/dx. What does the graph represent?

4-3   THE DERIVATIVE OF A FUNCTION: THE SINGLE MOST IMPORTANT CONCEPT IN MATHEMATICAL ECONOMICS

The derivative of a function is the single most important mathematical concept in economics. It gives not only the slope of a straight line but also the rate of change of y with respect to x at any point on a curve. We now have the means—the power rule— to find marginal y for any curve that can be expressed as $y = cx^n$. Derivatives of functions play a key role in three general areas in business and economics: (1) curve sketching of functions, (2) determining the elasticity of functions, (3) determining the marginals of functions. These areas will be considered in the following three sections.

4-4   THE DERIVATIVE: CURVE SKETCHING

Analogies can be made between the slope of linear functions and the derivative of $y = f(x)$. If $y = f(x)$ is increasing, then y' is positive; if $y = f(x)$ is decreasing, then y' is negative; if $y = f(x)$ levels off, then y' is 0; and if y is tangent to a vertical line, then y' is undefined.

Example 1:   If $y = f(x)$ is increasing, then the slope of the tangent line to a point is positive (y' is positive). (See Figure 4-12.)

Example 2:   Given that the cost function $C = x^3 - 3x^2 + 6x + 3$ and $C' = 3x^2 - 6x + 6$, notice that C' is positive for any positive value of x; therefore, C is increasing (see Figure 4-13).

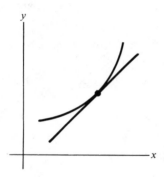

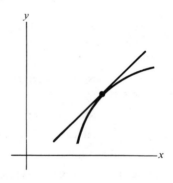

FIGURE 4-12

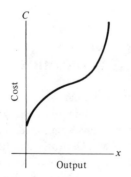

FIGURE 4-13

Example 3:   If $y = f(x)$ is decreasing, then y' is negative (see Figure 4-14).

Example 4:   Given that the demand expression $y = -x^3 + 8$, then $y' = -3x^2 < 0$. Notice that y' is negative for any value of $x > 0$; therefore, y is decreasing (see Figure 4-15).

Example 5:   If $y = f(x)$ levels off, then $y' = 0$ at this point. This point is the *critical point* and the curve has three possibilities here—concave up, concave down, and changing in concavity (see Figure 4-16).

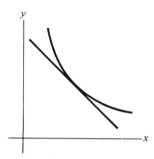
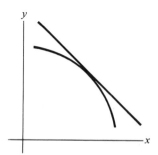

FIGURE 4-14

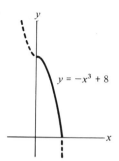

FIGURE 4-15

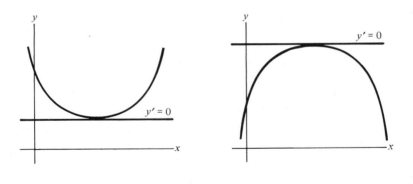

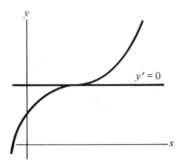

FIGURE 4-16

The Application of First Derivatives to Profit

Example 6:   Find the point of maximum profit for $P = (-x^3/3) + x^2 + 8x - 5$.

Solution.   The leading coefficient is negative, which means that the curve begins above the x axis and ends below the x axis with P-axis intercept at -5. Profit levels off when $P' = 0$:

$P' = -x^2 + 2x + 8$, and solving $-x^2 + 2x + 8 = 0$ gives

$x^2 - 2x - 8 = 0$ or $(x + 2)(x - 4) = 0$

and $P' = 0$ when $x = -2$ and $x = 4$. For $x = -2$, $P = -14.3$, and for $x = 4$, $P = 21.6$. The positive value of x is the point of maximum profit, so for output of $x = 4$ units the maximum profit is $P = 21.6$ units (see Figure 4-17).

Example 7: Find the point of maximum profit for $P = -x^3 + 3x^2 + x - 3$.

Solution. The leading coefficient is negative, which means that the curve begins above the x axis and ends below the x axis with $FC = -3$. This function factors, and the x-axis intercepts are $x = 1, x = 3$, and $x = -1$. Do not assume that maximum profit is at the midpoint of the BE points ($x = 2$), because P is not symmetrical with respect to the axis. Maximum profit is found by solving $P' = 0$:

$$P' = -3x^2 + 6x + 1 = 0$$

This expression does not factor, so the quadratic formula must be used to find the critical points. Solve $P' = -3x^2 + 6x + 1 = 0$ by formula (see Figure 4-18):

$$x = \frac{-6 \pm \sqrt{48}}{-6}$$

$x = -.15; \; x = 2.1$ (maximum profit)

The Application of First Derivatives to Total Cost and to Average Total Cost

Example 8: Given that $TC = x^3 - 2x^2 + 4x + 8$, sketch the graph of ATC and indicate minimum ATC.

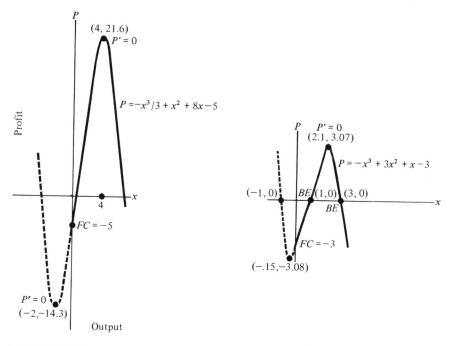

FIGURE 4-17   FIGURE 4-18

Solution. $ATC = TC/x = x^2 - 2x + 4 + (8/x)$, and the minimum point is found by solving $ATC' = 0$.

$$ATC = 2x - 2 - \frac{8}{x^2} = 0$$

$$x^3 - x^2 - 4 = 0$$

$$(x - 2)(x^2 + x + 2) = 0$$

which gives $x - 2$ and $ATC = 8$ as the minimum point for ATC (see Figure 4-19).

To the left of minimum ATC ($x = 2$), ATC' is negative, and thus the curve is decreasing. To the right of minimum ATC ($x = 2$), ATC' is positive, and thus ATC is increasing. We assume here that ATC is concave up and will consider the test for concavity shortly.

The Application of First Derivatives to the Production Function

Example 9:   A total product function is given by $X = 9U^2 - U^3$, where X represents the total product and U represents the units of input. Find maximum total product.

Solution. $dX/dU = X' = 18U - 3U^2$, and the derivative is 0 for $U = 0$ and $U = 6$. X is a third-degree polynomial with negative leading coefficients and zeros of $U = 0$ and $U = 9$. Maximum total product occurs at $(6, 108)$. (See Figure 4-20.)

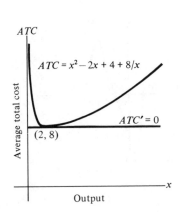

FIGURE 4-19

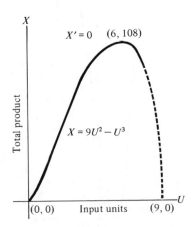

FIGURE 4-20

To the left of $U = 6$, dX/dU is positive, and thus $X = f(U)$ is increasing. To the right of $U = 6$, dX/dU is negative and thus $X = f(U)$ is decreasing. $X = f(U)$ changes from concave up to concave down, and this is appreciated by the fact that $X = f(U)$ is a third-degree polynomial whose behavior we have studied. Moreover, the first derivative tells us where a function is increasing, decreasing, or levels off but does not furnish information concerning concavity. We will consider concavity shortly.

The Application of First Derivatives to Revenue

Example 10:   If demand to an imperfectly competitive firm is given by $y = 16 - x^2$, then the revenue function is $R = yx - (16 - x^2)(x) = 16x - x^3$. The revenue function is a third-degree polynomial with a negative leading coefficient and zeros at $x = -4, 0$, and 4. The point of maximum revenue is found by solving $R' = 0$:

$$R' = 16 - 3x^2 = 0$$

which gives $x = \sqrt{16/3} = 2.3$ (see Figure 4-21).

Example 11:   If demand to an imperfectly competitive seller is given by $y = mx + b$ (when m is negative and b is positive), then the firm's revenue function is:

$$R = yx = (mx + b)x = mx^2 + bx$$

The point of maximum revenue is found by solving $R' = 0$:

$$R' = 2mx + b = 0$$

and $x = -b/2m$ is the x value for maximum revenue (see Figure 4-22).

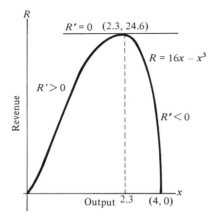

FIGURE 4-21

Example 12:   If demand to an imperfectly competitive seller is given by $y = 28 - x$ and the firm's total cost function is:

$$C = x^3 - x^2 + x + 1$$

then maximize the firm's revenue function, maximize the firm's profit function, and sketch a conclusion concerning the relationship of maximum profit to the elasticity of demand.

The firm's revenue function is:

$$R = yx = (28 - x)x = 28x - x^2$$

and maximum revenue is found by solving $R' = 28 - 2x = 0$ or $x = 14$ (see Figure 4-23).

The firm's profit function is $P = R - C$:

$$P = (28x - x^2) - (x^3 - x^2 + x + 1) = -x^3 + 27x - 1$$

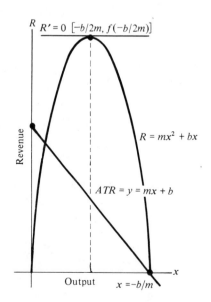

FIGURE 4-22

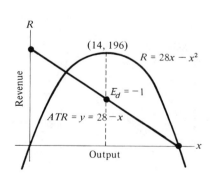

FIGURE 4-23

Maximum profit is found by solving $P' = -3x^2 + 27 = 0$; therefore, $x = 3$ (see Figure 4-24).

From the revenue function we know that, from $x = 0$ to $x = 14$, demand is relatively elastic (revenue is increasing). Profit is maximized at $x = 3$, which means that profit is maximized at a point at which demand is relatively elastic (revenue is increasing).

Example 13:   If $y = f(x)$ is tangent to a line parallel to the y axis, then y' is undefined (see Figure 4-25).

Example 14:   Given that supply is represented by $y = \sqrt{x} + 2$, then $y' = 1/2\sqrt{x}$, and at $x = 0$, $y' = 1/0$ (undefined). (See Figure 4-26.)

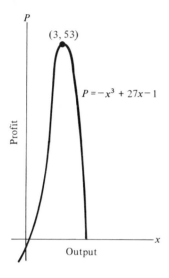

FIGURE 4-24

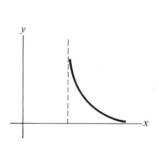

FIGURE 4-25

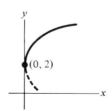

FIGURE 4-26

The Second Derivative and Concavity

Determining concavity using the first derivative is tedious and can be simplified by using the second derivative. The second derivative of $y = f(x)$ is obtained by taking the derivative of $y = f(x)$ twice and is symbolized by:

$$y'' = \frac{d^2 y}{dx^2}$$

We place the "2" in the numerator in this manner in order to avoid confusion with squaring the derivative. A few examples illustrate the second derivative:

$$y = x^5 ; \ y' = 5x^4 ; \ y'' = 20x^3$$
$$y = 3x; \ y' = 3; \ y'' = 0$$
$$y = 2x^2 - 2x - 2; \ y'' = 4$$

The second derivative at a point will be a specific number; in each case the number gives information concerning the concavity of $y = f(x)$ according to whether y'' is negative, zero, or positive.

Example 15:   If y'' is positive at a point, then $y = f(x)$ is concave up at the point. y'' measures the change of y'. If y is concave up, then as x increases, y' increases, and therefore y'' is positive, which makes the graph of $y = x^2$ concave up (see Figure 4-27).

Example 16:   If y'' is negative at a point, then $y = f(x)$ is concave down at the point. y'' measures the change in y'. If y is concave down, then as x increases, y' decreases, and therefore y'' is negative, which makes the graph of $y = -x^2$ concave down (see Figure 4-28).

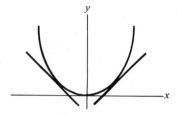

FIGURE 4-27

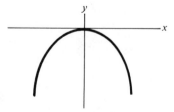

FIGURE 4-28

Example 17: If $y'' = 0$ at a point, then $y = f(x)$ has a *point of inflection*. A point of inflection demonstrates a change of concavity. For example, $y = x^3$ has a point of inflection at $x = 0$, because $y'' = 0$ for $y'' = 3x^2$. At the point of inflection concavity changes sense (see Figure 4-29).

The Application of Second Derivatives to Profit

Example 18: Determine the concavity of $P = -x^3 + 3x^2 + x - 3$ at the point where $P' = 0$ for positive x.

Solution. $P' = 0$ when $x = 2.1$. To test the concavity of P at the point $x = 2.1$, we find the second derivative:

$$P'' = -6x + 6$$

and at $x = 2.1$, $P'' = -6.6$, which means that profit is concave down at the critical point; profit is maximized at $P' = 0$ (see Figure 4-30).

The Application of Second Derivatives to Revenue

Example 19: Determine the concavity for $R = 20x - x^2$.

Solution. $R'' = -2$, which means that revenue is always concave down (see Figure 4-31).

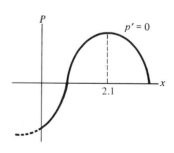

FIGURE 4-30

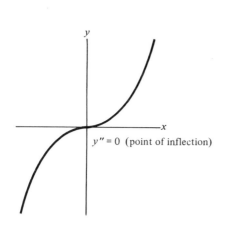

$y'' = 0$ (point of inflection)

FIGURE 4-29

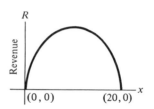

FIGURE 4-31

The Application of Second Derivatives to Average Total Cost

Example 20:   Determine the concavity of ATC for $TC = x^3 - 2x^2 + 4x + 8$.

Solution. $ATC = x^2 - 2x + 4 + 8/x$ ($ATC' = 0$ for $x = 2$, $ATC = 8$). The second derivative is $ATC'' = 2 + (16/x^3)$, which is always positive; thus ATC is concave up and $(2, 8)$ represents minimum ATC (see Figure 4-32).

The Application of Second Derivatives to Total Cost

Example 21:   Determine the concavity of $C = x^3 - 3x^2 + 6x + 3$.

Solution. $C' = 3x^2 - 6x + 6$ (C' is positive, which means that cost increases). $C'' = 6x - 6$, and C'' is 0 when $x = 1$ (point of inflection). If x is less than 1, then C'' is negative and C is concave down. If x is greater than 1, then C'' is positive and C is concave up (see Figure 4-33).

The Application of Second Derivatives to the Production Function

Example 22:   Plot the graph of the following total product function in which x represents total product and U represents units of input:

$$X = 9U^2 - U^3$$

$X' = 18U - 3U^2$, and X reaches a maximum at $U = 6$, $X = 108$. $X'' = 18 - 6U$ and the point of inflection is at $U = 3$, $X = 54$. To the left of $U = 3$, X'' is positive, and thus X is concave up. To the right of $U = 3$, X'' is negative, and thus X is concave down (see Figure 4-34).

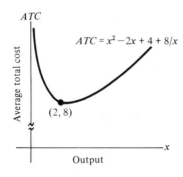

FIGURE 4-32

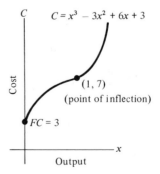

FIGURE 4-33

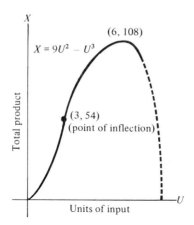

FIGURE 4-34

The Application of Second Derivatives to Consumption and Savings

Example 23:   Sketch the graphs of consumption and savings for consumption as given by:

$$C = 12 + .6I + 4\sqrt{I}$$

$C' = .6 + 2/\sqrt{I}$, and C' is positive, which means that consumption is increasing. $C'' = -1/\sqrt{I^3}$, and C'' is negative, which means that consumption is concave down (see Figure 4-35).

The savings function is determined by $S = I - C$:

$$S = I - (12 + .6I + .4\sqrt{I}) = -12 + .4I - .4\sqrt{I}$$

$S' = .4 - (.2/\sqrt{I})$, and S' is positive, which means that savings is increasing. $S'' = -(.1/\sqrt{I^3})$, and S'' is positive, which means that savings is concave up (see Figure 4-36).

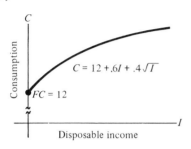

FIGURE 4-35

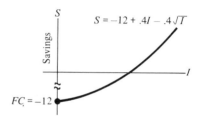

FIGURE 4-36

PROBLEMS 4-4

*1. For the following functions determine where $f'(x)$ is positive [y is increasing], $f'(x)$ is negative (y is decreasing), $f'(x) = 0$ (y levels off), $f'(x)$ is undefined (y is tangent to a vertical line). Interpret the results graphically:

*a. $y = x^4$ h. $y = -x^2 + 8x$ o. $y = x^3 + 3x^2 + 4x + 4$

*b. $y = x^3$ i. $y = 20x - x^2$ p. $y = \dfrac{5}{x}$

*c. $y = x^2 - 4x + 4$ j. $y = 12x - x^2$

d. $y = x^2 - 5x + 6$ k. $y = 20x - 2x^2$ q. $y = \dfrac{1}{x^2}$

e. $y = -2x^2 + 4x + 8$ l. $y = ax^2 + bx + c$

f. $y = 2x^2 - 4x - 4$ m. $y = -x^3 + 9$ r. $y = \sqrt{x}$

g. $y = -x^2 + 8x + 2$ n. $y = 4x^2 - x^3$

*2. For the following revenue functions determine where R' is positive', determine where R' is negative, determine where $R' = 0$. These points tell us where revenue increases, where revenue levels off, and where revenue decreases (x is positive). Plot the graphs.

*a. $R = 12x - 3x^2$ c. $R = 100x - x^2$ e. $R = -x^4 + 64x$

b. $R = 18x - 3x^2$ d. $R = 100x - 2x^2$ f. $R = 4x - x^{3/2}$

*3. Using the first derivative test determine for what values of x total cost is increasing in the following. Sketch the graphs of total cost and dC/dx, and explain the relationship between the graphs:

*a. $C = \dfrac{x^3}{3} - x^2 + 4x + 10$ b. $C = x^3 - 2x^2 + 8x + 10$

4. For total cost given by $C = 2x^3 - 4x^2 + 8x + 16$ sketch the graph of average total cost, indicating the values of x where ATC is decreasing and ATC is increasing. Also indicate the point of minimum ATC.

*5. Plot the graphs of the following profit functions, indicating the point of maximum profit:

*a. $P = \dfrac{-x^3}{3} + x^2 + 15x - 10$ c. $P = \dfrac{-x^3}{3} + 2x^2 + 12x - 10$

b. $P = \dfrac{-x^3}{3} + x^2 + 16x - 10$ d. $P = -x^3 + 2x^2 + 14x - 10$

6. Given that the consumption function $C = .5\sqrt{I} + .7I + 10$, use the first derivative to find the values of x where C is increasing. Also find the slopes of the tangent lines for $x = 1, x = 4$, and $x = 9$. Sketch the graph of consumption.

7. Given that the production function $x = 36U^2 - U^3$, determine where $x = f(U)$ is increasing, is decreasing, and levels off. Plot the graph of the production function, and indicate maximum total product.

*8. Use the second derivative to determine the concavity of the following functions for positive values of x. Sketch the graphs of the functions:

*a. $y = 16 - x^2$ (represents demand)

*b. $y = -x^3 + 27$ (represents demand)

c. $y = -\sqrt{x} + 4$ (represents demand)

d. $R = 12x - x^2$ (represents total revenue)

e. $R = 14x - 2x^2$ (represents total revenue)

f. $C = \dfrac{x^3}{3} - x^2 + 4x + 10$ (represents total cost)

g. $C = x^3 - 2x^2 + 8x + 10$ (represents total cost)

h. $C = .5\sqrt{I} + .7I + 10$ (represents consumption)

i. $ATC = \dfrac{2x + 6}{x}$ (represents average total cost)

j. $ATC = x^3 - 2x^2 + 8x + 10$ (represents average total cost)

k. $x = 36U^2 - U^3$ (represents the production function)

l. $y = ax^2 + bx + c$

9. Given that the total cost function $C = x^3/3 - x^2 + 4x + 10$, use the second derivative to find the point of inflection. Show graphically where total cost is concave up and concave down. Also sketch the graph of $MC = C'$ and relate the graph of C' to the graph of $C = f(x)$.

4-5   THE DERIVATIVE AND ELASTICITY

The Elasticity of Demand

Demand expressions are conventionally expressed as $y = f(x)$, where y represents price and x represents quantity demanded. The elasticity of demand was seen in Chapter 1, and for linear demand expressions the point *elasticity* was defined as:

$$E_d = \left(\frac{\Delta x}{\Delta y}\right)\left(\frac{y}{x}\right) \quad \text{where} \quad \frac{\Delta x}{\Delta y} = \frac{1}{\dfrac{\Delta y}{\Delta x}}$$

By extending the idea of the slope of a straight line to the derivative of $y = f(x)$ the elasticity of demand at a point (x, y) is:

$$E_d = \left(\frac{dx}{dy}\right)\left(\frac{y}{x}\right) \quad \text{where} \quad \frac{dx}{dy} = \frac{1}{\dfrac{dy}{dx}}$$

Example 1:   Given that demand is expressed by $y = -x^3 + 64$, sketch the graph of y and find E_d at the following points on the curve (see Figure 4-37):

a. $(0, 64)$ c. $(2, 56)$ e. $(4, 0)$
b. $(1, 63)$ d. $(3, 37)$

Solution.   By definition:

$$E_d = \left(\frac{dx}{dy}\right)\left(\frac{y}{x}\right)$$

where dx/dy is the reciprocal of dy/dx. For $y = -x^3 + 64$, $dy/dx = -3x^2$, and thus $dx/dy = -1/3x^2$, which gives:

$$E_d = \left(\frac{-1}{3x^2}\right)\left(\frac{y}{x}\right)$$

a. At $x = 0, E_d = (-1/0)(64/0) = -\infty$ (purely elastic).
b. At $x = 1, E_d = (-1/3)(63/1) = -63/3$ (relatively elastic).
c. At $x = 2, E_d = (-1/12)(56/2) = -56/24$ (relatively elastic).
d. At $x = 3, E_d = (-1/27)(37/3) = -37/81$ (relatively inelastic).
e. At $x = 4, E_d = (-1/48)(0/4) = 0$ (purely inelastic).

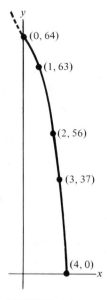

FIGURE 4-37

Notice that E_d is not unit elasticity at the midpoint of the x-axis intercept ($x = 2$). At the midpoint E_d is relatively elastic. Therefore, $E_d = -1$ to the right of the midpoint ($x = 2$).

Example 2:   Given that $y = -x^3 + 64$, find the point (x, y) where $E_d = -1$.

Solution.   By definition:

$$E_d = \left(\frac{dx}{dy}\right)\left(\frac{y}{x}\right)$$

and for $y = -x^3 + 64$:

$$E_d = \left(\frac{-1}{3x^2}\right)\left(\frac{y}{x}\right) = \left(\frac{-1}{3x^2}\right)\left(\frac{-x^3 + 64}{x}\right) = \frac{x^3 - 64}{3x^3}$$

To find the point at which $E_d = -1$ means to solve:

$$\frac{x^3 - 64}{3x^3} = -1$$
$$x^3 - 64 = -3x^3$$
$$4x^3 = 64$$
$$x^3 = 16$$
$$x = 2.5; \ y = 48$$

We can show that elasticity is -1 to the right of the midpoint of the x-axis intercept (see Figure 4-38).

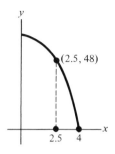

FIGURE 4-38

Example 3:   Given that demand is expressed by the polynomial $y = x^2 - 4x + 4$, where x varies from 0 to 2 units, find the point of unit elasticity.

Solution. $dy/dx = 2x - 4$, which means that $dx/dy = 1/(2x - 4)$ for x between 0 and 2. To find the point where $E_d = -1$ means to solve:

$$E_d = \left(\frac{1}{2x - 4}\right)\left(\frac{y}{x}\right) = \frac{(x - 2)(x - 2)}{2(d - 2)x} = \frac{x - 2}{2x} = -1$$

or $x - 2 = -2x$ and $3x = 2$, which gives $x = 2/3$, and $y = f(2/3) = 1.78$ (see Figure 4-39). $E_d = -1$ to the left of the midpoint of the x-axis intercept (2/3, 1.78).

Example 4:   We saw previously that the expression $y = 1/x^a$ (where a is positive) represents a reciprocal relationship between x and y and is therefore a good model to represent demand. This function generates a constant elasticity of demand: $E_d = -1/a$ (where a is positive). Find the elasticity of demand for $y = 1/x^a$ (where a is positive).

Solution.

$$E_d = \left(\frac{dx}{dy}\right)\left(\frac{y}{x}\right) = \frac{-(x^{a+1})}{a} \cdot \frac{\frac{1}{x^a}}{1} = \frac{-1}{a} \quad (a \text{ is positive})$$

$y = 1/x^a$ results in $E_d = -1/a$ (where a is positive). (See Figure 4-40.)

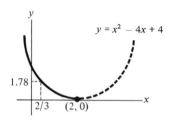

FIGURE 4-39

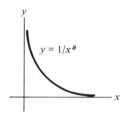

FIGURE 4-40

Elasticity and Revenue

The elasticity of demand to the individual firm can be understood in relation to the seller's revenue. If elasticity is relatively elastic, then the firm's revenue is increasing; if elasticity is relatively inelastic, then the firm's revenue is decreasing; if elasticity is unit, then the firm's revenue is maximum:

	relatively elastic	unit elasticity	relatively inelastic	
$-\infty$	revenue increasing	-1 maximum revenue	revenue decreasing	0

Example 5: In order to demonstrate the relationship between E_d and revenue, assume that demand is given by $y = 16 - x^2$. To find the point where $E_d = -1$, solve:

$$E_d = \left(\frac{dx}{dy}\right)\left(\frac{y}{x}\right) = \left(\frac{-1}{2x}\right)\left(\frac{16 - x^2}{x}\right) = -1$$

$$x = \sqrt{\frac{16}{3}} = 2.3$$

The revenue function is $R = yx = (16 - x^2)x = 16x - x^3$, and maximum revenue is found by solving (see Figure 4-41):

$$R' = 16 - 3x^2 = 0$$

$$x = \sqrt{\frac{16}{3}} = 2.3$$

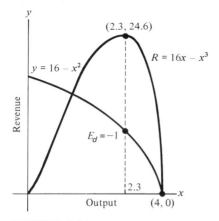

FIGURE 4-41

Example 6:   If demand to an imperfectly competitive firm is given by $y = mx + b$ (when m is negative and b is positive), then a firm's revenue function is maximized when $E_d = -1$. An algebraic proof of this was given in Chapter 2; here we will prove it with calculus. Assume that $y = mx + b$ represents the firm's demand curve; then revenue is:

$$R = yx = (mx + b)x = mx^2 + bx \text{ (} m \text{ is negative, } b \text{ is positive)}$$

Maximum revenue occurs when $MR = 0$:

$$MR = 2mx + b = 0$$

$$x = \frac{-b}{2m}$$

E_d is -1 at the same point; this is determined by:

$$E_d = \left(\frac{\Delta x}{\Delta y}\right)\left(\frac{y}{x}\right) = \left(\frac{1}{m}\right)\left(\frac{mx + b}{x}\right) = -1$$

or $mx + b = -mx$, which gives $x = -b/2m$ as the point where $E_d = -1$ (see Figure 4-42).

Elasticity and Profit

The revenue function of an imperfectly competitive firm is maximized when $R' = 0$ or $E_d = -1$. This does not mean that the firm's profit function is maximized at the same point, because profit is also dependent on cost. However, if demand to an imperfectly competitive firm is expressed by $y = mx + b$ (when m is negative and b is positive), then the firm's profit function is maximized at a point where E_d is relatively elastic (revenue is increasing).

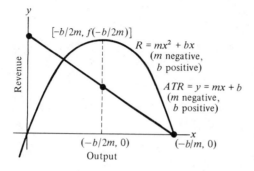

FIGURE 4-42

Example 7:   Assume that a firm's demand curve is given by $y = 22 - (3x/2)$ and its cost function is $TC = x^3 - 3x^2 + 4x + 4$. The profit function is determined by $P = R - C$, and profit is maximized when $P' = 0$:

$$P = \left(22x - \frac{3x^2}{2}\right) - (x^3 - 3x^2 + 4x + 4)$$

$$P' = (22 - 3x) - (3x^2 - 6x + 4) = 0$$

$$x = 3$$

The elasticity of demand is unit at the midpoint of the x-axis for $y = 22 - 3x/2$, and thus $E_d = -1$ at $x = 22/3$. Therefore, E_d is relatively elastic to the left of $22/3$, and the profit function is maximized at $x = 3$ (see Figures 4-43 and 4-44).

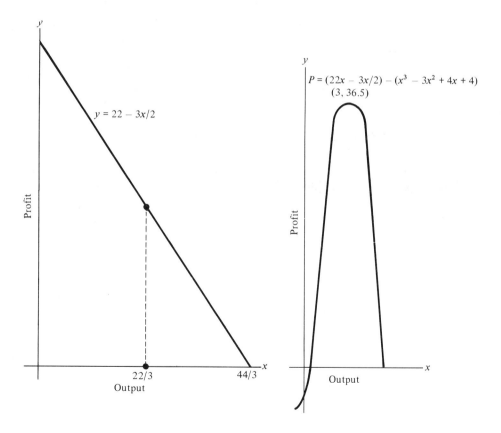

FIGURE 4-43   FIGURE 4-44

PROBLEMS 4-5

*1. Find E_d for all integer points on the graphs of the following demand curves. Sketch the graphs of $y = f(x)$, indicating elasticities:

   *a. $y = 16 - x^2$ b. $y = 125 - x^3$

2. If demand is represented by a linear function, then the elasticity of demand is -1 at the midpoint of the line. If demand is represented by a nonlinear expression, this is no longer true. For demand expressed by $y = 16 - x^2$, find the value for x where $E_d = -1$.

*3. Find expressions for E_d for the following demand curves:

   *a. $y = \dfrac{1}{x^2}$ b. $y = \dfrac{1}{y^3}$ c. $y = \dfrac{1}{\sqrt{x}}$

4. From the individual firm's viewpoint the elasticity of demand determines if the firm's revenue function increases, reaches a maximum, or decreases. For demand expressed by $y = 32 - x^2$ determine what values of x result in y's being relatively elastic, unit elasticity, and relatively inelastic. Sketch the graph of demand and indicate the values where demand is relatively elastic, unit elasticity, and relatively inelastic. Sketch the graph of total revenue, and indicate the point of maximum revenue $(R' = 0)$. Superimpose the graphs of demand and revenue. If demand is relatively elastic, what is the result of an increase in price?

4-6   THE DERIVATIVE AS MEANING MARGINAL

For $y = (x)$ the term "marginal y" is synonymous with the derivative of y. The derivative of y gives the rate of change of y with respect to x at a point on the curve. In the applied sense this means that we have an important method for measuring the change in economic variables at any point on $y = f(x)$. Stated in formula form:

$$\text{marginal } y = \frac{dy}{dx} = \lim_{x \to 0} \frac{\Delta y}{\Delta x}$$

The Marginal Propensities to Consume and to Save

If $C = f(\text{income}) = f(I)$ represents a consumption function, then C' represents the marginal propensity to consume (MPC); and if $S = f(I)$ represents a savings function, then S' represents the marginal propensity to save (MPS). It is also noted that $MPC + MPS = 1 = 100\%$. Stated in formula form:

$$MPC = C' = \lim_{I \to 0} \frac{\Delta C}{\Delta I}$$

$$MPS = S' = \lim_{I \to 0} \frac{\Delta S}{\Delta I}$$

In other words, C' represents the instantaneous change in consumption at a point. S' represents the instantaneous change in savings at a point.

The Multiplier

The multiplier effect that results from new spending was defined in Chapter 1 as $k = 1/(1 - MPC)$ or $k = 1/MPS$. By using derivatives the multiplier would be defined as:

$$k = \frac{1}{1 - C'} = \frac{1}{S'}$$

We can use derivatives to analyze consumption and savings functions that are not linear.

Example 1:   Given that consumption is represented by $C = 12 + .6I + .4\sqrt{I}$, sketch the graph of consumption, and find MPC at the consumer's break-even point.

Solution.   The derivative tests show that consumption is increasing and concave down. The *CBEP* is found by solving $C = I$:

$$12 + .6I + .4\sqrt{I} = I$$
$$I^2 - 61I + 900 = 0$$
$$(I - 36)(I - 25) = 0 \quad \text{and} \quad C = I$$
$$I = 36; \; I = 25$$

$I = 25$ is extraneous. The *CBEP* is $I = 36$:

$$MPC = .6 + \frac{.2}{\sqrt{I}} = .6 + \frac{.2}{\sqrt{36}}$$

$MPC = .633$, which implies that $MPS = .367$ (see Figure 4-45).

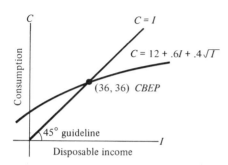

FIGURE 4-45

Example 2:   Given that $C = 12 + .6I + .4\sqrt{I}$, find the multiplier at *CBEP* ($I = 36$).

Solution.

$$k = \frac{1}{1 - C'} = \frac{1}{S'}$$

From Example 1, $MPC = .633$ and $MPS = .367$, and the multiplier at $I = 36$ becomes:

$$k = \frac{1}{1 - .633} = \frac{1}{.367} = 2.72$$

The interpretation of the multiplier was given in Chapter 1.

Example 3:   Given that $C = 12 + .6I + .4\sqrt{I}$, sketch the graph of savings, and find the *CBEP*.

Solution. $S = I - C$ and thus $S = -12 + .4I - .4\sqrt{I}$. The *CBEP* is found by solving $S = 0$ and this solution is the same as Example 1, giving $I = 36$ as $C = I$ or $S = 0$. The derivative tests indicate that savings is increasing and concave up; S' and S'' are positive (see Figure 4-46).

Example 4:   Given that $C = 12 + .6I + .4\sqrt{I}$, sketch the graphs of *MPC* and *MPS*, and show that $MPC + MPS = 100\%$ (see Figures 4-47 and 4-48).

Solution.

$$MPC = .6 + \frac{.2}{\sqrt{I}}$$

$$MPS = .4 - \frac{.2}{\sqrt{I}}$$

$MPC + MPS = 1$

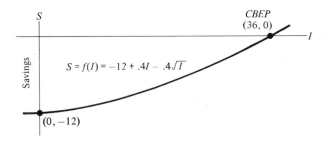

FIGURE 4-46

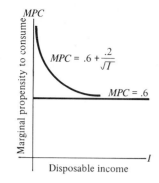

FIGURE 4-47

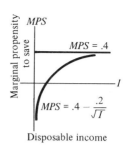

FIGURE 4-48

The Relationships of Total Cost, Marginal Cost, and Average Total Cost

If total cost is given by $C = f(x)$, then $C' = dC/dx$ represents marginal cost. MC represents the change in cost with respect to a change in output at some particular level of output. Stated in formula form:

$$MC = C' = \lim_{x \to 0} \frac{\Delta C}{\Delta X}$$

C' represents the instantaneous change in cost at a point.

We can demonstrate the use of derivatives to analyze cost functions represented by polynomials by pointing out relationships between C, MC, and ATC for general cases. We will consider first-degree, second-degree, and third-degree cost functions and will make general conclusions to relate these cost functions to MC and ATC. Although cost functions are generally represented by third-degree polynomials, first- and second-degree cases can also be examined for the sake of completion.

Example 5:   For a linear total cost function (see Figure 4-49), ATC meets MC at infinity.

$$TC = C = mx + b \ (m, b \text{ positive})$$

$$ATC = m + \frac{b}{x}$$

$$MC = m$$

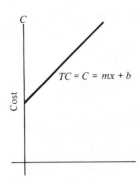
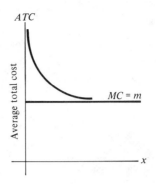

FIGURE 4-49

Example 6:   For second-degree total cost functions:

$$C = ax^2 + bx + c \ (a, b, c \text{ positive})$$

$$ATC = ax + b + \frac{c}{x} \text{ (reaches a minimum point)}$$

$$MC = 2ax + b \ (a, b, \text{ positive})$$

Conclusion.   If cost is a second-degree function, then marginal cost is a linear expression, and average total cost reaches a minimum. Another important conclusion is that MC intersects ATC at minimum ATC (see Figure 4-50):

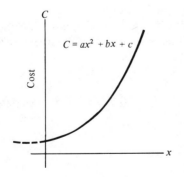
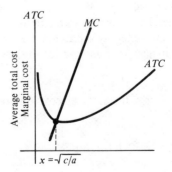

FIGURE 4-50

Proof.   The minimum point of ATC is found by solving $ATC' = 0$:

$$ATC = ax + b + \frac{c}{x}$$

$$ATC' = a - \frac{c}{x^2}$$

The point of intersection of MC and ATC is found by solving $MC = ATC$:

$$2ax + b = ax + b + \frac{c}{x^2}$$

$$x = \sqrt{\frac{c}{a}}$$

Thus, MC intersects ATC at minimum ATC.

Example 7:   Given that $C = 2x^2 + 4x + 8$, sketch the graphs of C and superimpose the graphs of ATC and MC, demonstrating that MC intersects ATC at the minimum point of ATC.

Solution.   Total cost $= C = 2x^2 + 4x + 8$ is a parabola, concave up, with its vertex to the left of the y axis (see Figure 4-51).

Marginal cost is the derivative of cost and is $C' = 4x + 4$. Average total cost is $ATC = 2x + 4 + 8/x$ and reaches its minimum point where $ATC' = 0$. $ATC' = 2 - 8/x^2 = 0$ gives $x = 2$, and $ATC = 12$. MC intersects ATC at the point where $MC = ATC$; where $4x + 4 = 2x + 4 + 8/x$ (see Figure 4-52).

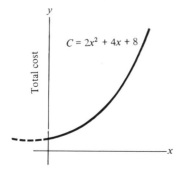

FIGURE 4-51

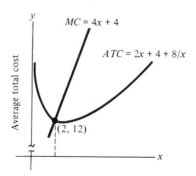

FIGURE 4-52

Recall from Chapter 3 that total cost functions are related to production functions and thus are typically third-degree functions that go from concave down to concave up, while the function is continually increasing. The coefficients of TC must meet certain conditions in order that the function behave in the desired manner. First, the coefficient of the third-degree term must be positive to ensure that TC starts below the x axis and ends above the x axis. Moreover, the constant term must be positive, because this quantity represents fixed cost. Second, TC is continually increasing, and thus TC' must be positive. For $TC = ax^3 + bx^2 + cx + d$ (when a and d are positive):

$$TC' = MC = 3ax^2 + 2bx + c$$

must be positive, which means that the discriminant of MC must be negative:

$$(2b)^2 - 4(3a)c = 4b^2 - 12ac < 0$$
$$b^2 - 3ac < 0$$

Third, TC must have a point of inflection in the first quadrant; therefore, TC'' must be 0 in the first quadrant:

$$TC'' = MC' = 6ax + 2b = 0$$
$$x = \frac{-2b}{6a}$$

is the x value for the point of inflection. This value must be positive, so it follows that b must be negative in order that the fraction $-2b/6a$ be positive. Because total cost must go from concave down to concave up, marginal cost must be a concave-up parabola with its vertex in the first quadrant. This means that the derivative of MC is negative to the left of the vertex of MC ($TC'' = MC' < 0$), and the derivative of MC is positive to the right of the vertex of MC ($TC'' = MC' > 0$).

Example 8:   Given that $TC = ax^3 + bx^2 + cx + d$ (when a, c, and d are positive; b is negative; and $b^2 < 3ac$), then:

$$MC = 3ax^2 + 2bx + c$$

which is a parabola that is concave up with its vertex in the first quadrant:

$$ATC = \frac{TC}{x} = ax^2 + bx + c + \frac{d}{x}$$

If TC is represented by a third-degree function that goes from concave down to concave up (see Figure 4-53), then MC is a parabola that is concave up with its vertex in the first quadrant (see Figure 4-54).

In Figure 4-54, when $C = f(x)$ is concave down, $C' = MC$ is decreasing and $C'' < 0$. When $C = f(x)$ is concave up, $C' = MC$ is increasing at an increasing rate, and $C'' > 0$. At the bottom of the parabola, $C'' = MC = 0$, which means that at the vertex of MC there is a point of inflection in $C = f(x)$. $C' = MC$ is always positive for $x > 0$, which means that $C = f(x)$ is increasing.

We can also demonstrate that ATC reaches a minimum point and that MC intersects ATC at minimum ATC (see Figure 4-55).

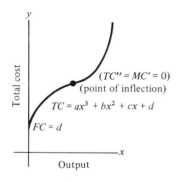

FIGURE 4-53

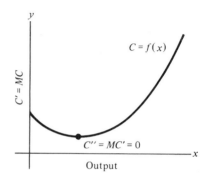

FIGURE 4-54

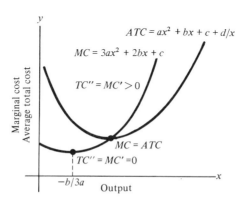

FIGURE 4-55

Example 9:   Given that $TC = x^3 - 2x^2 + 4x + 8$, sketch the graph of TC, and indicate concavity. Superimpose the graphs of MC and ATC, and indicate that MC intersects ATC at minimum ATC.

Solution. $TC' = MC = 3x^2 - 4x + 4$ and $TC'' = 6x - 4$, which gives $x = 2/3$ as the x-value for the vertex of MC. To the left of $x = 2/3$, TC'' is negative, and therefore TC is concave down. To the right of $x = 2/3$, TC'' is positive, and thus TC is concave up (see Figure 4-56).

The point of minimum ATC is found by solving $ATC' = 0$:

$$ATC = x^2 - 2x + 4 + \frac{8}{x}$$

$$ATC' = 2x - 2 - \frac{8}{x^2}$$

which reduces to $x^3 - x^2 - 4 = 0$. The factors are $(x - 2)(x^2 + x + 2) = 0$, which gives $x = 2$ and $ATC = 8$ as the minimum point for ATC. ATC intersects MC when:

$$ATC = MC \text{ or } x^2 - 2x + 4 + \frac{8}{x} = 3x^2 - 4x + 4$$

which reduces to $x^3 - x^2 - 4 = 0$. This gives $x = 2$ and $ATC = MC = 8$ as the solution (see Figure 4-57).

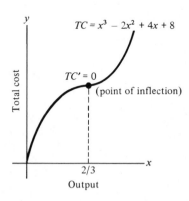

FIGURE 4-56

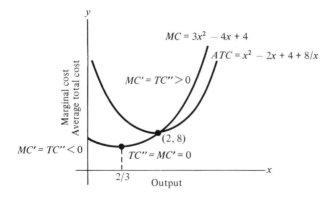

FIGURE 4-57

Marginal Revenue

If revenue is given by $R = f(x)$, then R' represents marginal revenue. MR represents the change in revenue with respect to output at some particular point:

$$MR = R' = \lim_{x \to 0} \frac{\Delta R}{\Delta x}$$

In other words, R' represents the instantaneous change in revenue at some point.

Example 10:   This example illustrates marginal revenue to an imperfectly competitive firm. Given that demand is represented by the linear function $y = mx + b$ (when m is negative, b is positive, with zero at $x = -b/m$), then $R = yx = (mx + b)x = mx^2 + bx$ (a parabola that is concave down with zeros at $x = -b/m$, $x = 0$). Marginal revenue is the derivative of revenue or $MR = R' = 2mx + b$ (when m is negative, b is positive, with zero at $x = -b/2m$). The slope of marginal revenue ($2m$) is twice that of demand (m). (See Figure 4-58.)

Example 11:   Given that demand is represented by $y = 20 - x$ (this is also ATR):

$$R = 20x - x^2$$
$$MR = 20 - 2x$$

Revenue reaches a maximum point when $R' = MR = 0$, which is at $x = 10$ and $R = 100$. After we superimpose the graphs of y (also ATR), R, and MR, we observe some general conclusions: Demand and revenue have a common x-axis intercept; MR will pass through the x value where $E_d = -1$ (10, 0), which is the point at which revenue is maximized; $MR = 0$ at the point of maximum revenue. Remember that the slope of MR is twice that of the demand curve (see Figure 4-59).

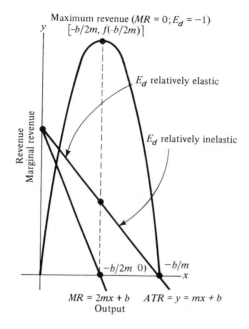

FIGURE 4-58

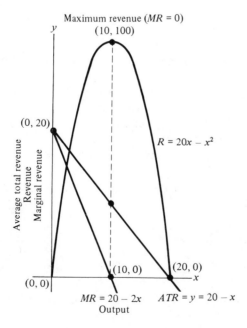

FIGURE 4-59

Example 12:   Given that demand is represented by $y = 16 - x^2$, then:

$$R = yx = (16 - x^2)(x) = 16x - x^3$$
$$MR = 16 - 3x^3$$

$MR = 0$ for $x = \sqrt{16/3} = 2.3$. When $R' = MR = 0$, we obtain maximum revenue. Maximum revenue also occurs at the point at which $E_d = -1$, and this is determined by:

$$E_d = \left(\frac{\Delta x}{\Delta y}\right)\left(\frac{y}{x}\right) = \left(\frac{-1}{2x}\right)\left(\frac{16 - x^2}{x}\right) = -1$$

for $x = 2.3$. The revenue function $R = 16x - x^3$ is a third-degree polynomial with leading coefficient of -1 and zeros of $x = -4$, $x = 0$, and $x = 4$ (see Figure 4-60).

The Oligopoly

The *oligopoly*, or *kinked demand curve*, is a special case of demand to an imperfectly competitive firm. The analysis of demand, revenue, and marginal revenue is much the same as demand given by $y = mx + b$, but in this situation we deal with two linear demand curves (see Figure 4-61).

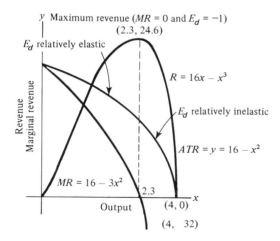

FIGURE 4-60

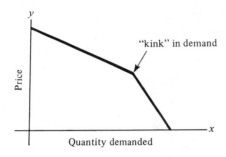

FIGURE 4-61

Because there is a kink in demand, there is also a kink in the revenue function. We might also suspect that there is a kink in marginal revenue. This is not exactly the case, because at the point in demand at which the kink occurs, there is a *gap* in marginal revenue. We can demonstrate the relationship of revenue and marginal revenue to the kinked demand curve.

Example 13:   If the kink in demand is at a point at which E_d is *relatively elastic*, then *MR* has a gap at the x value at which the kink occurs. Moreover, the gap will be in the first quadrant (see Figures 4-62, 4-63, 4-64).

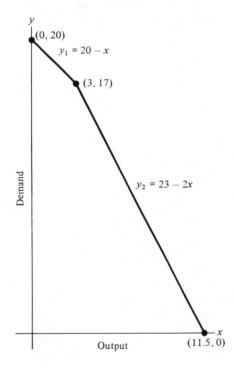

FIGURE 4-62

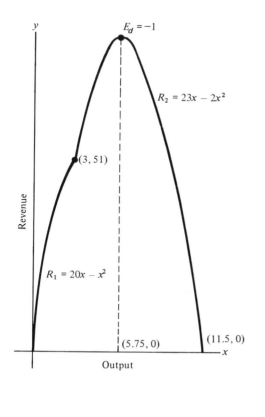

FIGURE 4-63

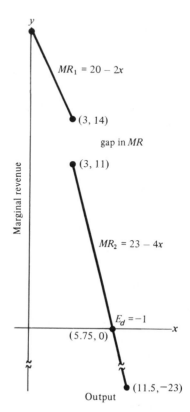

FIGURE 4-64

Example 14: If the kink in demand is at a point at which E_d is *relatively inelastic*, then *MR* has a gap at the x value at which the kink occurs. Moreover, the gap will be in the fourth quadrant (see Figures 4-65, 4-66, 4-67).

Example 15: If the kink in demand is at a point at which E_d is *unit elasticity*, then the gap in *MR* will begin (or end) on the x axis where $E_d = -1$ according to whether $E_d = -1$ for y_1 or y_2 at the kink (see Figures 4-68, 4-69, 4-70).

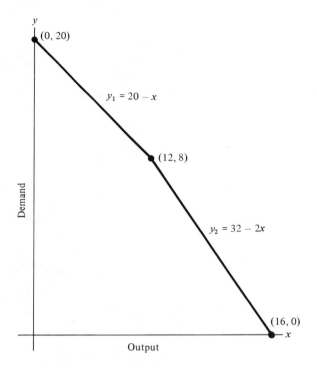

FIGURE 4-65

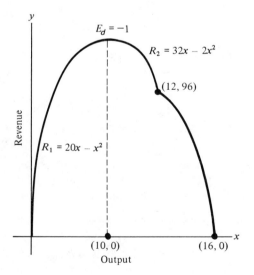

FIGURE 4-66

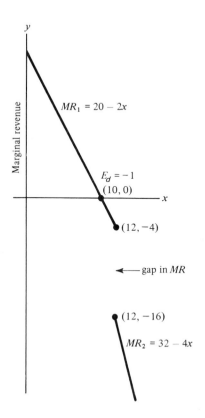

FIGURE 4-67

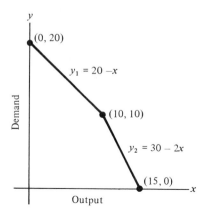

FIGURE 4-68

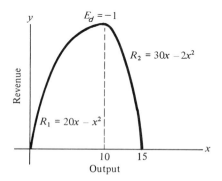

FIGURE 4-69

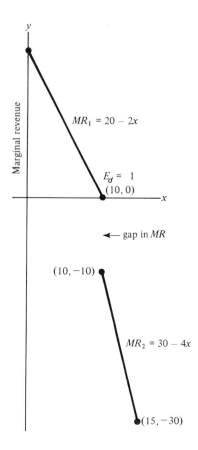

FIGURE 4-70

Marginal Profit: Profit Maximization Using Marginal Cost and Marginal Revenue

Total profit is defined as $TP = TR - TC$. Marginal profit is defined as P'; in formula form:

$$MP = P' = \lim_{x \to 0} \frac{\Delta P}{\Delta x}$$

In this section we will study profit maximization in the case of TC represented by third-degree polynomials and TR characterized by purely competitive and by imperfectly competitive firms.

An *important theorem* states that: given that $P = f(x)$ and profit reaches a maximum point, then the point x at which $MC = MR$ will maximize profits.

Proof.

$$P = R - C$$
$$P' = R' - C'$$

Total profit reaches a maximum point for $P' = 0$:

$$P' = R' - C' = 0 \text{ (for maximum } P)$$
If $R' = C'$ then $P' = 0$
or $MR = MC$ (for maximum P)

The following examples show that maximum profit exists when $MC = MR$. They also include the method of maximizing profits by maximizing the profit function itself.

Example 16:   For $C = x^3/3 - 2x^2 + 6x + 8$ and $R = 38x$ the point of maximum profit can be found by two methods. In the first method we maximize the profit function by finding the point at which $MP = 0$ ($P' = 0$). (See Figure 4-71.)

$$P = R = C = 38x - \left(\frac{x^3}{3} - 2x^2 + 6x + 8 \right) = \frac{-x^3}{3} + 2x^2 + 32x - 8$$

$$P' = -x^2 + 4x + 32 = 0$$

when $x = 8$ and $P = 206$.

We can also find the point of maximum profit by finding the x value at which $MR = MC$ (see Figure 4-72).

$$MC = x^2 - 4x + 6$$
$$MR = 38$$

Solving for $MC = MR$ (when $x = 8$):

$$x^2 - 4x + 6 = 38$$

When $x = 8$, $P = 206$ and $MC = MR = 38$.

Example 17:   For $C = x^3 - 3x^2 + 4x + 4$ and $R = 22x - 3x^2/2$ the point of maximum profit can be found by two methods. In the first method we maximize the profit function by finding the point where $P' = 0$. (See Figure 4-73.)

$$P = R - C = \left(22x - \frac{3x^2}{2}\right) - (x^3 - 3x^2 + 4x + 4)$$

$$P' = -3x^2 + 3x + 18 = 0$$

$P' = 0$ for $x = 3$, and thus maximum profit occurs at $x = 3$ and $P = 36.5$.

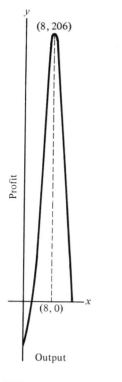

FIGURE 4-71

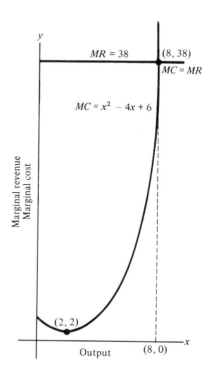

FIGURE 4-72

We can also find the point of maximum profit by finding the x value at which $MR = MC$ (see Figure 4-74).

$$MC = 3x^2 - 6x + 4$$
$$MR = 22 - 3x$$

Solving for $MC = MR$ (when $x = 3$):

$$3x^2 - 6x + 4 = 22 - 3x$$

When $x = 3, MC = MR = 13$.

The preceding examples demonstrate that profit analysis with respect to marginal revenue and marginal cost can be made without using the profit function itself. In the usual case the profit function is a third-degree function, because TC is typically a third-degree polynomial.

If the marginal revenue of a purely competitive firm is greater than its marginal cost, then dP/dx is positive, which means that the profit function is increasing. On the other hand, if $MC > MR$, then the profit function is decreasing. Maximum profit results when $MR = MC$ ($dP/dx = 0$). (See Figure 4-75.)

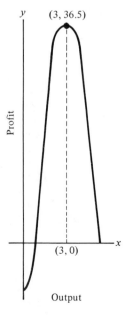

FIGURE 4-73

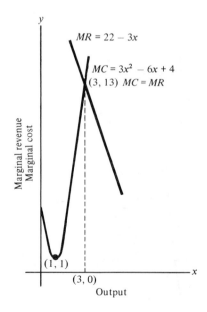

FIGURE 4-74

Likewise, if the marginal revenue of an imperfectly competitive firm is greater than marginal cost, then $P' = MR - MC$ is positive, and the profit function is increasing. On the other hand, if marginal cost is greater than marginal revenue, then $P' = MR - MC$ is negative, and the profit function is decreasing. Maximum profit results when $MR = MC$ ($dP/dx = 0$). (See Figure 4-76.)

PROBLEMS 4-6

*1. If the consumption function is given by $C = 5 + .5I + .5\sqrt{I}$, find MPC and MPS at the following income levels: $I = 4, I = 9, I = 16$. What is the multiplier at these incomes? Sketch the graph of $C = f(I)$ and indicate MPC for the given income levels.

2. Given that consumption is represented by $C = 5 + .5I + .5\sqrt{I}$, show that at any income level that $MPC + MPS = 100\%$. Sketch the graphs of MPC and MPS.

3. Given that consumption is represented by $C = 5 + .5I + .5\sqrt{I}$, sketch the graph of consumption, and find the consumer's break-even point.

*4. For the following total cost functions, sketch the graphs of total cost and marginal cost:

   *a. $C = 4x + 100$ *b. $C = 2x^2 + 3x + 4$ c. $C = \dfrac{x^3}{3} - 2x^2 + 8x + 10$

*5. For the following total cost functions, superimpose the graphs of MC and ATC, and indicate the point of intersection of MC with ATC. Show that MC intersects ATC at minimum ATC.

   *a. $C = 2x^2 + 8x + 18$ b. $C = 2x^3 - 4x^2 + 8x + 16$

6. Costs in the long run result from all costs becoming variable and thus the constant in the cost functions is not included. For the long-run cost functions given below sketch the graphs of total cost, marginal cost, and average total cost:

   a. $C = x^2 + x$ b. $C = x^3 - 2x^2 + 8x$

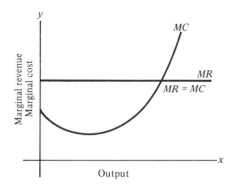

FIGURE 4-75

FIGURE 4-76

7. If total cost is represented by $C = ax^3 + bx^2 + cx + FC$ (fixed cost), what are the conditions for the coefficients a, b, and c such that MC appears concave up with its vertex in the first quadrant (see Figure 4-77)?

If the vertex of MC is in the first quadrant and MC is concave up, this will ensure that total cost will increase while it changes from concave down to concave up (see Figure 4-78). Why does total cost appear as it does if marginal cost behaves in this manner? Also prove that the x value for the vertex of MC and the x value at the point of inflection of TC are the same.

*8. For the following total revenue functions, sketch the graphs of revenue, marginal revenue, and average total revenue on the same axis. What is an equivalent expression for average total revenue?

*a. $R = 6x$ c. $R = 14x - 2x^2$ e. $R = 125x - x^4$

*b. $R = 20x - 2x^2$ d. $R = 16x - x^3$

*9. For the following demand expressions, show that $MR = 0$ when $E_d = -1$. Superimpose the graphs of demand, marginal revenue, and revenue. If demand is relatively elastic, what is the result of increasing price? If demand is relatively inelastic, what is the result of decreasing price?

*a. $y = 20 - 2x$ b. $y = 14 - 2x$ c. $y = 16 - x^2$

*10. Given that the points given in Figures 4-79, 4-80, 4-81 determine oligopolies, find the linear expressions that represent demand, and sketch the graphs of revenue and of marginal revenue. Determine whether the kink occurs at a relatively elastic point, at a relatively inelastic point, or at the point of unit elasticity.

*11. For the following cost and revenue functions, determine maximum profits by using two methods. First, sketch the graph of profit, and indicate maximum profit by finding the point at which $MP = P' = 0$. Second, maximize profits by finding the x value at which $MR = MC$. Sketch the graphs of MR and MC, and indicate the point of intersection.

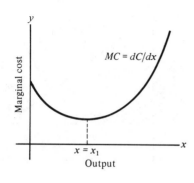

FIGURE 4-77

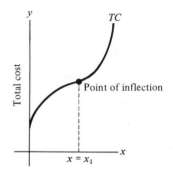

FIGURE 4-78

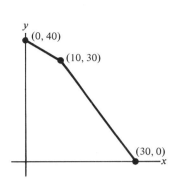

a. FIGURE 4-79

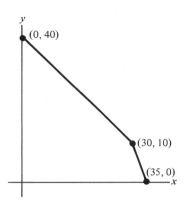

b. FIGURE 4-80

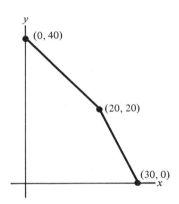

c. FIGURE 4-81

*a. $C = 2x^2 + 3x + 4$; $R = 15x$ (the revenue function indicates that revenue represents a purely competitive firm)

b. $C = 2x^2 + 3x + 4$; $R = 16x$

c. $C = x^2 + 3x + 2$; $R = 20x - 3x^2$ (the revenue function indicates that revenue represents an imperfectly competitive firm)

*d. $C = \dfrac{x^3}{3} - x^2 + 4x + 10$; $R = 19x$

e. $C = \dfrac{x^3}{3} - x^2 + 4x + 10$; $R = 28x$

f. $C = \dfrac{x^3}{3} - x^2 + 4x + 10$; $R = 20x - x^2$

g. $C = \dfrac{x^3}{3} - 2x^2 + 8x + 10; R = 40x$

h. $C = \dfrac{x^3}{3} - 3x^2 + 8x + 10; R = 20x - x^2$

i. $C = x^3 - 2x^2 + 8x + 10; R = 20x$

j. $C = x^3 - 2x^2 + 8x + 10; R = 20x - x^2$

12. If demand is represented by $y = mx + b$ (when m is negative and b is positive) and total cost is represented by a typical third-degree polynomial, give a simple geometrical argument that profit is maximized at a point at which demand is relatively elastic.

4-7   PRODUCTION FUNCTIONS

Total Product

The production function expresses a firm's total product as a function of its units of input and was discussed initially in Chapter 3:

total product = f(units of input)

Labor and capital are units commonly used to represent input variables. At this point we are restricted to functions of a single independent variable. Therefore, the production function must be expressed in terms of one input variable, and the remaining variables will be fixed.

If all other input variables remain fixed except the quantity of labor (L), then a firm's total product (X) can be expressed as a function of labor:

total product = $X = f(L)$

average product of labor = $APL = \dfrac{X}{L}$

marginal product of labor = $MPL = \dfrac{dX}{dL}$

Similarly, if the input variable is capital, then the total product can be expressed as a function of capital. The average total product uses capital as the divisor. The derivative of the total product is the marginal product of capital.

The production function states that, as the employment of labor increases, the *total product* increases first at an increasing rate (concave up) and then at a decreasing rate (concave down). The total product curve eventually turns down (see Figure 4-82).

The third-degree polynomial is best suited to represent the product function, because it is the simplest algebraic expression whose concavity can be controlled from one sense to another.

The Production Function

Output (X) is a function of labor (L) and is expressed by:

$$X = 9L^2 - L^3$$

The leading coefficient is negative, so the graph begins above the L axis and ends below it. The L-axis intercepts are $L = 0$ (double root) and $L = 9$. The production function reaches a maximum where $dX/dL = 0$ or $18L - 3L^2 = 0$, which gives $L = 6$ and $X = 108$ (see Figure 4-83). The second derivative gives us information concerning concavity. The second derivative is:

$$\frac{d^2 X}{dL^2} = 18 - 6L$$

The second derivative is 0 for $L = 3$ (point of inflection). The second derivative is positive for $L < 3$ (concave up). The second derivative is negative for $L > 3$ (concave down).

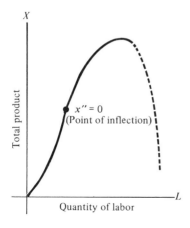

FIGURE 4-82

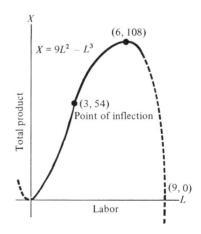

FIGURE 4-83

The Average Product of Labor

By definition, $APL = X/L$. For the total product function expressed by $X = 9L^2 - L^3$:

$$APL = \frac{9L^2 - L^3}{L} = 9L - L^2$$

which is a parabola, concave down, with intercepts of $L = 0$ and $L = 9$ and vertex at $L = 4.5, X = 24.75$ (see Figure 4-84).

The Marginal Product of Labor

By definition, $MPL = dX/dL$. For the total product function expressed by $X = 9L^2 - L^3$:

$$MPL = 18L - 3L^2$$

which is a parabola, concave down, with intercepts of $L = 0$ and $L = 6$ and vertex at $L = 3, MPL = 27$ (see Figure 4-85).

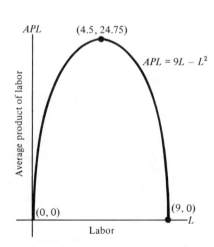

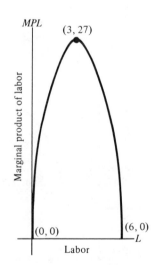

FIGURE 4-84   FIGURE 4-85

The Relationship of Average Total Product to Marginal Product

The marginal product curve and the average total product curve intersect at the point of maximum average total product. For $X = 9L^2 - L^3$ the point of maximum average total product is (4.5, 24.75). (See Figure 4-86.) The point of intersection of ATP and MPL is found by solving:

$$ATP = MPL$$
$$9L - L^2 = 18L - 3L^2$$
$$L = 4.5$$

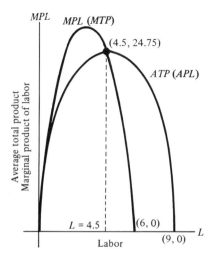

FIGURE 4-86

Production Functions and Total Cost Functions

We can draw many analogies between production functions and total cost functions. Third-degree production functions with negative leading coefficients result in second-degree, concave-down marginal product curves, where MPL and APL intersect at maximum APL (see Figure 4-87). Third-degree cost functions with positive leading coefficients result in second-degree, concave-up marginal cost curves, where MC and ATC intersect at minimum ATC (see Figure 4-88).

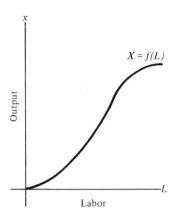

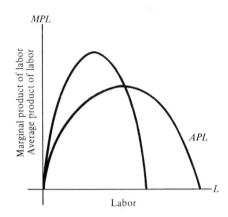

FIGURE 4-87

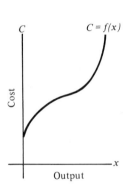

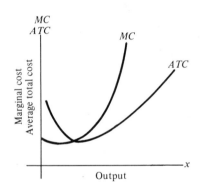

FIGURE 4-88

PROBLEMS 4-7

*1. By using first and second derivatives, sketch the graphs of the following production functions, and indicate concavity and the point of maximum total product:

   *a. $X = f(\text{labor}) = 32L^2 - L^3$ b. $X = f(\text{capital}) = 64K^2 - K^3$

2. Given that $X = f(\text{labor}) = 32L^2 - L^3$, superimpose the graphs of average total product and marginal product of labor, and indicate that MPL and APL intersect at maximum APL.

3. Given that $X = f(\text{capital}) = 64K^2 - K^3$, superimpose the graphs of average total product and marginal product of capital, indicating that APK and MPK intersect at maximum APK.

4-8   THE ECONOMIC ORDER QUANTITY

The *economic order quantity* is used in cost accounting to minimize the total cost to order and to carry a firm's inventory over a specified period of time. Assuming that a firm has uniform demand and batch arrival for a stock item, its inventory can be expressed as a function of time. For example, if the annual required units of a stock item is 2400 and the economic order quantity is 600 units, then 4 orders placed over equal time intervals during the year will yield 2400 required annual units. For time $t = 3$, $t = 6$, $t = 9$, $t = 12$ months, the inventory is 0. At each time a batch arrival of 600 units brings the inventory level up to the required 600 units (see Figure 4-89).

The formula used to determine the *annual economic order quantity* is:

$$EOQ = \sqrt{\frac{2(ARU)(CO)}{(CU)(CC)}}$$

where EOQ is economic order quantity (minimizes the total annual cost of inventory), ARU is annual required units, CO is cost per order, CU is cost per unit of material, and CC is carrying cost (based on a percentage of average inventory value).

Example 1:   Find the EOQ for:

annual required units = 6000
cost per order   = \$30
cost per unit   = \$5
carrying cost   = 20%

Solution.

$$EOQ = \sqrt{\frac{2(ARU)(CO)}{(CU)(CC)}} = \sqrt{\frac{2(6000)(30)}{5(20\%)}} = \sqrt{\frac{180,000}{.50}} = \sqrt{360,000}$$

= 600 units

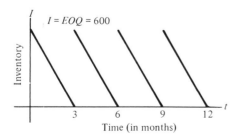

FIGURE 4-89

The *EOQ* is 600 units or 10 orders per year (see Figure 4-90).

The yearly interval is broken into 10 equal parts. Ten orders per year, each of 600 units, result in the annual required units of 6000. At times $t_1, t_2, \ldots, t_{10}$ the inventory is 0. At that time a batch arrival of 600 units brings the inventory level up to the required 600 units.

The Economic Order Quantity Formula

As we stated earlier, the economic order quantity will minimize the total annual cost to order and to carry inventory. The total annual cost to order and carry inventory can be expressed by:

total cost to order and carry inventory = annual cost of placing orders

+ annual carrying cost

$$TC = ACO + ACC$$

In order to express *TC* in terms of order quantity, we express both *ACO* and *ACC* in terms of order quantity:

$$ACO = \frac{(\text{annual required units})(\text{cost per order})}{\text{economic order quantity}} = \frac{(ARU)(CO)}{EOQ}$$

$$ACC = (\text{cost per unit})(\text{carrying cost})\left(\frac{\text{economic order quantity}}{2}\right)$$

$$= (CU)(CC)\left(\frac{EOQ}{2}\right)$$

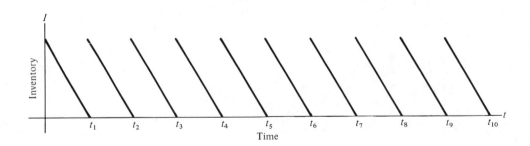

FIGURE 4-90

where $EOQ/2$ represents the average number of units in inventory at a particular time. Therefore:

$$TC = f(EOQ) = \frac{(ARU)(CO)}{EOQ} + \frac{(CU)(CC)}{2} (EOQ)$$

where ARU, CO, CU, and CC are constants.

Minimum TC is found by solving $TC' = 0$:

$$TC' = \frac{(-ARU)(CO)}{EOQ^2} + \frac{(CU)(CC)}{2} = 0$$

Solving for EOQ:

$$\frac{(CU)(CC)}{2} = \frac{(ARU)(CO)}{EOQ^2}$$

$$EOQ^2 = \frac{(2ARU)(CO)}{(CU)(CC)}$$

$$EOQ = \sqrt{\frac{(2ARU)(CO)}{(CU)(CC)}}$$

The graph of TC can be appreciated by analyzing:

$$TC = ACO + ACC = \frac{(ARU)(CO)}{EOQ} + (CU)(CC)\left(\frac{EOQ}{2}\right)$$

where ARU, CO, CC, and CU are constants.
The graph of ACO is the model reciprocal function, and the graph of ACC is a linear function. Furthermore, the graph of TC is concave up, because TC'' is positive:

$$TC' = \frac{(-ARU)(CO)}{EOQ^2} + \frac{(CU)(CC)}{2}$$

$$TC'' = \frac{(2ARU)(CO)}{EOQ^3}$$

TC'' is always positive.

We can further demonstrate that the graph of ACO intersects the graph of ACC at the economic order quantity (see Figure 4-91). Minimum TC occurs at $TC' = 0$. We first solve $ACO = ACC$:

$$\frac{(ARU)(CO)}{EOQ} = \frac{(CU)(CC)}{2} \quad (EOQ)$$

$$EOQ^2 = \frac{(2ARU)(CO)}{(CU)(CC)}$$

$$EOQ = \sqrt{\frac{(2ARU)(CO)}{(CU)(CC)}}$$

Example 2:   On the same axis sketch the graphs of annual carrying cost of inventory, annual cost of placing inventory orders (this is the model reciprocal function), annual total cost to order and carry inventory. The company's annual required units is 6000, the cost per order is $30, the cost per unit is $5, and the carrying cost is 20 percent of inventory (see Figure 4-92).

Solution.

$$\text{annual carrying cost} = (\text{cost per unit})(\text{carrying cost}) \left(\frac{\text{order quantity}}{2} \right)$$

$$ACC = \frac{(5)(20\%)}{2} \ (OQ) = \frac{OQ}{2}$$

$$\text{annual cost of ordering} = \frac{(\text{annual required unit})(\text{cost per order})}{\text{order quantity}}$$

$$AC = f(OQ) = \frac{180,000}{OQ}$$

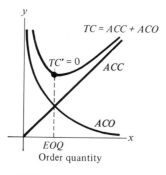

FIGURE 4-91

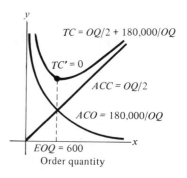

FIGURE 4-92

$$\text{total cost to order and carry} = ACC + ACD = \frac{OQ}{2} + \frac{180{,}000}{OQ}$$

Minimum TC is found by solving $TC' = 0$:

$$TC' = \frac{1}{2} - \frac{180{,}000}{OQ^2} = 0$$

which gives $OQ = EOQ = 600$ units. The point of intersection of ACC and ACO is found by solving $ACC = ACO$:

$$\frac{180{,}000}{OQ} = \frac{OQ}{2}$$

$$OQ = 600 \text{ units} = EOQ$$

PROBLEMS 4-8

*1. Determine the economic order quantity for a computer component manufacturer who uses 7200 units of a certain material per year, whose cost of ordering is $20 per order, whose cost per unit of the material is $3, and whose carrying cost (as a percent of inventory) is 20 percent.

2. For the data given in Problem 1, sketch the graphs of annual carrying cost (*ACC*), annual cost of ordering (*ACO*), total cost to order and to carry (*TC*). Indicate the point of minimum *TC*, and show that this is also the same value as determined by the intersection of *ACP* and *ACC*. The point of minimum *TC* is the economic order quantity.

4-9 INTEGRAL CALCULUS: THE ANTIDERIVATIVE OF A FUNCTION

If the derivative of a function is given, we can reconstruct the original function through the process of *antidifferentiation* or *integral calculus*. Instead of finding the derivative of a function, we must now find the *antiderivative* of a function. For example, if $y' = 2$, then the antiderivative is $y = 2x + c$ (c is constant). The value of the constant is not known without further information that relates to the function. When we find the antiderivative, we must always include the constant that was lost when we took the derivative. In applied problems initial conditions on the function will be given. This will determine the constant to be included when the antiderivative of a function is found.

The symbol that indicates the antiderivative of a function $y = f(x)$ is:

$$\int f(x) \quad \text{or} \quad \int f(x)\, dx$$

We include the dx notation in order to identify the independent variable. The notation dx is called the *differential* of x. For example:

$$\int 2 = \int 2\, dx = 2x + c$$

The symbol $\int$ is the *integral*. Finding the antiderivative of a function is often referred to as finding the integral of the function. The terms *antidifferentiation* and *integration* can be used interchangeably.

The antiderivative is obtained by using the inverse steps of differentiation. When the derivative was found, we brought down the exponent of x and multiplied the exponent by the coefficient of x; the exponent of x was reduced by 1. In order to find the antiderivative, we reverse the process. The exponent of x is increased by 1, and the coefficient of x is divided by the new exponent. Stated as a theorem:

$$\int cx^n = \frac{cx^{n+1}}{n+1} + k \ (n \neq -1)$$

This theorem is proved by taking the derivative of:

$$y = \frac{cx^{n+1}}{n+1} + k$$

which is $y' = cx^n$. The theorem gives antiderivatives of algebraic functions only of the specific form of the variable raised to an exponent where the exponent is not -1. As in the case of derivatives, the antiderivative of a sum (or difference) is the sum (or difference) of the antiderivatives.

This example demonstrates the mechanics of finding antiderivatives.

Example 1:

a. $\int 3 = 3x + c$

b. $\int 2x = x^2 + c$

c. $\int x = \dfrac{x^2}{2} + c$

d. $\int x^3 + 4x^5 = \dfrac{x^4}{4} + \dfrac{2x^6}{3} + c$

e. $\int x^4 + x^{-3} - x^6 = \dfrac{x^5}{5} - \dfrac{x^{-2}}{2} - \dfrac{x^7}{7} + c$

f. $\int x^{1/2} = \dfrac{2}{3} x^{3/2} + c$

g. $\int \dfrac{1}{x} = $ (cannot be found by the theorem)

h. $\int x^{10} \, dx \; n = \dfrac{x^{11}}{11} + k$ (differential used)

i. $\int c \, dx = cx + k$ (differential used)

j. $\int ab \, dx = abx + k$ (differential used)

k. $\int a^2 b^2 \, db = \dfrac{a^2 b^3}{3} + k$ (differential used)

l. $\int x^2 z^2 \, dz = \dfrac{x^2 z^3}{3} + k$ (differential used)

When differential notation is used, the independent variable is given in the notation. Thus the theorem can be applied to the variable, and the remaining quantities are assumed to be constants.

We can reconstruct functions when the derivatives are known. The techniques that we use are important, because changes in economic variables are frequently more readily obtainable than the original functions themselves.

Reconstructing Consumption Functions from the Marginal Propensity to Consume

If *MPC* is known, then:

$$C = \int MPC$$

The constant in integration is found by determining consumption when disposable income is 0.

Example 2:   Given that $MPC = .2 + 1/2\sqrt{x}$ and fixed consumption = 28, find the consumption function.

Solution.

$$C = \int MPC = \int .2 + \frac{1}{2\sqrt{x}} = .2x + \sqrt{x} + 28$$

Reconstructing Revenue Functions from Marginal Revenue

If *MR* is known, then:

$$R = \int MR$$

The constant in integration is found by determining revenue when $x = 0$. Revenue at this level of production = 0.

Example 3:   Given that $MR = 20 - 2x$, find revenue.

Solution.

$$R = \int MR = \int 20 - 2x = 20x - x^2 + c \text{ (fixed revenue = 0)}$$

$$R = 20x - x^2$$

The revenue function is obtainable from *MR*. Moreover, the demand expression is also derived from revenue by $R = xy = x(20 - x)$. To review, marginal revenue was given (see Figure 4-93), and then total revenue was reconstructed (see Figure 4-94).

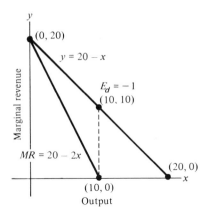

FIGURE 4-93

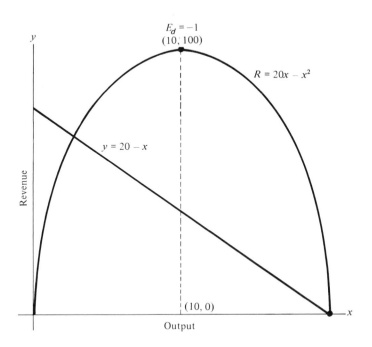

FIGURE 4-94

Example 4:   Given that $MR = 64 - 4x^3$, find the expression for revenue and demand.

Solution.

$$R = \int MR = 64 - 4x^3 = 64x - x^4 \text{ (constant} = 0)$$

By definition $R = xy = x(64 - x^3)$, which means that $y = 64 - x^3$.

Reconstructing Cost Functions from Marginal Cost

If MC is known, then:

$$C = \int MC$$

The constant in integration is found by determining cost when $x = 0$. This value is fixed cost. The following examples illustrate important general conclusions regarding cost and marginal cost.

Example 5:   If marginal cost is a straight line parallel to the x axis, then the total cost function is linear. Given that $MC = 2$ and fixed cost $= 60$, find the total cost function, and sketch the graphs of cost and marginal cost.

Solution.

$$C = \int MC = \int 2 = 2x + 60$$

To review, marginal cost was given (see Figure 4-95), and total cost was reconstructed (see Figure 4-96).

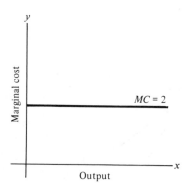

FIGURE 4-95

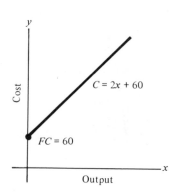

FIGURE 4-96

Example 6:   If marginal cost is a linear function of the form $MC = mx + b$, then total cost is a second-degree function of the form $TC = C = mx^2/2 + bx + FC$. Given that $MC = 4x + 4$ and $FC = 8$, reconstruct the total cost function.

Solution.

$$TC = \int MC = \int 4x + 4 = 2x^2 + 4x + 8$$

To review, marginal cost was given (see Figure 4-97), and total cost was reconstructed (see Figure 4-98).

Example 7:   If marginal cost is a second-degree function, then total cost is a third-degree function. Given that $MC = 3x^2 - 4x + 4$ and $FC = 8$, find the cost function.

Solution.

$$C = \int MC = \int 3x^2 - 4x + 4 = x^3 - 2x^2 + 4x + 8$$

To review, marginal cost was given (see Figure 4-99), and total cost was reconstructed (see Figure 4-100).

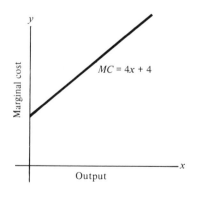

FIGURE 4-97

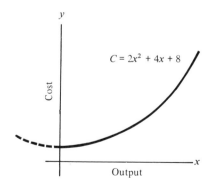

FIGURE 4-98

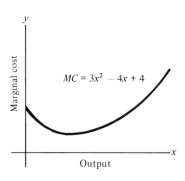

FIGURE 4-99

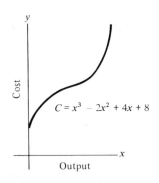

FIGURE 4-100

Example 8:   In Chapter 2 the formula for the best-fitting curve for a scatter diagram was given. If marginal cost is best fit by $MC = ax^2 + bx + c$, then:

$$TC = C = \frac{ax^3}{3} + \frac{bx^2}{2} + cx + FC$$

where FC represents fixed cost. A table for X, TC, and ΔC can be constructed and sufficient observations made to obtain a scatter diagram to represent MC. After we apply the statistical techniques of the best-fitting curve (Chapter 2), we can find MC (see Figure 4-101).

By using antidifferentiation, we can reconstruct total cost (see Figure 4-102).

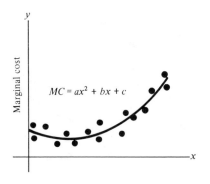

FIGURE 4-101

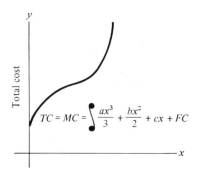

FIGURE 4-102

PROBLEMS 4-9

*1. Find the antiderivatives of the following:

*a. $\displaystyle\int 6$

d. $\displaystyle\int 2x^3 - 3x^2 + 8x + 9$

g. $\displaystyle\int (8x^2 + 3)\, dx$

b. $\displaystyle\int m \ (m \text{ fixed})$

e. $\displaystyle\int \frac{13}{x^2}$

h. $\displaystyle\int (8w^2 + 3)\, dw$

*c. $\displaystyle\int 3x - 4$

f. $\displaystyle\int \sqrt{3x}$

i. $\displaystyle\int (8w^2 x^2 + z)\, dw$

2. Reconstruct the consumption function if $MPC = .3 + 1/4\sqrt{x}$ and fixed consumption = 30.

*3. Reconstruct the following revenue and demand expressions from MR:

  *a. $MR = 10 - 2x$ (constant = 0)   d. $MR = 14 - 4x$ g. $MR = 16 - 3x^2$

  b. $MR = 10 - 4x$ e. $MR = 18 - 6x$ h. $MR = 27 - 4x^3$

  c. $MR = 14 - 2x$ f. $MR = 18 - 10x$ i. $MR = 4 - 1.5\sqrt{x}$

*4. Reconstruct the following cost functions from MC:

  *a. $MC = 4; \ FC = 10$ d. $MC = x^2 - 2x + 4; \ FC = 10$

  b. $MC = 8x; \ FC = 10$ e. $MC = 3x^2 - 4x + 8; \ FC = 10$

  c. $MC = 8x + 2; \ FC = 8$

4-10   THE DEFINITE INTEGRAL

The notation $\int f(x)$ represents the antiderivative of $f(x)$ and is called the *indefinite integral*, because the result of integration is in variable form. The *definite integral* is represented by:

$$\int_a^b f(x)$$

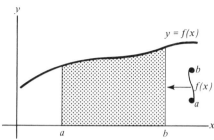

FIGURE 4-103

The definite integral represents the "definite" area bounded by $y = f(x)$ and the x axis from $x = a$ to $x = b$ (see Figure 4-103). This area is shaded in the figure.

The following theorem states how the area bounded by the function $y = f(x)$ and the x axis from $x = a$ to $x = b$ is determined: If $F(x)$ is the antiderivative of $f(x)$, then the area bounded by $y = f(x)$ and the x axis from $x = a$ to $x = b$ is given by:

$$\int_a^b f(x) = F(b) - F(a) = F(x) \Big|_a^b$$

This theorem is stated without proof; however the student can easily verify the theorem for a particular case is $f(x)$ is linear.

Example 1:   Find the area bounded by $y = x^2$ and the x axis from $x = 1$ to $x = 3$.

Solution.   The antiderivative of $f(x) = x^2$ is $F(x) = x^3/3 + c$. The constant in the antiderivative is not needed in evaluating the definite integral, because it will simply be added and then subtracted (see Figure 4-104):

$$\int_1^3 x^2 = \frac{x^3}{3} \Big|_1^3 = \frac{27}{3} - \frac{1}{3} = \frac{26}{3}$$

The shaded area in the figure is equal to $26/3$.

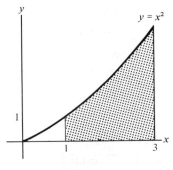

FIGURE 4-104

Application of the Definite Integral to the Consumers' Surplus

The definite integral in mathematical economics is commonly used in determining the consumers' surplus. If the point of *ME* for supply and demand is (x_1, y_1), then the shaded area represents the consumers' surplus (see Figure 4-105).

Example 2:   Assume that supply and demand are given by:

$y = x^2 + 1$ (represents supply)
$y = 19 - x^2$ (represents demand)

Solution.   The point of *ME* is found by solving $S = D$ or:

$$x^2 + 1 = 19 - x^2$$

which gives $x = 3$ (quantity) and $y = 10$ (price). The consumers' surplus is found by determining the area bounded by the curve $y = 19 - x^2$ and the x axis between $x = 0$ and $x = 3$ and then by subtracting the area bounded by $y = 10$ and the x axis between $x = 0$ and $x = 3$ (see Figure 4-106):

$$\text{consumers' surplus} = \int_0^3 (19 - x^2) - \int_0^3 10$$

$$= 19x - \frac{x^3}{3}\Big|_0^3 - 10x\Big|_0^3 = 48 - 30 = 18 \text{ (units of money)}$$

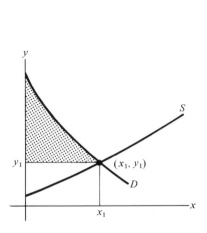

FIGURE 4-105

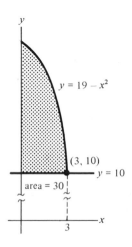

FIGURE 4-106

The interpretation of the consumers' surplus for Example 2 follows. The point of ME is (3, 10), which means that consumers pay 30 (units of money) for a quantity of 3. This represents the total cost to the consumer. The total cost to the consumer at the point of ME is the area of a rectangle (see Figure 4-107).

The demand curve shows that consumers would have been willing to pay more than 10 (units of money) for quantities of x up to $x = 3$. The shaded area represents how much more consumers would have been willing to pay for the commodity. This area is the consumers' surplus (see Figure 4-108).

The surplus can also be appreciated by the fact that, instead of paying 10 (units of money), the consumer would have been willing to pay 18 (units of money) for commodity of $x = 1$, 15 (units of money) for commodity of $x = 2$, and so on. The consumer receives a "surplus" on each unit of commodity up to $x = 3$, because the consumer has to pay only 10 (units of money) for each unit.

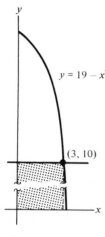

FIGURE 4-107

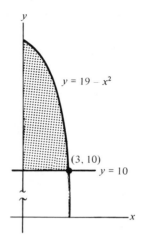

FIGURE 4-108

PROBLEMS 4-10

*1. Evaluate the following integrals and give a geometrical interpretation of your answer:

*a. $\displaystyle\int_0^4 3x$

d. $\displaystyle\int_0^4 x$

g. $\displaystyle\int_{-2}^2 x^3$

*b. $\displaystyle\int_0^4 3x + 2$

e. $\displaystyle\int_{-2}^0 x^3$

c. $\displaystyle\int_0^4 x^2$

f. $\displaystyle\int_0^2 x^3$

2. Find the consumers' surplus for demand expressed by $y = 16 - x^2$ and supply given by $y = 8$. Interpret the result graphically.

3. Find the consumers' surplus for demand expressed by $y = 19 - x^2$ and supply given by $y = x^2 + 1$. Interpret the result graphically.

4-11   DERIVATIVES AND ANTIDERIVATIVES OF ALGEBRAIC FUNCTIONS

The following rules for finding derivatives of algebraic functions are stated for the sake of completion and are given without proof.

The Power Rule

Given that $y = cx^n$, then

$$y' = ncx^{n-1}$$

The Chain Rule

The chain rule exhibits two forms. In the first, given that $y = f(u)$ and $u = g(x)$, then

$$\frac{dy}{dx} = \frac{dy}{du}\frac{du}{dx}$$

Example 1:   Given that $y = \sqrt{25 - x^2} = (25 - x^2)^{1/2}$, then

$$y' = \frac{1}{2}(25 - x^2)^{-1/2}(2x) = \frac{x}{\sqrt{25 - x^2}}$$

In the second form of the chain rule, given that $y = u^n$ and $u = g(x)$, then

$$\frac{dy}{dx} = nu^{n-1}\frac{du}{dx}$$

Example 2:   Given that $y = (x^3 + 5)^{10}$, then

$$y' = 10(x^3 + 5)^9(3x^2)$$

The Product Rule

Given that $y = (u)(v)$, when u and v are functions of x, then

$$y' = uv' + vu'$$

Example 3:   Given that $(x^2 + 3)(x^4 + 5)$, then

$$y' = (x^2 + 3)(4x^3) + (x^4 + 5)(2x)$$

The Quotient Rule

Given that $y = u/v$ (when u and v are functions of x), then

$$y' = \frac{vu' - uv'}{v^2}$$

Example 4:   Given that $y = (x^2 + 3)/(x^3 + 2)$:

$$y' = \frac{(x^3 + 2)(2x) - (x^2 + 3)(3x^2)}{(x^3 + 2)^2}$$

The Implicit Function Rule

An implicit function is one in which y is not given directly in terms of x. We use the chain rule on each term to find the derivative of an implicit function.

Example 5:   Given that $x^2 + y^2 = 25$, the derivative is:

$$2x \frac{dx}{dx} + 2y \frac{dy}{dx} = 0$$

$$2x + 2y \frac{dy}{dx} = 0$$

$$y' = \frac{-x}{y}$$

Antiderivatives of Algebraic Functions

One of the most commonly used rules for integrating algebraic functions in mathematical economics is:

$$\int cx^n \, dx = \frac{cx^{n+1}}{n + 1} + c \ (n \neq -1)$$

Example 6:

$$\int 5x^3 \, dx = \frac{5x^4}{4} + c$$

Another commonly used rule is:

$$\int (k)(u^n) \frac{du}{dx} = (k) \frac{u^{n+1}}{n + 1} + c \ (n \neq -1; u = f(x))$$

Example 7:

$$\int (3x^2 + 6)^5 (6x) = \frac{(3x^2 + 6)^6}{6} + c$$

Example 8:

$$\int (4x^3 - 7)^{20} (12x^2) = \frac{(4x^3 - 7)^{21}}{21} + c$$

Example 9:   If the proper constant is not found in du/dx, it can be introduced, as long as the reciprocal of the constant multiplies the integral. In effect we are multiplying the integral by 1:

$$\int (2x^3 + 20)^{10} (x^2) = \frac{1}{6} \int (2x^3 + 20)^{10} (6x^2) = \frac{(2x^3 + 20)^{11}}{66} + c$$

PROBLEMS 4-11

*1. Find the derivatives of the following functions by using the chain rule:
  *a. $y = (3x + 10)^4$ c. $y = \sqrt{36 - x^2}$
   b. $y = (3x^2 + 8x + 5)^{10}$ d. $y = (x + 1)^2$

*2. Find the derivatives of the following functions by using the product rule:
  *a. $y = (x^2)(x^3)$
   b. $y = (x^2 + 1)(\sqrt{x})$
   c. $y = (3x^2 + 8x + 3)(3x^4 - 6x + 8)$

*3. Find the derivatives of the following functions by using the quotient rule:

  *a. $y = \dfrac{x^5}{x^3}$

   b. $y = \dfrac{x^2 + 2}{x^3 + 5}$

*4. Find the derivatives of the following functions by using the implicit function rule:
  *a. $x^2 + y^2 = 36$
   b. $y^2 = x$

   c. $\dfrac{x^2}{9} + \dfrac{y^2}{16} = 1$

MATRIX ALGEBRA

5-1 INTRODUCTION AND DEFINITION OF A MATRIX

Many areas in business and economics are concerned with setting up arrays of numbers that can be subjected to mathematical analysis. For example, a firm's financial statement contains numbers in an array that represent such items as sales, operating expenses, capital, assets, and liabilities. The figures are analyzed horizontally by rows, vertically by columns, by position, and by selected ratios. *Matrix algebra* is that branch of mathematics concerned with arrays of numbers arranged in rows and columns.

A *matrix* is a rectangular array of numbers enclosed by parentheses or brackets. The usual convention is that upper-case letters refer to matrices, and corresponding lower-case letters refer to elements within matrices. A matrix is presented in two dimensions so the use of two subscripts is desirable in the notation. A matrix forms a rectangle with rows and columns; conventional notation indicates the row first and the column second with a double subscript notation. For example, a matrix with two rows and three columns is called a 2 by 3 matrix (2 X 3) and is represented as:

$$A = \begin{pmatrix} a_{11} & a_{12} & a_{13} \\ a_{21} & a_{22} & a_{23} \end{pmatrix}$$

In general a matrix with m rows and n columns is expressed as:

$$A = \begin{pmatrix} a_{11} & a_{12} & a_{13} & \cdots & a_{1n} \\ a_{21} & a_{22} & a_{23} & \cdots & a_{2n} \\ \cdot & \cdot & \cdot & \cdot & \cdot \\ \cdot & \cdot & \cdot & \cdot & \cdot \\ \cdot & \cdot & \cdot & \cdot & \cdot \\ a_{m1} & a_{m2} & a_{m3} & \cdot & a_{mn} \end{pmatrix}$$

The element a_{jk} is located in row j and column k. If more than single digits are needed to locate the row-column position, commas must be used to avoid confusion. For example, the element $a_{23,99}$ is the element in the 23rd row and 99th column. A few examples of matrices of different sizes follow:

$$A = \begin{pmatrix} -1 & 0 & 3 \\ 3 & -7 & 5 \end{pmatrix}_{2 \times 3}$$

Matrix A has two rows and three columns.

$$B = \begin{pmatrix} 1 & 0 \\ 0 & 1 \end{pmatrix}_{2 \times 2}$$

Matrix B is square.

$$C = \begin{pmatrix} 2 \\ 3 \\ 4 \end{pmatrix}_{3 \times 1}$$

Matrix C has three rows and one column and is called a *column vector*.

$$D = (2 \quad 3 \quad 4)_{1 \times 3}$$

Matrix D has one row and three columns and is called a *row vector*.

Matrix algebra forms an algebra in the classical sense of the word, and the intent of the algebra is similar at times. One of the main problems in algebra is in solving equations. Likewise in matrix algebra the solution of equations is equally important. Analogies between classical algebra and matrix algebra are useful in understanding the solutions to matrix equations. For example, when we solve algebraic equations, we must define such basic operations as addition, subtraction, and multiplication, Furthermore, we must have a zero, a multiplicative identity (the number 1), and an inverse. The *inverse* is the reciprocal and is denoted by $1/a$ or a^{-1} for the number a.

Matrix algebra will be developed in much the same manner as classical algebra. Section 5-2 will consider matrix operations and special types of matrices; Section 5-3 will find the inverse of a matrix. These sections will be foundational to Section 5-4, in which matrix equations will be studied.

PROBLEMS 5-1

1. If matrix A is square, then the main diagonal consists of those elements that lie on the line determined by the a_{11} and a_{nn} elements:

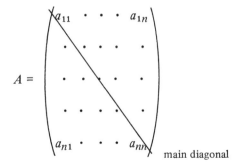

$$A = \begin{pmatrix} a_{11} & \cdots & a_{1n} \\ & & \\ & & \\ & & \\ a_{n1} & \cdots & a_{nn} \end{pmatrix}$$

main diagonal

Use sigma notation to find an expression that represents the sum of the elements on the main diagonal.

*2. Assume that matrix A has 30 rows and 50 columns:

   *a. Use sigma notation to find an expression for the sum of the elements in the tenth row.

   b. Use sigma notation to find an expression for the sum of the elements in the twentieth column.

   c. Use sigma notation to find an expression for the sum of the elements in column j.

3. The product of a set of n numbers $x_1, x_2, \ldots, x_n$ can be represented in *product notation*:

$$\prod_{k=1}^{n} X_k = x_1 x_2 \ldots x_n$$

If matrix A is a square matrix with 100 rows and 100 columns, use product notation to find an expression for the product of the elements on the main diagonal. What is the expression for $A_{n \times n}$?

5-2   MATRIX OPERATIONS AND SPECIAL MATRICES

Operations in matrix algebra are restricted to addition (subtraction) and multiplication. In this respect the algebra is considerably simplified. The following operations will be defined and supported by examples.

Addition (Subtraction) of Matrices

The sum (or difference) of two matrices is determined by adding (or subtracting) corresponding elements of the matrices. The matrices must be of the same size—that is, they must have an equal number of rows and columns—in order to *conform* to addition.

Example 1:

$$\begin{pmatrix} 1 & 2 & 5 \\ 3 & 4 & -1 \end{pmatrix}_{2 \times 3} + \begin{pmatrix} -1 & 0 & 2 \\ 3 & -4 & -2 \end{pmatrix}_{2 \times 3} = \begin{pmatrix} 0 & 2 & 7 \\ 6 & 0 & -3 \end{pmatrix}_{2 \times 3}$$

Example 2:

$$\begin{pmatrix} 4 & 6 \\ 8 & 10 \end{pmatrix}_{2 \times 2} - \begin{pmatrix} 2 & -6 \\ 8 & -20 \end{pmatrix}_{2 \times 2} = \begin{pmatrix} 2 & 12 \\ 0 & 30 \end{pmatrix}_{2 \times 2}$$

Example 3:

$$(1 \quad 2 \quad 3)_{1 \times 3} + (5 \quad 6 \quad 7)_{1 \times 3} = (6 \quad 8 \quad 10)_{1 \times 3}$$

Example 4:

$$(1 \quad 2 \quad 3)_{1 \times 2} + \begin{pmatrix} 5 \\ 6 \\ 6 \end{pmatrix}_{3 \times 1}$$

This example does not conform to addition.

Multiplication of a Matrix by a Scalar

To multiply a matrix by a *scalar* (real number) means to multiply every element in the matrix by the scalar. The definition can be used in reverse to "factor" a matrix. Conformability is not involved with this operation.

Example 5:

$$2 \begin{pmatrix} 2 & -4 \\ 3 & -5 \end{pmatrix} = \begin{pmatrix} 4 & -8 \\ 6 & -10 \end{pmatrix}$$

In this example the scalar = 2.

Example 6:

$$\begin{pmatrix} \dfrac{3}{5} & -\dfrac{2}{5} \\[2ex] \dfrac{7}{5} & \dfrac{9}{5} \end{pmatrix} = \dfrac{1}{5} \begin{pmatrix} 3 & -2 \\ 7 & 9 \end{pmatrix}$$

Matrix Multiplication

The multiplication of one matrix by another matrix is accomplished by the *row-column method*: First, multiply a row in the first matrix (on the left) by a column of a second matrix (on the right). In other words, multiply corresponding row-column elements, and then sum the products. This must be done for all rows and columns (starting at the top for the first matrix and moving left to right for the second matrix). *Conformability* for multiplication means, again, that the number of elements in the rows of the first matrix must equal the number of elements in the columns of the second matrix.

Example 7:

$$(1 \quad 3 \quad 5)_{1 \times 3} \cdot \begin{pmatrix} 2 \\ 4 \\ 6 \end{pmatrix}_{3 \times 1} = (44)_{1 \times 1}$$

Multiply corresponding row-column elements, and sum the products:

$$(1)(2) = 2$$
$$(3)(4) = 12$$
$$(5)(6) = \underline{30}$$
$$44$$

Conformability and the size of the product of two matrices is given in the notation of the matrix itself:

$$(1 \quad 3 \quad 5)_{1 \times 3} \cdot \begin{pmatrix} 2 \\ 4 \\ 6 \end{pmatrix}_{3 \times 1} = (44)_{1 \times 1}$$

size of product

Check for conformability.

Example 8:   For larger matrices the procedure is carried out for all possible rows and columns. Multiply the first row by the first column and proceed to multiply the first row by all columns (moving from left to right). Follow the same steps for subsequent rows.

$$\begin{pmatrix} 1 & 2 \\ 3 & 4 \end{pmatrix}_{2\times 2} \cdot \begin{pmatrix} 1 & 2 & 1 \\ 2 & 3 & 3 \end{pmatrix}_{2\times 3} = \begin{pmatrix} 5 & 8 & 7 \\ 11 & 18 & 15 \end{pmatrix}_{2\times 3}$$

Check for conformability and size of product.

Solution.   The first row times the first column yields $(1)(1) + (2)(2) = 5$. The first row times the second column yields $(1)(2) + (2)(3) = 8$. The first row times the third column yields $(1)(1) + (2)(3) = 7$. The second row times the first column yields $(3)(1) + (4)(2) = 11$. The second row times the second column yields $(3)(2) + (4)(3) = 18$. The second row times the third column yields $(3)(1) + (4)(3) = 15$.

Example 9:   Matrix multiplication is not necessarily commutative:

$$\begin{pmatrix} 1 & 2 \\ 3 & 4 \end{pmatrix}_{2\times 2} \cdot \begin{pmatrix} 2 & 1 \\ 1 & 1 \end{pmatrix}_{2\times 2} = \begin{pmatrix} 4 & 3 \\ 10 & 7 \end{pmatrix}_{2\times 2}$$

Interchanging the order of multiplication gives:

$$\begin{pmatrix} 2 & 1 \\ 1 & 1 \end{pmatrix}_{2\times 2} \cdot \begin{pmatrix} 1 & 2 \\ 3 & 4 \end{pmatrix}_{2\times 2} = \begin{pmatrix} 5 & 8 \\ 4 & 6 \end{pmatrix}_{2\times 2}$$

Example 10:   Special matrices are commutative:

$$\begin{pmatrix} 1 & 0 \\ 0 & 1 \end{pmatrix}_{2\times 2} \cdot \begin{pmatrix} 1 & 2 \\ 3 & 4 \end{pmatrix}_{2\times 2} = \begin{pmatrix} 1 & 2 \\ 3 & 4 \end{pmatrix} \cdot \begin{pmatrix} 1 & 0 \\ 0 & 1 \end{pmatrix} = \begin{pmatrix} 1 & 2 \\ 3 & 4 \end{pmatrix}_{2\times 2}$$

Example 11:

$$\begin{pmatrix} 2 \\ 1 \\ 3 \end{pmatrix}_{3\times 1} \cdot (4 \quad 5)_{1\times 2} = \begin{pmatrix} 8 & 10 \\ 4 & 5 \\ 12 & 15 \end{pmatrix}_{3\times 2}$$

Example 12:   The following matrices do not conform to multiplication:

$$\begin{pmatrix} 1 & 2 & 1 \\ 2 & 3 & 3 \end{pmatrix}_{2 \times 3} \cdot \begin{pmatrix} 3 & 4 \\ 5 & 6 \end{pmatrix}_{2 \times 2}$$

The conformability for multiplication of matrices can be generalized:

$$A_{m \times n} \cdot B_{n \times p} = C_{m \times p}$$

Check for conformability $(n = n)$ and size of product $(m \times p)$

Equality of Matrices

Two matrices are equal if corresponding elements are equal:

$$\begin{pmatrix} a & 2b \\ 3c & 4d \end{pmatrix} = \begin{pmatrix} 4 & 6 \\ -3 & 12 \end{pmatrix}$$

The above matrices are equal if $a = 4$, $b = 3$, $c = -1$, and $d = 3$.

Identity Matrix

The *identity matrix* (symbolized by I) is a square matrix with 1's along the main diagonal and 0's everywhere else. The identity matrix is commutative and is the matrix that performs the same function as the number 1 in algebra.

2 × 2 Identity (I)

minor diagonal

$$\begin{pmatrix} 1 & 0 \\ 0 & 1 \end{pmatrix}_{2 \times 2}$$

main diagonal

3 × 3 Identity (I)

$$\begin{pmatrix} 1 & 0 & 0 \\ 0 & 1 & 0 \\ 0 & 0 & 1 \end{pmatrix}_{3 \times 3}$$

4 × 4 Identity (I)

$$\begin{pmatrix} 1 & 0 & 0 & 0 \\ 0 & 1 & 0 & 0 \\ 0 & 0 & 1 & 0 \\ 0 & 0 & 0 & 1 \end{pmatrix}_{4\times4}$$

Example 13:   In general, $A_{n\times n}I_{n\times n} = I_{n\times n}A_{n\times n} = A_{n\times n}$. This can be verified for $I_{3\times3}$:

$$\begin{pmatrix} 1 & 2 & 3 \\ 4 & 5 & 6 \\ 7 & 8 & 9 \end{pmatrix}\begin{pmatrix} 1 & 0 & 0 \\ 0 & 1 & 0 \\ 0 & 0 & 1 \end{pmatrix} = \begin{pmatrix} 1 & 0 & 0 \\ 0 & 1 & 0 \\ 0 & 0 & 1 \end{pmatrix}\begin{pmatrix} 1 & 2 & 3 \\ 4 & 5 & 6 \\ 7 & 8 & 9 \end{pmatrix} = \begin{pmatrix} 1 & 2 & 3 \\ 4 & 5 & 6 \\ 7 & 8 & 9 \end{pmatrix}$$

Zero Matrix

The *zero matrix* is a matrix of any size all of whose elements are zeros. A 2 × 2 zero matrix is expressed as:

$$\begin{pmatrix} 0 & 0 \\ 0 & 0 \end{pmatrix}$$

A 1 × 3 zero matrix is expressed as:

$$(0 \quad 0 \quad 0)$$

$$\begin{pmatrix} 1 & 2 \\ 3 & 4 \end{pmatrix} + \begin{pmatrix} 0 & 0 \\ 0 & 0 \end{pmatrix} = \begin{pmatrix} 1 & 2 \\ 3 & 4 \end{pmatrix}$$

Transpose of a Matrix

The *transpose* of a matrix A, written A^T, is obtained by making rows of A into columns in the transpose.

$$A = \begin{pmatrix} 1 & 2 & 3 \\ 4 & 5 & 6 \end{pmatrix}_{2\times3}$$

$$A = \begin{pmatrix} 1 & 4 \\ 2 & 5 \\ 3 & 6 \end{pmatrix}_{3 \times 2}$$

PROBLEMS 5-2

Perform the indicated operations:

*1. $\begin{pmatrix} 1 & -7 & 4 \\ 0 & 3 & 4 \end{pmatrix} + \begin{pmatrix} 2 & 4 & -6 \\ 1 & -3 & 5 \end{pmatrix}$

2. $(-1 \quad 2 \quad 5) + (1 \quad -2 \quad 7)$

3. $\begin{pmatrix} 2 \\ 5 \\ -3 \end{pmatrix} + \begin{pmatrix} 0 \\ 3 \\ 7 \end{pmatrix}$

4. $\begin{pmatrix} 1 & 4 \\ 3 & 7 \end{pmatrix} + \begin{pmatrix} 0 & 0 \\ 0 & 0 \end{pmatrix}$

5. $\begin{pmatrix} 1 & 2 \\ 3 & 4 \end{pmatrix} + \begin{pmatrix} 5 \\ 2 \end{pmatrix}$

*6. $2 \begin{pmatrix} 5 & 6 \\ -1 & 3 \end{pmatrix} - 2 \begin{pmatrix} 3 & -4 \\ 3 & 7 \end{pmatrix}$

*7. $\begin{pmatrix} -3 & 4 \\ -5 & 2 \end{pmatrix} \cdot \begin{pmatrix} 3 & 7 \\ 1 & -5 \end{pmatrix}$

8. $(1 \quad 3 \quad 7) \cdot \begin{pmatrix} 7 \\ -2 \\ 5 \end{pmatrix}$

9. $\begin{pmatrix} 1 \\ 7 \\ 8 \\ 4 \end{pmatrix} \cdot (1 \quad 3 \quad 8 \quad 2)$

*10. $\begin{pmatrix} 3 & 5 \\ 4 & 9 \end{pmatrix} \cdot \begin{pmatrix} 0 & 0 \\ 0 & 0 \end{pmatrix}$

11. $\begin{pmatrix} 3 & 7 \\ -5 & 6 \end{pmatrix} \cdot \begin{pmatrix} 1 & 0 \\ 0 & 1 \end{pmatrix}$

12. $\begin{pmatrix} 1 & 0 \\ 0 & 1 \end{pmatrix} \cdot \begin{pmatrix} 3 & 7 \\ -5 & 6 \end{pmatrix}$

13. $\begin{pmatrix} 1 & 0 & 0 \\ 0 & 1 & 0 \\ 0 & 0 & 0 \end{pmatrix} \cdot \begin{pmatrix} 2 & 4 & 6 \\ 8 & 7 & 5 \\ 1 & 3 & 5 \end{pmatrix}$

14. $\begin{pmatrix} 0 & 0 & 1 \\ 0 & 1 & 0 \\ 1 & 0 & 0 \end{pmatrix} \cdot \begin{pmatrix} 1 & 2 & 3 \\ 4 & 5 & 6 \\ 7 & 8 & 9 \end{pmatrix}$

15. $\begin{pmatrix} 1 & 2 & 3 \\ 4 & 5 & 6 \end{pmatrix} \cdot \begin{pmatrix} 1 & 2 \\ 3 & 4 \\ 5 & 6 \end{pmatrix}$

18. $(4 \quad 5 \quad 7) \cdot \begin{pmatrix} -4 \\ -2 \\ 1 \end{pmatrix}$

19. $\begin{pmatrix} 3 & 4 \\ 5 & 6 \end{pmatrix} \cdot \begin{pmatrix} 3 & 4 \\ 6 & 7 \\ 6 & 2 \end{pmatrix}$

*16. $\begin{pmatrix} 1 & 2 \\ 5 & 7 \\ 3 & 8 \end{pmatrix} \cdot \begin{pmatrix} 7 \\ 6 \end{pmatrix}$

17. $\begin{pmatrix} 4 & 8 \\ 4 & 10 \end{pmatrix} \cdot \begin{pmatrix} 5/4 & -1 \\ -1/2 & 1/2 \end{pmatrix}$

20. Solve the following matrix equation for the unknowns:

$$\begin{pmatrix} 2x & 4y \\ 5z & 8w \end{pmatrix} = \begin{pmatrix} 4 & -8 \\ 17 & -13 \end{pmatrix}$$

*21. Find the transpose of the following matrices:

*a. $\begin{pmatrix} 1 & 2 & 3 & 4 \\ 2 & 4 & 6 & 8 \end{pmatrix}$

d. $(1 \quad 2 \quad 3)$

b. $\begin{pmatrix} 4 & 8 \\ 4 & 8 \end{pmatrix}$

e. $\begin{pmatrix} 3 & 4 & 5 \\ 1 & 3 & 5 \\ 3 & 5 & 7 \end{pmatrix}$

c. $\begin{pmatrix} 1 & 0 \\ 0 & 1 \end{pmatrix}$

f. $\begin{pmatrix} 1 \\ 2 \\ 3 \\ 4 \end{pmatrix}$

5-3   INVERSE OF A MATRIX

The *inverse* of a square matrix $A_{n \times n}$ is represented by $A_{n \times n}^{-1}$ and:

$$(A_{n \times n}^{-1})(A_{n \times n}) = (A_{n \times n})(A_{n \times n}^{-1}) = I_{n \times n}$$

where I is the identity matrix.

Before you study the procedure for finding the inverses of matrices, review the section on determinants in Chapter 1. Recall that:

$$D = \begin{vmatrix} a & b \\ c & d \end{vmatrix} = ad - bc$$

Inverse of a 2 × 2 Matrix

Three steps are involved in finding the inverse of a 2 × 2 matrix. To find the inverse of a 2 × 2 matrix A, first, interchange the positions of the elements on the main diagonal. Next, negate the elements on the minor diagonal. Finally, divide each element by the determinant of the matrix A.

The above three steps can be stated as a formula: The inverse of:

$$A = \begin{pmatrix} a & b \\ c & d \end{pmatrix}$$

is:

$$A^{-1} = \begin{pmatrix} \dfrac{d}{D} & -\dfrac{b}{D} \\ -\dfrac{c}{D} & \dfrac{a}{D} \end{pmatrix}$$

where D is the determinant of matrix A and $D \neq 0$.

The proof of the above procedure can be obtained by carrying out the multiplication $(A)(A^{-1}) = (A^{-1})(A) = I_{2 \times 2}$.

Example 1:   Find the inverse of:

$$A = \begin{pmatrix} 5 & 13 \\ 1 & 3 \end{pmatrix}$$

Solution.   First, interchange the positions of the elements of the main diagonal (5 and 3). Then negate the elements on the minor diagonal (becomes -13 and -1). Finally, divide each element by the determinant of the matrix:

$$\begin{vmatrix} 5 & 13 \\ 1 & 3 \end{vmatrix} = 2$$

The inverse is:

$$A^{-1} = \begin{pmatrix} \dfrac{3}{2} & -\dfrac{13}{2} \\ -\dfrac{1}{2} & \dfrac{5}{2} \end{pmatrix}$$

Verify that $(A)(A^{-1}) = (A^{-1})(A) = I_{2 \times 2}$.

Example 2:   The inverse of:

$$B = \begin{pmatrix} 2 & 5 \\ 1 & 3 \end{pmatrix}$$

is:

$$B^{-1} = \begin{pmatrix} 3 & -5 \\ -1 & 2 \end{pmatrix}$$

Example 3:   The inverse of:

$$I = \begin{pmatrix} 1 & 0 \\ 0 & 1 \end{pmatrix}$$

is:

$$I^{-1} = \begin{pmatrix} 1 & 0 \\ 0 & 1 \end{pmatrix}$$

Example 4:   The matrix:

$$\begin{pmatrix} 2 & 3 \\ 4 & 6 \end{pmatrix}$$

has no inverse, because:

$$\begin{vmatrix} 2 & 3 \\ 4 & 6 \end{vmatrix} = 0$$

and division by 0 is undefined.

Inverse of a 3 × 3 Matrix

The inverse of a 3 × 3 matrix is obtained by the following steps (these steps can also be used to find the inverse of an $n \times n$ matrix): (1) for the inverse of $A_{3 \times 3}$ replace a_{ij} by the cofactors, symbolized by c_{ij}; (2) take the transpose of the result in (1); (3) divide each element by the value of the determinant of the matrix (represented by D).

The above steps can be stated as a formula for finding the inverse of $A_{n \times n}$:

$$A_{n \times n}^{-1} = (1/D)(\text{transpose of the cofactors})_{n \times n}, \text{ where } D \neq 0.$$

Example 5:   Find the inverse of:

$$A = \begin{pmatrix} 1 & 2 & 3 \\ 4 & 2 & 2 \\ 1 & 3 & 3 \end{pmatrix}$$

Solution.   First, find the cofactors of each position (see Chapter 1):

$$\begin{aligned}
c_{11} &= 0 & c_{12} &= -10 & c_{13} &= 10 \\
c_{21} &= 3 & c_{22} &= 0 & c_{23} &= -1 \\
c_{31} &= -2 & c_{32} &= 10 & c_{33} &= -6
\end{aligned}$$

Next, take the transpose of the above cofactors to form the following matrix:

$$\begin{pmatrix} 0 & 3 & -2 \\ -10 & 0 & 10 \\ 10 & -1 & -6 \end{pmatrix}$$

The transpose of the cofactors forms the *adjoint* matrix.
   Finally:

$$\begin{vmatrix} 1 & 2 & 3 \\ 4 & 2 & 2 \\ 1 & 3 & 3 \end{vmatrix} = 10$$

The inverse of:

$$A = \begin{pmatrix} 1 & 2 & 3 \\ 4 & 2 & 2 \\ 1 & 3 & 3 \end{pmatrix}$$

is:

$$A^{-1} = \frac{1}{10} \begin{pmatrix} 0 & 3 & -2 \\ -10 & 0 & 10 \\ 10 & -1 & -6 \end{pmatrix}$$

Verify that $(A)(A^{-1}) = (A^{-1})(A) = I_{3 \times 3}$.

Example 6:   Find the inverse of:

$$A = \begin{pmatrix} 1 & 1 & 1 \\ 3 & 1 & -1 \\ -2 & -2 & 3 \end{pmatrix}$$

Solution.   The cofactors of the elements in A are:

$$c_{11} = 1 \qquad c_{12} = -7 \qquad c_{13} = -4$$
$$c_{21} = -5 \qquad c_{22} = 5 \qquad c_{23} = 0$$
$$c_{31} = -2 \qquad c_{32} = 4 \qquad c_{33} = -2$$

The transpose of these numbers forms the matrix:

$$\begin{pmatrix} 1 & -5 & -2 \\ -7 & 5 & 4 \\ -4 & 0 & -2 \end{pmatrix}$$

The determinant of matrix A is:

$$\begin{vmatrix} 1 & 1 & 1 \\ 3 & 1 & -1 \\ -2 & -2 & 3 \end{vmatrix} = -10$$

The inverse of:

$$A = \begin{pmatrix} 1 & 1 & 1 \\ 3 & 1 & -1 \\ -2 & -2 & 3 \end{pmatrix}$$

is:

$$A^{-1} = \frac{-1}{10} \begin{pmatrix} 1 & -5 & -2 \\ -7 & 5 & 4 \\ -4 & 0 & -2 \end{pmatrix}$$

Verify that $(A)(A^{-1}) = (A^{-1})(A) = I_{3 \times 3}$.

PROBLEMS 5-3

*1. Find the inverses of the following 2 X 2 matrices:

*a. $\begin{pmatrix} 2 & 5 \\ 7 & -1 \end{pmatrix}$ b. $\begin{pmatrix} -4 & 8 \\ -3 & 2 \end{pmatrix}$ c. $\begin{pmatrix} 1 & 0 \\ 0 & 1 \end{pmatrix}$

d. $\begin{pmatrix} 10 & 9 \\ 1 & 1 \end{pmatrix}$ f. $\begin{pmatrix} 10 & 10 \\ 1 & 2 \end{pmatrix}$ h. $\begin{pmatrix} 3 & -5 \\ -2 & 4 \end{pmatrix}$

e. $\begin{pmatrix} 2 & 4 \\ 4 & 8 \end{pmatrix}$ g. $\begin{pmatrix} -3 & -5 \\ -2 & -4 \end{pmatrix}$ i. $\begin{pmatrix} 0 & 5 \\ -1 & 4 \end{pmatrix}$

*2. Find the inverses of the following 3 × 3 matrices by using the adjoint (transpose of the cofactors) technique.

*a. $\begin{pmatrix} 2 & 2 & 6 \\ 4 & 2 & 6 \\ 8 & 4 & 4 \end{pmatrix}$ c. $\begin{pmatrix} 1 & 0 & 0 \\ 0 & 1 & 0 \\ 0 & 0 & 1 \end{pmatrix}$ e. $\begin{pmatrix} -1 & 3 & -2 \\ -3 & 1 & 4 \\ 1 & -2 & 5 \end{pmatrix}$

b. $\begin{pmatrix} 1 & 1 & 1 \\ 3 & 2 & 1 \\ 4 & 3 & 1 \end{pmatrix}$ d. $\begin{pmatrix} 2 & 2 & 2 \\ 4 & 4 & 4 \\ 2 & 2 & 2 \end{pmatrix}$

5-4   SOLVING MATRIX EQUATIONS

Matrix algebra can be used to solve systems of n equations in n unknowns. The principles involved are the same as in solving an equation in classical algebra. In understanding the procedure, keep in mind the algebraic process of solving the following equation for the variable Z:

$AZ = B$ (solve for Z)

$AA^{-1}Z = A^{-1}B$ (basic assumption)

$1Z = A^{-1}B$ (existence of 1)

$Z = A^{-1}B$ (property of 1)

The same steps will be used to solve systems of equations with matrix algebra where A, B, and Z represent matrices and the identity element is matrix identity I.

Solving Systems of Two Equations in Two Unknowns

Given that:

$$ax + by = c$$
$$dx + ey = f$$

then the solution to the system is:

$$\begin{pmatrix} x \\ y \end{pmatrix}_{2 \times 1} = \text{inverse of} \begin{pmatrix} a & b \\ d & e \end{pmatrix}_{2 \times 2} \cdot \begin{pmatrix} c \\ f \end{pmatrix}_{2 \times 1}$$

In the above equation it is important to place the inverse matrix to the left of the column of constants to obtain conformability for multiplication.

The proof of the above solution follows:

Given that:

$$ax + by = c$$
$$dx + ey = f$$

The equations can be written in matrix algebra form as:

$$\begin{pmatrix} ax + by \\ dx + ey \end{pmatrix}_{2 \times 1} = \begin{pmatrix} c \\ f \end{pmatrix}_{2 \times 1} \quad \text{or} \quad \begin{pmatrix} a & b \\ d & e \end{pmatrix}_{2 \times 2} \begin{pmatrix} x \\ y \end{pmatrix}_{2 \times 1} = \begin{pmatrix} c \\ f \end{pmatrix}_{2 \times 1}$$

Multiplying both sides of the above equation by the inverse of:

$$\begin{pmatrix} a & b \\ d & e \end{pmatrix}$$

gives the solution to the system:

$$\begin{pmatrix} x \\ y \end{pmatrix}_{2 \times 1} = \text{inverse of} \begin{pmatrix} a & b \\ d & e \end{pmatrix}_{2 \times 2} \cdot \begin{pmatrix} c \\ f \end{pmatrix}_{2 \times 1}$$

where the inverse of:

$$\begin{pmatrix} a & b \\ d & e \end{pmatrix}$$

is:

$$\begin{pmatrix} \dfrac{e}{D} & -\dfrac{b}{D} \\ -\dfrac{d}{D} & \dfrac{a}{D} \end{pmatrix} ; \; D \neq 0$$

When we multiply the inverse by the column of constants, we must place the inverse on the left to ensure conformability for multiplication.

Example 1:   Solve the system of equations:

$$2x + 5y = 4$$
$$x + 3y = 6$$

Solution.

$$\begin{pmatrix} x \\ y \end{pmatrix} = \text{inverse} \begin{pmatrix} 2 & 5 \\ 1 & 3 \end{pmatrix} \cdot \begin{pmatrix} 4 \\ 6 \end{pmatrix} = \begin{pmatrix} 3 & -5 \\ -1 & 2 \end{pmatrix} \cdot \begin{pmatrix} 4 \\ 6 \end{pmatrix}$$

$$\begin{pmatrix} x \\ y \end{pmatrix} = \begin{pmatrix} -18 \\ 8 \end{pmatrix}$$

which means that $x = -18$ and $y = 8$ are the solutions to the system of equations.

Example 2:   Solve the system of equations:

$$-x - 5y = 2$$
$$7x + 2y = 4$$

Solution.

$$\begin{pmatrix} x \\ y \end{pmatrix} = \text{inverse} \begin{pmatrix} -1 & -5 \\ 7 & 2 \end{pmatrix} \cdot \begin{pmatrix} 2 \\ 4 \end{pmatrix} = \begin{pmatrix} \dfrac{2}{33} & \dfrac{5}{33} \\ \dfrac{-7}{33} & \dfrac{-1}{33} \end{pmatrix} \cdot \begin{pmatrix} 2 \\ 4 \end{pmatrix}$$

$$\begin{pmatrix} x \\ y \end{pmatrix} = \begin{pmatrix} \dfrac{24}{33} \\ \dfrac{-18}{33} \end{pmatrix}$$

The solutions are $x = 24/33$ and $y = -18/33$.

Solving Systems of Three Equations in Three Unknowns

The solution of three equations in three unknowns would follow the same technique as the solution of a system of two equations in two unknowns.

Given that:

$$ax + by + cz = c_1$$
$$dx + ey + fz = c_2$$
$$gx + hy + iz = c_3$$

then

$$\begin{pmatrix} x \\ y \\ z \end{pmatrix}_{3 \times 1} = \frac{1}{D} \cdot \begin{pmatrix} \text{transpose of cofactors} \\ \text{of coefficient matrix} \end{pmatrix}_{3 \times 3} \cdot \begin{pmatrix} c_1 \\ c_2 \\ c_3 \end{pmatrix}_{3 \times 1} \quad ; D \neq 0$$

The proof of the solution is the same as the previous proof for a system of two equations in two unknowns. The transpose of the cofactors forms the adjoint matrix.

Example 3: Solve the following systems of equations:

$$x + y + z = 6$$
$$3x + y - z = 2$$
$$-2x - 2y + 3z = 3$$

Solution.

$$\begin{pmatrix} x \\ y \\ z \end{pmatrix} = \frac{1}{-10} \begin{pmatrix} 1 & -5 & -2 \\ -7 & 5 & 4 \\ -4 & 0 & -2 \end{pmatrix} \cdot \begin{pmatrix} 6 \\ 2 \\ 3 \end{pmatrix}$$

$$\begin{pmatrix} x \\ y \\ z \end{pmatrix} = \begin{pmatrix} 1 \\ 2 \\ 3 \end{pmatrix}$$

The solutions are $x = 1$, $y = 2$, and $z = 3$.

Solving Systems of n Equations in n Unknowns

A system of n equations in n unknowns can be solved in the same manner as the previously seen systems.

Given that:

$$a_{11}x_1 + a_{12}x_2 + \quad \cdot \quad \cdot \quad \cdot \quad + a_{1n}x_n = c_1$$
$$a_{21}x_1 + a_{22}x_2 + \quad \cdot \quad \cdot \quad \cdot \quad + a_{2n}x_n = c_2$$
$$a_{n1}x_1 + a_{n2}x_2 + \quad \cdot \quad \cdot \quad \cdot \quad + a_{nn}x_n = c_n$$

then:

$$\begin{pmatrix} x_1 \\ x_2 \\ x_3 \\ \cdot \\ \cdot \\ \cdot \\ x_n \end{pmatrix}_{n \times 1} = \frac{1}{D} \cdot \begin{pmatrix} \text{transpose of cofactors} \\ \text{of coefficient matrix} \end{pmatrix}_{n \times n} \cdot \begin{pmatrix} c_1 \\ c_2 \\ c_3 \\ \cdot \\ \cdot \\ \cdot \\ c_n \end{pmatrix}_{n \times 1} \quad ; D \neq 0$$

Many computer languages have built-in matrix operations or library subroutines that find the inverse of a matrix. In this case a system of n equations in n unknowns can be solved by the single operation of multiplying the inverse of the matrix making up the coefficients by the column vector of constants.

Solving Systems of Equations Using Elementary Row Operations

Three elementary row operations can be applied to matrices for solving systems of equations. These operations have their basis in algebra, where solving systems was given by using the basic assumption of algebra to eliminate a variable (see Chapter 1). The three elementary row operations include:

1. Multiplication of each element in a row of a matrix by the same number.
2. Addition or subtraction of each element in a row of a matrix by the corresponding element of another row.
3. Interchanging of two rows.

The symbol "$\sim$" is used to indicate that an elementary row transformation has taken place. The following demonstrates interchanging rows 1 and 2, then multiplying the first row by 2, and finally adding row 1 to row 2:

$$\begin{pmatrix} 2 & 3 \\ 5 & 7 \end{pmatrix} \sim \begin{pmatrix} 5 & 7 \\ 2 & 3 \end{pmatrix} \sim \begin{pmatrix} 10 & 14 \\ 2 & 3 \end{pmatrix} \sim \begin{pmatrix} 10 & 14 \\ 12 & 17 \end{pmatrix}$$

Example 4: Elementary row transformation can be used to solve systems of equations. Consider the system:

row 1: $2x + 3y = 8$

row 2: $4x + 5y = 6$

First, multiply row 1 by 1/2:

$$x + \frac{3}{2} y = 4$$

$$4x + 5y = 6$$

Next, multiply row 1 by -4, and add the result to row 2:

$$x + \frac{3}{2} y = 4$$

$$0 - y = -10$$

Then multiply row 2 by (3/2), and add the result to row 1:

$$x + 0 = 6$$
$$0 - y = -10$$

Finally, multiply row 2 by -1:

$$x + 0 = 6$$
$$0 + y = 10$$

The solutions are $x = 6$ and $y = 10$. The above steps can be expressed in matrix form. The system of equations can be represented by:

$$\begin{pmatrix} 2 & 3 \\ 4 & 5 \end{pmatrix} \cdot \begin{pmatrix} x \\ y \end{pmatrix} = \begin{pmatrix} 8 \\ 6 \end{pmatrix}$$

coefficient   constant
matrix   matrix

Step 1.

$$\begin{pmatrix} 1 & \dfrac{3}{2} \\ 4 & 5 \end{pmatrix} \cdot \begin{pmatrix} x \\ y \end{pmatrix} = \begin{pmatrix} 4 \\ 6 \end{pmatrix}$$

Step 2.

$$\begin{pmatrix} 1 & \dfrac{3}{2} \\ 0 & -1 \end{pmatrix} \cdot \begin{pmatrix} x \\ y \end{pmatrix} = \begin{pmatrix} 4 \\ -10 \end{pmatrix}$$

Step 3.

$$\begin{pmatrix} 1 & 0 \\ 0 & -1 \end{pmatrix} \cdot \begin{pmatrix} x \\ y \end{pmatrix} = \begin{pmatrix} 6 \\ 10 \end{pmatrix}$$

Step 4.

$$\begin{pmatrix} 1 & 0 \\ 0 & 1 \end{pmatrix} \cdot \begin{pmatrix} x \\ y \end{pmatrix} = \begin{pmatrix} 6 \\ 10 \end{pmatrix}$$

The above example will be used to develop the following algorithm, which is used to solve systems of equations by using elementary row transformations.

Algorithm.   To solve a system of equations by using elementary row operations, write the coefficients of the variables in columns as they are met from the equations. Assume that the same variables are given in columns. This forms the coefficient matrix. Draw a vertical line to the right of these elements, and place the columns of constants to the right of this line.

The coefficient matrix to the left of the vertical line is the *augmented matrix*. The algorithm states to reduce the coefficient matrix to the identity matrix by using elementary row operations. The reduction is usually made by working in columns to form the identity, and the solutions will appear in the constant matrix. If the variables in the system are in order $x_1, x_2, \ldots, x_n$, then the constant matrix represents respective solutions from the variables by starting from the top of the constant matrix and working down in that column.

Example 5:   Solve the following system of equations by using elementary row operations:

$$2x + 3y = 4$$
$$-2x + y = 12$$

Solution.   First, form the augmented matrix:

$$\left(\begin{array}{cc|c} 2 & 3 & 4 \\ -2 & 1 & 12 \end{array} \right)$$

coefficient constant
matrix   matrix

Use the algorithm to form the identity by columns by using elementary row operations. In doing this the solutions appear where the constant matrix has been formed. The top element in the constant matrix is the value of x, and the bottom element is the value of y.

Now divide row 1 by row 2:

$$\left(\begin{array}{cc|c} 2 & 3 & 4 \\ -2 & 1 & 12 \end{array} \right) \sim \left(\begin{array}{cc|c} 1 & \dfrac{3}{2} & 2 \\ -2 & 1 & 12 \end{array} \right)$$

Next, multiply row 1 by row 2, and add the result to row 2:

$$\sim \begin{pmatrix} 1 & \dfrac{3}{2} & \bigg| & 2 \\ 0 & 4 & \bigg| & 16 \end{pmatrix}$$

Then divide row 2 by 4:

$$\sim \begin{pmatrix} 1 & \dfrac{3}{2} & \bigg| & 2 \\ 0 & 1 & \bigg| & 4 \end{pmatrix}$$

Finally, multiply row 2 by $(-3/2)$, and add the result to row 1:

$$\sim \begin{pmatrix} 1 & 0 & \bigg| & -4 \\ 0 & 1 & \bigg| & 4 \end{pmatrix}$$

The solutions for x and y appear in order to the right of the vertical line: $x = -4$ and $y = 4$.

Example 6:   Solve the following system of equations by using elementary row operations:

$$x + y + z = 6$$
$$3x + y + 2z = 11$$
$$4x + 3y + z = 13$$

Solution.   Form the augmented matrix:

$$\begin{pmatrix} 1 & 1 & 1 & \bigg| & 6 \\ 3 & 1 & 2 & \bigg| & 11 \\ 4 & 3 & 1 & \bigg| & 13 \end{pmatrix}$$

$$\underbrace{\qquad\qquad}_{\substack{\text{coefficient} \\ \text{matrix}}} \quad \underbrace{\qquad}_{\substack{\text{constant} \\ \text{matrix}}}$$

Use elementary row operations to reduce the coefficient matrix to the identity matrix. Work in columns.

First, work from left to right and obtain the identity matrix by columns. The 3 and 4 in the first column must be eliminated, and zeros must appear in these positions. This is done by multiplying row 1 by -3 and adding this to row 2 and then by multiplying row 1 by -4 and adding this to row 3. These results appear in the first matrix; rows 2 and 3 are then interchanged to give the second-row equivalent matrix:

$$\begin{pmatrix} 1 & 1 & 1 & | & 6 \\ 0 & -2 & -1 & | & -7 \\ 0 & -1 & -3 & | & -11 \end{pmatrix} \sim \begin{pmatrix} 1 & 1 & 1 & | & 6 \\ 0 & -1 & -3 & | & -11 \\ 0 & -2 & -1 & | & -7 \end{pmatrix} \sim$$

Adding row 2 to row 1 and multiplying row 2 by -1 gives:

$$\begin{pmatrix} 1 & 0 & -2 & | & -5 \\ 0 & 1 & 3 & | & 11 \\ 0 & -2 & -1 & | & -7 \end{pmatrix} \sim$$

Multiplying row 2 by 2 and adding to row 3 gives:

$$\begin{pmatrix} 1 & 0 & -2 & | & -5 \\ 0 & 1 & 3 & | & 11 \\ 0 & 0 & 5 & | & 15 \end{pmatrix}$$

Dividing row 3 by 5 gives:

$$\begin{pmatrix} 1 & 0 & -2 & | & -5 \\ 0 & 1 & 3 & | & 11 \\ 0 & 0 & 1 & | & 3 \end{pmatrix}$$

Multiplying row 3 by 2 and adding to row 1 gives:

$$\begin{pmatrix} 1 & 0 & 0 & | & 1 \\ 0 & 1 & 3 & | & 11 \\ 0 & 0 & 1 & | & 3 \end{pmatrix}$$

Multiplying row 3 by -3 and adding to row 2 gives:

$$\begin{pmatrix} 1 & 0 & 0 & | & 1 \\ 0 & 1 & 0 & | & 2 \\ 0 & 0 & 1 & | & 3 \end{pmatrix}$$

The solutions appear in order: $x = 1$, $y = 2$, and $z = 3$.

PROBLEMS 5-4

*1. Solve the following systems of two equations in two unknowns:

*a. $2x - y = 4$ e. $-2x + 3y = -7$ i. $2x + 3y = 4$
  $3x + y = 6$ $3x - 2y = 8$ $6y + 4x = 8$

*b. $2x + 3y = 7$ f. $3x_1 + 4x_2 = 7$ j. $-2x + 3y + 7 = 0$
  $5x + 6y = 12$ $-2x_1 + 3x_2 = -5$ $3x = 2y + 8$

c. $-x + y = 7$ g. $3w - 5r = 8$ k. $2y + 4x = 8$
  $x + 2y = 14$ $8w + r = -3$ $3y - 7 = 0$

d. $-5x + 8y = -7$ h. $2s - 5p = 7$
  $6x - 8y = 12$ $3p + 5s + 4 = 0$

*2. Solve the following systems of three equations in three unknowns by using the adjoint (transpose of the cofactors):

*a. $x + y + z = 6$ b. $x + y + z = 12$ c. $x + y + z = 10$
  $3x + 2y + z = 10$ $-y + 2x - 18 = -3z$ $2x + 2y + 2z = 20$
  $4x + 3y + x = 13$ $6x + z - 3y = 6$ $3x + 3y + 3z = 30$

*3. Solve the following systems of equations by using elementary row operations:

*a. $2x - 3y = 4$ c. $x + y + z = 6$ d. $x + y + z = 12$
  $4x + 3y = 8$ $3x + 2y + z = 10$ $2x - y + 3z = 18$

b. $4x + 2y = 6$ $4x + 3y + z = 11$ $6x - 3y + z = 6$
  $-2x + 4y = 12$

5-5   APPLICATIONS OF MATRIX ALGEBRA

Business problems frequently involve the use of arrays. The examples here involve relatively small arrays simply for the sake of expediting the calculations. Regard the examples as being extendable to large arrays that would lend themselves to computerization.

Application to Production and Cost

A firm produces three types of computers, which are classified as small, medium, and large. Demand for the computers is such that 100 small, 200 medium, and 300 large machines must be scheduled for production to satisfy orders. These data can be represented by a row vector called *production*:

$$\text{production} = (100 \qquad 200 \qquad 300)_{1 \times 3}$$
$$\qquad\qquad\quad \text{small} \quad\;\; \text{medium} \quad\; \text{large}$$

Certain units of direct materials and direct labor go into the production of each of the computers. This can be expressed as follows:

$$\text{units} = \begin{pmatrix} 2 & 1 \\ 4 & 3 \\ 6 & 5 \end{pmatrix}_{3 \times 2} \begin{matrix} \text{small computers} \\ \text{medium computers} \\ \text{large computers} \end{matrix}$$
$$\quad\;\; \text{direct} \quad\; \text{direct}$$
$$\quad\;\; \text{materials} \quad \text{labor}$$

The unit cost of direct materials and direct labor is given by the following column vector:

$$\text{cost} = \begin{pmatrix} \$2,000 \\ \$3,000 \end{pmatrix}_{2 \times 1} \begin{matrix} \text{direct materials (per unit)} \\ \text{direct labor (per unit)} \end{matrix}$$

The above matrices were given according to a specific shape to satisfy conformability.

Example 1: The total number of units of direct materials and direct labor needed to meet production requirements can be represented by matrix multiplication as follows:

$$(\text{production})_{1 \times 3} \cdot (\text{units})_{3 \times 2} = (\text{total units})_{1 \times 2}$$

$$(100 \quad 200 \quad 300)_{1 \times 3} \cdot \begin{pmatrix} 2 & 1 \\ 4 & 3 \\ 6 & 5 \end{pmatrix}_{3 \times 2} = \underset{\substack{\text{units of direct} \\ \text{material needed}}}{(2,800} \quad \underset{\substack{\text{units of direct} \\ \text{labor needed}}}{22,000)_{1 \times 2}}$$

Example 2:   The firm's total cost of direct materials and direct labor is represented by:

$$(\text{total units})_{1 \times 2} \cdot (\text{cost})_{2 \times 1} = (\text{total cost})_{1 \times 1}$$

$$(2,800 \quad 2,200)_{1 \times 2} \cdot \begin{pmatrix} \$2,000 \\ \$3,000 \end{pmatrix}_{2 \times 1} = (\$12,200,000)_{1 \times 1}$$

$12,200,000 is the total cost of direct materials and direct labor.

Notice that the numbers had to be properly set up for meaningful conformability. For example, if the production matrix were set up as a column vector (3 × 1), it would not conform to multiplication with units. Moreover, if the cost matrix were set up as a row vector, conformability would not be satisfied with total units.

Application to Allocation of Overhead

A firm has two service departments that are symbolized by S_1 and S_2 and two production departments that are symbolized by P_1 and P_2. The firm allocates the total overhead to production departments by means of a primary and secondary distribution process as follows:

The *primary overhead* to be allocated to all departments is given by the following table:

S_1	S_2	P_1	P_2	Total
$9,700	$19,400	$30,000	$40,000	$99,100

The *secondary distribution* of overhead is made from the service department to the production departments on an exchange basis to ensure that all service costs are allocated to the production departments. The secondary distribution table below also reflects the fact that services are interchanged among service departments themselves:

	Percentages to be allocated			
Service departments	S_1	S_2	P_1	P_2
S_1	0%	30%	30%	40%
S_2	10%	0%	40%	50%

The service departments' overhead allocations in the secondary distribution process can be represented by the following equations:

$$S_1 = \$9,700 + .10S_2$$
$$S_2 = \$19,400 + .30S_1$$

which can be rewritten as:

$$S_1 - .10S_2 = \$9,700$$
$$-.30S_1 + S_2 = \$19,400$$

The solution to these equations can be obtained by using matrix algebra:

$$\begin{pmatrix} 1 & -.10 \\ -.30 & 1 \end{pmatrix} \cdot \begin{pmatrix} S_1 \\ S_2 \end{pmatrix} = \begin{pmatrix} \$9,700 \\ \$19,400 \end{pmatrix}$$

$$\begin{pmatrix} S_1 \\ S_2 \end{pmatrix} = \begin{pmatrix} \dfrac{1}{.97} & \dfrac{.10}{.97} \\ \dfrac{.30}{.97} & \dfrac{1}{.97} \end{pmatrix} \cdot \begin{pmatrix} 9,700 \\ 19,400 \end{pmatrix} = \begin{pmatrix} \$12,000 \\ \$23,000 \end{pmatrix}$$

$S_1 = \$12,000$ represents the amount of overhead allocated to service department 1 after receiving the allocation from service department 2. $S_2 = \$23,000$ represents the amount of overhead allocated to service department 2 after receiving the allocation from service department 1.

The total amount of overhead allocated to the production departments are:

$$P_1 = \$30,000 + (.30)\,(\$12,000) + (.40)\,(\$23,000) = \$24,800$$
$$P_2 = \$40,000 + (.40)\,(\$12,000) + (.50)\,(\$23,000) = \underline{\$56,300}$$
$$\text{Total} = \$99,100$$

Application to Computer Programming

Matrix algebra was developed about 100 years ago, and yet one of the algebra's most significant area of application is in computer programming. Computer programming frequently involves the use of subscripted variables or arrays. Although our consideration of matrices was limited to a maximum of two-dimensional arrays, the definition of a matrix could easily be extended to three or more dimensions simply by including more subscripts. In computer programming single and double subscripts are generally used, but up to seven subscripts are permitted by some computer languages such as

FORTRAN (*FOR*mula *TRAN*slation). This computer language uses the word DIMEN-SION to indicate that a matrix is involved in a program. The following examples demonstrate how matrices can use the FORTRAN language in the computer's memory.

Example 3:   For one-dimensional matrices (single subscripts), the FORTRAN statement DIMENSION A(4) sets up four variable storage locations in one dimension in the computer's memory (see Figure 5-1).

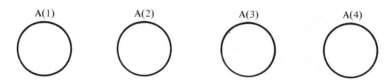

FIGURE 5-1

Example 4:   For two-dimensional matrices (double subscripts), The FORTRAN statement DIMENSION A(2, 3) sets up six variable storage locations in two dimensions in the computer's memory (see Figure 5-2).

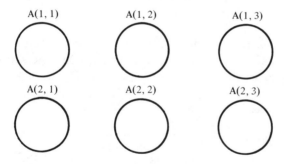

FIGURE 5-2

Example 5:   For three-dimensional matrices (triple subscripts) the FORTRAN statement DIMENSION A(2, 2, 2) sets up eight variable storage locations in three dimensions in the computer's memory (see Figure 5-3).

Example 6:   For seven-dimensional arrays (seven subscripts) the FORTRAN statement DIMENSION A(10, 10, 10, 10, 10, 10, 10) sets up $10^7 = 10,000,000$ variable storage locations in the computer's memory in seven dimensions.

    Some computer languages have built-in matrix operations or matrix subroutines in the computer's library. These subroutines are designed for two-

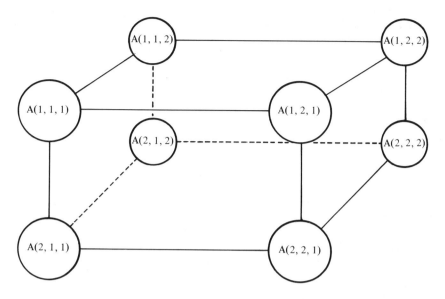

FIGURE 5-3

dimensional matrices. The following list gives some matrix subroutines found in the computer language **BASIC**, which stands for Beginners All-purpose Scientific Instruction Code:

TRN(A) finds the transpose for matrix A
A + B adds conformable matrices A and B
A*B multiplies conformable matrices A and B
INV(A) finds the inverse of $A_{n \times n}$ (DET $\neq 0$)
DET(A) finds the determinant of $A_{n \times n}$

The BASIC language can solve a system of n equations in n unknowns in a single operation by multiplying the inverse of the coefficient matrix by the constant matrix.

PROBLEMS 5-5

1. A firm manufactures four different computer components. Orders are such that 10 units of component A, 20 units of component B, 30 units of component C, and 40 units of component D are needed to be scheduled for production over a specified

period of time. The numbers of units of materials and labor that go into the production of each component are:

	Component			
	A	B	C	D
Plastic	1	1	1	1
Fiber glass	1	0	2	1
Metals	0	1	1	2
Labor	1	1	3	3

The unit costs of materials and labor are:

	Cost (in dollars)
Plastic	20
Fiber glass	20
Metals	40
Labor	100

Set up a matrix solution that gives the total number of units of materials and labor needed to meet production requirements. Then set up a matrix solution that gives the firm's total cost of materials and labor.

2. A firm has two service departments S_1 and S_2 and two production departments P_1 and P_2. The firm allocates its total overhead to production departments by means of a primary and secondary distribution process:

Primary overhead allocation
(to all departments)

S_1	S_2	P_1	P_2
$9,900	$19,800	$90,100	$100,200

Secondary overhead allocation
(to service departments)
Allocations (in percent)

	S_1	S_2	P_1	P_2
S_1	0	10	40	50
S_2	10	0	30	60

Represent the service departments' overhead allocation in the secondary distribution process in matrix form, and solve the system of two equations in two unknowns for S_1 and S_2. (The value of S_1 represents the amount of overhead allocated to service department 1 after receiving the allocation from service department 2. The value for S_2 represents the amount of overhead allocated to service department 2 after receiving the allocation from service department 1.) Then find the total amount of overhead to be allocated to production departments.

5-6   LINEAR PROGRAMMING: SIMPLEX METHOD

The graphic approach to linear programming was introduced in Chapter 1; however, the method was suited to systems consisting of two unknowns and was not extendable to systems of n unknowns. The simplex method overcomes this problem and uses ordinary algebraic techniques with matrix tables to solve systems including any number of unknowns.

In this section we will maximize or minimize *objective functions* that are subjected to certain restrictions, or *restraints*. The method supposes that the variables used are nonnegative. If the problem is one of maximization, then inequalities used to represent the restraints are set less than or equal to constants. If the problem is one of minimization, then inequalities used to represent the restraints are set greater than or equal to constants. [Methods exist to solve systems that have mixed inequalities (greater and less than both), but they will not be considered here.]

To introduce the simplex algorithm the profit maximization problem that was seen in Chapter 1 will be revisited. The production chart for the firm producing standard-use and special-use calculators is:

	Department A	*Department B*
Standard-use (x)	1 hour/case	3 hours/case
Special-use (y)	2 hours/case	4 hours/case
	8 hours available	20 hours available

The objective function (profit) to be maximized is:

$$P = 50x + 80y$$

Chapter 1 demonstrated graphically that the objective function is maximized for $x = 4$ (cases of standard-use calculators) and for $y = 2$ (cases of special-use calculators), which results in a maximum profit of:

$$P = 50(4) + 80(2) = \$360$$

The first step in the simplex method is to introduce *slack variables*. These hypothetical variables represent unused resources and are introduced to convert the system of inequalities to equalities. In our example from Chapter 1 we introduce the slack variables s_1 and s_2 and convert the restraints to equalities:

System of inequalities (restraints) $x + 2y \leqslant 8$
$$3x + 4y \leqslant 20$$
$$x \geqslant 0, y \geqslant 0$$

System of equalities (obtained by
  introducing the slack variables
  s_1, s_2)

$$x + 2y + s_1 = 8$$
$$3x + 4y + s_2 = 20$$

We are now ready to introduce the simplex algorithm for the maximization problem just reviewed.

Simplex Algorithm to Maximize the Objective Function

Example 1:   Maximize $P = 50x + 80y$ (objective function) subject to the following restraints:

$$x + 2y < 8$$
$$3x + 4y < 20$$

Solution.   First, introduce slack variables. Maximize $P = 50x + 80y$ subjected to:

$$x + 2y + s_1 = 8$$
$$3x + 4y + s_2 = 20$$

The objective function can be written as $-50x - 80y + P = 0$, and the above equations can be written as:

$$x + 2y + s_1 = 8$$
$$3x + 4y + s_2 = 20$$
$$-50x - 80y + P = 0$$

(The objective function is placed in the bottom row.)

Next, transform step 1 to matrix form: Form the augmented matrix from the system of equations in step 1. Partition the matrix accordingly:

x	y	s_1	s_2	P	Constants
1	2	1	0	0	8
3	4	0	1	0	20
-50	-80	0	0	1	0

Then find the *privileged column*: Find the smallest negative number in the bottom row; this position gives the privileged column. The elements in the bottom row are −50, −80, 0, 0, 1, 0, and the smallest number is −80, which means that the second column is the privileged column:

$$
\left(
\begin{array}{ccccc|c}
1 & 2 & 2 & 0 & 0 & 8 \\
3 & 4 & 0 & 1 & 0 & 20 \\
\hline
-50 & -80 & 0 & 0 & 1 & 0
\end{array}
\right)
$$

Note: If there are two or more equally small negative numbers, select one.

Now find the *pivotal element*: Form all ratios by dividing each *positive* element in the privileged column into the element in that same row and last column on the right. The element in the privileged column that generates the smallest ratio is the pivotal element. The ratios are: $8/2 = 4$ and $20/4 = 5$. $8/2 = 4$ is the smaller ratio, and thus 2 is the pivotal element. Note that the ratio $0/-80$ was not used, because only positive elements in the privileged column are considered.

Note: If all the elements in the privileged column are negative, the problem will not have a solution. If there are two or more ratios that are equally small, choose one.

Next, reduce columns by using elementary row transformations. Use elementary row transformations to convert the pivotal element to 1 and to reduce all other elements in the privileged column to 0. Divide the first row by 2 to reduce the pivotal element to 1:

$$
\left(
\begin{array}{ccccc|c}
\frac{1}{2} & 1 & \frac{1}{2} & 0 & 0 & 4 \\
3 & 4 & 0 & 1 & 0 & 20 \\
\hline
-50 & -80 & 0 & 0 & 1 & 0
\end{array}
\right)
$$

Multiply row 1 by −4, and add the result to row 2 to obtain:

$$
\left(
\begin{array}{ccccc|c}
\frac{1}{2} & 1 & \frac{1}{2} & 0 & 0 & 4 \\
1 & 0 & -2 & 1 & 0 & 4 \\
\hline
-50 & -80 & 0 & 0 & 1 & 0
\end{array}
\right)
$$

Multiply row 1 by 80, and add the result to row 3 to obtain:

$$
\left(
\begin{array}{ccccc|c}
\frac{1}{2} & 1 & \frac{1}{2} & 0 & 0 & 4 \\
1 & 0 & -2 & 1 & 0 & 4 \\
\hline
-10 & 0 & 40 & 0 & 1 & 320
\end{array}
\right)
$$

When the pivotal element is 1, and the remaining elements in the privileged column are 0's, then this is a *reduced column*.

Now eliminate negative numbers in the bottom row: Repeat the preceding steps until no negative numbers appear in the bottom row. The smallest negative number in the bottom row is -10, so the first column becomes the privileged column, and the ratios are $4/(1/2) = 8$ and $4/1 = 4$, which means that 1 is the pivotal element:

$$\left(\begin{array}{ccccc|c} \dfrac{1}{2} & 1 & \dfrac{1}{2} & 0 & 0 & 4 \\[2mm] 1 & 0 & -2 & 1 & 0 & 4 \\ \hline -10 & 0 & 40 & 0 & 1 & 320 \end{array}\right)$$

To obtain the reduced column, multiply row 2 by $(-1/2)$, and add the result to row 1, which will place a 0 in the first-row, first-column position. To place a 0 in the third-row, first-column position and complete the reduced column, multiply row 2 by 10, and add the result to the third column:

$$\left(\begin{array}{ccccc|c} 0 & 1 & -\dfrac{1}{2} & -\dfrac{1}{2} & 0 & 2 \\[2mm] 1 & 0 & -2 & 1 & 0 & 4 \\ \hline 0 & 0 & 20 & 10 & 1 & 360 \end{array}\right)$$

No negative quantities appear in the bottom row. The process is terminated.

Now, use the reduced columns to obtain the solution. The corresponding variable heading a reduced column (using the coefficient of 1) is matched with the element in the last column on the right. Moreover, maximum profit is the quantity in the last column and bottom element. If variables do not correspond to a reduced column, they will be assigned the value 0.

$$\begin{array}{ccccc} x & y & s_1 & s_2 & P \end{array}$$
$$\left(\begin{array}{ccccc|c} 0 & 1 & -\dfrac{1}{2} & -\dfrac{1}{2} & 0 & 2 \\[2mm] 1 & 0 & -2 & 1 & 0 & 4 \\ \hline 0 & 0 & 20 & 10 & 1 & 360 \end{array}\right)$$

When $x = 4$ and $y = 2$, maximum profit $= 360$.

Conclusion.   Maximum profit occurs for $x = 4$ cases of standard-use calculators and $y = 2$ cases of special-use calculators. Maximum profit is (as mentioned earlier):

$$P = 50x + 80y = 50(4) + 80(2) = 360$$

The algorithm can be shortened by eliminating the column under the variable P, which remains fixed throughout all the steps.

Note: If the integer 1 appears in the same row of more than one reduced column, there is no solution. For example, if the algorithm resulted in the following matrix, the problem would have no solution, because the integer 1 appears twice in column 1.

$$\left(\begin{array}{ccccc|c} 1 & 1 & -\dfrac{1}{2} & -\dfrac{1}{2} & 0 & 2 \\[2mm] 1 & 0 & -2 & 1 & 0 & 4 \\[2mm] \hline 0 & 0 & 20 & 10 & 1 & 320 \end{array}\right)$$

PROBLEMS 5-6

*1. The production chart below depicts a firm that produces both standard-use and special-use calculators; the firm uses two departments in the assembling process. Find the number of cases of standard-use calculators (x) and special-use calculators (y) that is necessary to schedule for production in order to maximize the profit function, if profit for each case of standard-use calculators is 60 and profit for each case of special-use calculators is 30.

	Department A	Department B
Standard-use	1 hour/case	5 hours/case
Special-use	1 hour/case	1 hour/case
Available hours	12 hours	20 hours

2. Repeat Problem 1 if the profit for each case of standard-use calculators is 30, and the profit for each case of special-use calculators is 60.

3. Repeat Problem 1 if the profit for each case of standard-use calculators is 80, and the profit for each case of special-use calculators is 10.

4. The production chart below depicts a firm that produces standard-use and special-use calculators; the firm uses three departments in the assembling process. Find the number of cases of standard-use calculators (x) and special-use calculators (y) that is necessary to schedule for production in order to maximize the profit function, if profit for each case of standard-use calculators is 100 and the profit for each case of special-use calculators is 100.

	Department A	Department B	Department C
Standard-use	1 hour/case	5 hours/case	5 hours/case
Special-use	1 hour/case	1 hour/case	1 hour/case
Available hours	12 hours	20 hours	10 hours

THE MATHEMATICS OF FINANCE

6

In this chapter we derive and apply some of the more commonly used formulas in the mathematics of finance. The first five sections of the chapter are concerned with interest problems, and the final section looks at the problem of depreciation.

6-1 SIMPLE INTEREST

The concept of simple interest is fundamental to all interest problems. The formula for determining simple interest is:

$$I = Prt$$

where:

I = simple interest
P = principal
r = yearly interest rate
t = time

Ordinary and Exact Interest, Ordinary and Exact Time

The value of t can be used in different ways. If the denominator of the fraction representing time is 365, we have *exact interest*, whereas if the denominator is 360 (based on 30 days in each month), we have *ordinary interest*. This presents four different cases for time:

$$\text{exact interest and exact time} = \frac{\text{exact number of days}}{365}$$

This case is commonly used by the U.S. government.

$$\text{exact interest and ordinary time} = \frac{\text{based on 30-day month}}{365}$$

This case is not commonly used.

$$\text{ordinary interest and ordinary time} = \frac{\text{based on 30-day month}}{360}$$

This case is commonly used.

$$\text{ordinary interest and exact time} = \frac{\text{exact number of days}}{360}$$

This case is commonly used and is called the banker's rule.

Example 1:   Find the interest for a principal of $1,000, a yearly rate of 10%, where the time goes from May 10 to September 20 using (1) exact interest and exact time, (2) exact interest and ordinary time, (3) ordinary interest and ordinary time, and (4) ordinary interest and exact time.
The exact number of days is:

May	21 days
June	30 days
July	31 days
August	31 days
September	20 days
Total	133 days (exact)

The ordinary number of days is:

May	20 days
June	30 days
July	30 days
August	30 days
September	20 days
Total	130 days (ordinary)

Solution.   For exact interest and exact time:

$$I = Prt = 1,000(.10) \ \frac{133}{365} \ = \$36.44$$

For exact interest and ordinary time:

$$I = Prt = 1,000(.10) \ \frac{130}{365} \ = \$35.62$$

For ordinary interest and ordinary time:

$$I = Prt = 1{,}000(.10) \; \frac{130}{360} \; = \$36.12$$

For ordinary interest and exact time:

$$I = Prt = 1{,}000(.10) \; \frac{133}{360} \; = \$36.95$$

The formula $I = Prt$ involves four variable quantities. Given three quantities, we can solve for the fourth:

$$I = Prt \quad \text{or} \quad P = \frac{I}{rt} \quad \text{or} \quad r = \frac{I}{Pt} \quad \text{or} \quad t = \frac{I}{Pr}$$

Example 2:   Given that $I = \$50$, $r = 10\%$ and days $= 180$, find P by using ordinary interest.

Solution.

$$P = \frac{I}{rt} = \frac{\$50}{(.10)(180/360)} = \$1{,}000$$

Example 3:   Given that $I = \$50$, $P = \$1{,}000$, and days $= 180$, find r by using ordinary interest.

Solution.

$$r = \frac{I}{Pt} = \frac{\$50}{\$1{,}000(180/360)} = .10$$

Example 4:   Given that $I = \$50$, $P = \$1{,}000$, and $r = 10\%$, find t by using ordinary interest.

Solution.

$$t = \frac{I}{Pr} = \frac{\$50}{\$1{,}000(.10)} = \frac{1}{2} \text{ year} = 180 \text{ days}$$

Amount Due

The *amount due* for simple interest is the principal plus the interest:

$$S = P + Prt = P(1 + rt)$$

Frequently the amount due is termed *future value* and is symbolized by F_v. For simple interest the future value is:

$$F_v = P(1 + rt)$$

Example 5: Find the amount due for simple interest where $P = \$1,000$, $r = 10\%$, and days $= 180$ by using ordinary interest.

Solution.

$$S = P(1 + rt) = \$1,000 \left[1 + .10 \left(\frac{180}{360} \right) \right] = \$1,050.00$$

Example 6: Given $S = \$1,050$, $P = \$1,000$, and days $= 180$, find r by using ordinary interest.

Solution.

$$S = P + Prt$$

$$r = \frac{S - P}{Pt} = \frac{\$1,050 - \$1,000}{\$1,000(180/360)} = 10\%$$

Present Value

The *present value* for simple interest is the principal (P). The present value of an interest problem means what principal (P) is involved to result in the amount due (S) for the given time period and interest rate. The present value for simple interest is obtained by solving the amount due formula for P:

$$S = P(1 + rt)$$

means:

$$P = \frac{S}{1 + rt} = S(1 + rt)^{-1}$$

where:

P = present value (frequently symbolized by P_v)
S = amount due (frequently symbolized by F_v)
r = yearly interest rate
t = fraction of a year

Example 7:   Find the present value for an amount due = $1,050, r = 10%, and days = 180 by using ordinary interest.

Solution.

$$P = \frac{S}{1 + rt} = \frac{\$1,050}{1 + .10(180/360)} = \$1,000$$

If a principal of $1,000 is borrowed (or invested) *now* at r = 10% for 180 days under ordinary interest, then the amount due will be $1,050. Stated another way, the present value of $1,050 due in 180 days, by using ordinary interest, at an interest rate of 10% is $1,000.

PROBLEMS 6-1

Use a pocket calculator for many of the problems in this chapter.

*1. Find the simple interest for a principal of $1,000, a yearly rate of 10%, and a time of from April 2 to August 20. Use:

  *a. exact interest and exact time

  b. exact interest and ordinary time

  c. ordinary interest and ordinary time

  d. ordinary interest and exact time

  Find the amount due for simple interest for the above problems.

*2. Given that I = $80, r = 12%, and t = 240 days, find P by using ordinary interest.

3. Given that I = $40, P = $1,000, t = 120 days, find r by using ordinary interest.

4. Given that I = $80, P = $2,000, r = 12%, find t by using ordinary interest.

5. Find the present value for simple interest for an amount due = $1,080, r = 16%, and t = 180 days by using *both* exact and ordinary interest.

6. Find the present value of simple interest for an amount due = $1,100, r = 15%, and t = 200 days by using *both* exact and ordinary interest.

6-2   COMPOUND INTEREST

Amount Due

The formula for the amount due for compound interest is:

$$S = P(1 + i)^n$$

where:

F_v = future value
S = amount due for compound interest
P = principal
i = interest rate per conversion period
n = number of conversion periods

The formula for the amount due for compound interest can be derived inductively:

first period	$S = P(1 + i)^1$
second period	$S = P(1 + i)^2$
third period	$S = P(1 + i)^3$
.	.
.	.
.	.
nth period	$S = P(1 + i)^n$

Example 1:   Find the amount due for compound interest where P = $1,000, yearly interest rate = 12%, time = 2 years, and interest is compounded monthly. In this problem the interest rate per conversion period is i = 12%/12 = .01, and the number of conversion periods is $n = (12)(2) = 24$ (see Table 2).

Solution.

$$S = \$1,000(1 + .01)^{24} = \$1,000(1.26973465) = \$1269.73$$

Example 2:   Find the amount due for compound interest where P = $1,000, yearly interest rate = 12%, for a time interval of five years, and compounded monthly (see Table 2).

Solution.

$$S = P(1 + i)^n = \$1,000(1 + .01)^{60} = \$1,816.69$$

Example 3:   Find the amount due for compound interest where P = $1,000, yearly interest rate = 12%, for a time period of ten years, and compounded monthly.

Solution.

$$S = P(1 + i)^n = \$1{,}000(1 + .01)^{120}$$

and $(1 + .01)^{120}$ exceed the limits in Table 2, so S is expressed as:

$$S = \$1{,}000(1 + .01)^{60}(1 + .01)^{60} = \$1{,}000(1.8166967)(1.8166967)$$

$$= \$3{,}300.38$$

Example 4:   Given that $S = \$1{,}816.69$, $P = \$1{,}000$, and a time period = 5 years (compounded monthly), find i. From $S = P(1 + i)^n$ the interest can be isolated as:

$$(1 + 1)^n = \frac{S}{P}$$

or:

$$(1 + i)^{60} = \frac{1816.69}{1000} = 1.81669$$

and from Table 2:

$$i = .01$$

Alternate solution.   With sufficiently large and complete tables the value of i can be found by searching for the value of $(1 + i)^n$ for the appropriate n. Otherwise i can be found algebraically by taking the log of both sides of the equation:

$$(1 + i)^n = \frac{S}{P}$$

and then applying the third law of logarithms:

$$(1 + i)^{60} = 1.81669$$
$$\log (1 + i)^{60} = \log (1.81669) \quad \text{or}$$
$$60 \log (1 + i) = \log (1.81669) \quad \text{or}$$

$$\log (1 + i) = \frac{\log (1.81669)}{60} = \frac{.2577}{60} = .0043$$

The antilog of .0043 is 1.01, which means $i = 1\%$ and the yearly rate is 12%.

Compound Interest and Daily Compounding

The formula for the amount due for daily compounding is:

$$S = P(1 + i)^n$$

where:

S = amount due
P = principal

$$i = \frac{\text{yearly rate}}{365} \qquad \text{(for exact interest)}$$

$$i = \frac{\text{yearly rate}}{360} \qquad \text{(for ordinary interest)}$$

n = number of compounds that can be determined by using exact or ordinary time

This leads to four cases:

Daily compounding may be based on *exact interest and exact time* (n = number of periods based on 365 days per year):

$$S = P \left(1 + \frac{\text{yearly rate}}{365}\right)^n$$

Daily compounding may be based on *exact interest and ordinary time* (n = number of periods based on 360 days per year):

$$S = P \left(1 + \frac{\text{yearly rate}}{365}\right)^n$$

Daily compounding may be based on *ordinary interest and ordinary time* (n = number of periods based on 360 days per year):

$$S = P \left(1 + \frac{\text{yearly rate}}{360}\right)^n$$

Daily compounding may be based on *ordinary interest and exact time* (n = number of periods based on 365 days per year):

$$S = P \left(1 + \frac{\text{yearly rate}}{360}\right)^n$$

Example 5:   Find the amount due for daily compounding where $P = \$1000$, yearly interest rate is 12%, for a time of ten years using (1) exact interest and exact time, (2) exact interest and ordinary time, (3) ordinary interest and ordinary time, (4) ordinary interest and exact time.

Solution.   For exact interest and exact time (result derived by pocket calculator):

$$S = P(1 + i)^n = 1,000\left(1 + \frac{.12}{365}\right)^{3,650} = \$3,318.65$$

For exact interest and ordinary time:

$$S = P(1 + i)^n = 1,000\left(1 + \frac{.12}{365}\right)^{3,600} = \$3,264.56$$

For ordinary interest and ordinary time:

$$S = P(1 + i)^n = 1,000\left(1 + \frac{.12}{360}\right)^{3,600} = \$3,319.05$$

For ordinary interest and exact time:

$$S = P(1 + i)^n = 1,000\left(1 + \frac{.12}{360}\right)^{3,650} = \$3,374.82$$

Present Value

The present value for compound interest is obtained by solving the amount due formula for the principal. From:

$$S = P(1 + i)^n$$

the principal is:

$$P = \frac{S}{(1 + i)^n} = S(1 + i)^{-n}$$

where:

P_y = present value
P = present value
S = amount due
i = interest rate per conversion period
n = number of conversion periods

Example 6:   Find the present value of $1,816.69 due in five years, at a yearly interest rate of 12%, compounded monthly (use Table 3).

Solution.

$$P = S(1 + i)^{-n} = \$1816.69(1 + .01)^{-60}$$

$$P = \$1,816.69(.55044962) = \$1,000.00$$

Example 7:   Find the present value of $1,000,000 due in two years, at a yearly interest rate of 12%, compounded monthly (use Table 3).

$$P = S(1 + .01)^{-24} = \$1,000,000(.7876613) = \$787,566.13$$

Example 8:   Find the present value of $1,000 due in two years, at a yearly rate of 10% using daily compounding and ordinary interest with exact time (result derived by pocket calculator).

Solution.

$$P = \frac{S}{(1 + i)^n} = \frac{1000}{(1 + .10/360)^{730}} = \$816.53$$

PROBLEMS 6-2

*1. Find the amount due for compound interest where P = $1,000, yearly interest rate = 12%, compounded monthly for:

*a. 1 year   d. 4 years
 b. 18 months   e. 8 years
 c. 2 years   f. 10 years

*2. Find the amount due for daily compounding where P = $1,000, yearly interest rate = 12%, a time of 2 years by using:

   *a. exact interest and exact time

   b. exact interest and ordinary time

   c. ordinary interest and ordinary time

   d. ordinary interest and exact time

3. Find the number of periods (time) if the amount due for monthly compounding is $1,430.77 for a principal of $1,000 and yearly interest rate of 12%.

*4. Find the present value of $100,000 due in 3 years at a yearly interest rate of 12% compounded monthly.

5. Find the present value of $100,000 due in 20 years at a yearly interest rate of 12% compounded monthly.

6. Find the number of periods (time) if the present value of $1,000 is $620.26, and the interest is 12% per year compounded monthly.

7. A bank advertises that if $1,000 is put in a savings account with a yearly interest rate of 8% for 2 years, then the amount due will be $1,173.42. What type of daily compounding is used to obtain this amount (find the combination of exact or ordinary interest with exact or ordinary time)?

8. If a bank compounds monthly with a yearly rate of 12%, in how many years will a given principal double?

6-3   COMPOUND INTEREST: THE CONTINUOUS CASE

The formula for determining compound interest for the continuous case involves the constant e; refer to Appendix A (Algebra Review) before you attempt to derive the expression for the amount due.

Amount Due

The formula for determining the *amount due* for *continuous* compounding is:

$$S = Pe^{rt}$$

where:

     $e = 2.71828 \ldots$
     S = amount due for continuous compounding
     P = principal
     r = yearly interest rate
     t = time in years

Proof.   The amount due formula is:

$$S = P(1 + i)^n$$

where $i = r/k$ and $n = kt$ for k representing the number of compounds per year. By making substitutions:

$$S = P\left(1 + \frac{r}{k}\right)^{kt}$$

$$S = P\left(1 + \frac{r}{k}\right)^{k(r/r)t}$$

$$S = P\left[\left(1 + \frac{r}{k}\right)^{k/r}\right]^{rt}$$

for the continuous cases:

$$k \to \infty; \quad \left(1 + \frac{r}{k}\right)^{k/r} \to e = 2.71828 \ldots$$

Therefore, the amount due for continuous compound is:

$$S = Pe^{rt}$$

Example 1:   Find the amount due for continuous compounding where $P = \$1,000$, $r = 12\%$, for a time of 10 years (use Table 4).

Solution.

$$S = Pe^{rt}$$

$$S = \$1,000(e^{1.2}) = \$1,000(3.20) = \$3,320$$

Compare this result with the same problem that uses the four cases of daily compounding.

Example 2:   Given that $S = \$3,320$, $P = \$1,000$, and $t = 10$ years, find the yearly rate of interest (r) for continuous compounding.

Solution.

$$S = Pe^{rt}$$

$$3{,}320 = 1{,}000(e^{10r})$$

$$e^{10r} = \frac{3{,}320}{1{,}000} = 3.320$$

Searching Table 4 gives:

$$r = 12\%$$

Alternate solution.   Given $e^{10r} = 3.320$. Then:

$$\log e^{10r} = \log (3.320)$$

and for $e = 2.71$ this becomes:

$$10r \log (2.71) = \log (3.320) \text{ or } 10r = \frac{\log 3.320}{\log 2.71}$$

which gives:

$$r = \left(\frac{1}{10}\right)\left(\frac{.5211}{.4330}\right) = .12 = 12\%$$

Present Value

The present value for continuous compounding can be obtained by solving the amount due formula for the principal $(P) \cdot S = Pe^{rt}$ means that:

$$P = \frac{S}{e^{rt}} = Se^{-rt}$$

where:

$e = 2.71828 \ldots$
P = present value
S = amount due
r = yearly interest rate
t = time in years

Example 3:   Find the present value of $3,320.00 due in ten years with yearly interest rate of 12% compounded continuously (use Table 4).

Solution.

$$P = Se^{-rt}$$

$$P = \$3,320(e^{-1.2}) = \$3,320(.301) = \$1,000$$

PROBLEMS 6-3

1. Find the amount due for continuous compounding where $P = \$1,000$, $i = 12\%$, and $t = 2$ years. (Use a pocket calculator for your answer; the tables are not adequate for this example.) Compare the results of this problem with those of monthly compounding and daily compounding.

*2. Find the amount due for continuous compounding where $P = \$1,000$, yearly interest rate is 10%, and time intervals of:

    *a. 1 year   c. 10 years   e. 32 years

    b. 5 years   d. 15 years

3. Find the amount due for continuous compounding where $P = \$1,000$, yearly interest rate is 10.5% and a time interval of 10 years. Use tables and interpolation to arrive at an approximate answer, and compare the result with that from a pocket calculator.

*4. Find the present value of $1,000 due in 5 years for a yearly interest rate of 10%.

5. Find the present value of $1,500 due in 15 years for a yearly interest rate of 10%.

6-4   ANNUAL PERCENTAGE RATE AND BANK DISCOUNTING

Annual Percentage Rate

The interest rate used in compound interest problems can be equivocated to simple interest terms by determining the annual percentage rate. The stated interest rate for a particular problem is the *nominal rate*. The *annual percentage rate (APR)* is the true rate of simple interest that will generate in one year the same amount of interest as would compound interest. The annual percentage rate, effective yield, and effective rate can be used synonymously.

Annual Percentage Rate for Compound Interest and Continuous Compounding

The formula used to determine the annual percentage rate for compound interest problems based on the formula $S = P(1 + i)^n$ is:

$$APR = (1 + i)^n - 1$$

where

APR = annual percentage rate
  i = interest per period
  n = total number of compounding periods

Proof.   The amount of interest for compound interest is:

$I = S - P$
$I = P(1 + i)^n - P$
$I = P[(1 + i)^n - 1]$

Simple interest is $I = Prt$ and for $t = 1$ year:

$Pr(1) = P(1 + i)^n - 1$
     or
$APR = r = (1 + i)^n - 1$

Example 1:   Find the annual percentage rate for a bank that advertises a nominal rate of 12% per year compounded monthly (use Table 2).

Solution.

$APR = (1 + i)^n - 1$
$APR = (1 + .01)^{12} - 1$
$APR = 1.12682503 - 1 = 12.6825\%$

Example 2:   Find the annual percentage rate for a bank that advertises a nominal rate of 12% per year compounded daily (use ordinary interest and exact time).

Solution.

$APR = (1 + i)^n - 1$
$APR = \left(1 + \dfrac{.12}{360}\right)^{365} - 1$
$APR = 1.12934 = 1 = 12.934\%$

The formula used to determine the annual percentage rate for continuous compounding problems based on the formula $S = Pe^{rt}$ is:

$APR = e^r - 1$

where:

$$APR = \text{annual percentage rate}$$
$$r = \text{nominal interest rate}$$
$$e = 2.71828 \ldots$$

Proof.   The amount of interest is:

$$I = S - P$$
$$I = Pe^{rt} - P$$

Simple interest is determined by $I = Prt$ and for a time of $t = 1$ year:

$$Pr(1) = Pe^{r(1)} - P$$
$$APR = r = e^r - 1$$

Example 3:   Find the annual percentage rate for a bank that advertises a nominal rate of 10% per year compounding continuously (use Table 4):

Solution.

$$APR = e^r - 1$$
$$APR = e^{.1} - 1$$
$$APR = 1.105 = 1 = 10.5\%$$

Example 4:   Find the annual percentage rate for a bank that advertises a nominal rate of 12% per year compounding continuously (result derived by pocket calculator).

Solution.

$$APR = e^r - 1 = e^{.12} - 1$$
$$APR = 1.1275 - 1 = 12.75\%$$

Bank Discounting

· Bank discounting is frequently used with loans and installment payments. When interest is deducted before money is lent, then we have *discounting interest* in advance or *bank discounting*. The stated rate is the nominal rate or *discount rate,* and the annual percentage rate is the true simple interest rate and is determined by the formula:

$$APR = \frac{P-A}{At}$$

$$P = \frac{A}{1-rt}$$

where:

APR = annual percentage rate
A = amount of loan (proceeds)
P = effective principal (principal used to determine interest)
r = discount rate (nominal rate)
t = ordinary time

Proof.

proceeds = effective principal − interest
$$A = P - Prt = P(1-rt)$$

$$P = \frac{A}{1-rt}$$

The true rate of simple interest is:

interest = (principal)(rate)(time)

$$rate = \frac{interest}{(principal)(time)}$$

$$APR = rate = \frac{P-A}{At}$$

Example 5:   Find the annual percentage rate and effective principal on a loan of $1,000 discounted at 10% for eight months.

Solution.   The effective principal is obtained by using:

$$P = \frac{A}{1-rt} = \frac{\$1,000}{1-.10(8/12)} = \$1,071.43$$

The annual percentage rate is found by using:

$$APR = \frac{P-A}{At} = \frac{1,071.43 - 1,000}{1,000(8/12)} = 10.71\%$$

Some banks deduct interest from the amount of the desired loan, in which case the effective principal is the amount requested by the borrower. However, the actual proceeds are the effective principal minus the interest. In this situation the formula to determine the annual percentage rate is:

$$APR = \frac{r}{1 - r}$$

where:

APR = annual percentage rate
r = discount rate

Proof.   By definition the simple interest rate for one year is:

$$\text{interest rate} = \frac{\text{interest}}{\text{principal (1)}} \quad \text{or}$$

$$APR = \frac{PR}{P - Pr} = \frac{r}{1 - r}$$

Example 6:   Find the proceeds and the annual percentage rate if an individual requests a loan of $1,000 where the discount rate is 10%. In this problem the $1,000 represents the effective principal which is discounted immediately.

Solution.   If the bank deducts the interest immediately then the proceeds are:

$$A = 1,000 - 1,000(.10) = \$900$$

The annual percentage rate is found using:

$$APR = \frac{r}{1 - r} = \frac{.10}{.90} = 11\%$$

PROBLEMS 6-4

*1. Find the annual percentage rates for banks that advertise monthly compounding for the following nominal rates:

   *a. 10%   b. 9%   c. 8.75%

2. Find the annual percentage rate for a bank that advertises a nominal rate of 8%, compounded daily, by using exact interest and exact time.

3. A bank advertises a nominal rate of 8% and an annual percentage rate of 8.45% by using daily compounding. What type of daily compounding is used to determine this annual percentage rate (find the combination of exact or ordinary interest with exact or ordinary time)?

*4. Find the annual percentage rates for banks that advertise the following nominal rates by using continuous compounding.

   *a. 10%   b. 9%   c. 8%

*5. Find the annual percentage rate and effective principal on a loan of $10,000 discounted at 12% for 6 months.

6. Find the annual percentage rate and nominal rate, if the effective principal of a $1,000 loan is $1,063.83.

7. Find the proceeds and annual percentage rate if an individual requests a loan of $3,000 when the discount rate is 12%. (In this problem the loan of $3,000 represents the effective principal that is discounted immediately.)

6-5   ORDINARY ANNUITY

In the general sense an annuity represents a series of periodic payments. In this section we will study annuities with fixed payments made at fixed time intervals. Before we discuss specific annuity problems, we give a general classification of annuities for the sake of completion.

   For an *annuity certain* the term is represented by a fixed time interval. A *perpetuity* begins at a fixed time but never ends. A *contingent* annuity is represented by a term that is not fixed in advance.

   Annuities can also be classified by payment dates. For an *ordinary* annuity periodic payments are made at the end of each payment interval. For an *annuity due*, payments are made at the beginning of each payment interval. An ordinary annuity whose term does not begin until after a specific amount of time is a deferred annuity.

   Annuities can also be classified as *simple* or *complex*. For a simple annuity the payment interval agrees with the interest rate of the payment interval whereas for a complex annuity the interest rate does not agree with the payment interval's interest.

Amount of an Ordinary Annuity

The *ordinary annuity* (simple and certain) is a series of equal payments made at the end of each payment interval. The amount of the annuity is obtained by finding the total compound amounts of each payment by using:

$$S = P(1 + i)^n$$

The formula for the amount of the annuity will be given shortly, but first an example will serve as a basis for understanding and deriving the formula for the ordinary annuity.

Example 1:   Find the amount of an ordinary annuity if the size of each payment is $100 and the payments are made monthly for four months with a yearly interest rate of 12%.

	1 month	2 months	3 months	4 months

| | $100 | $100 | $100 | $100 |

Solution.   The interest for the first month is accumulated for three periods, which is $100(1 + .01)^3 = \$103.03$. Interest on the second month's $100 payment is accumulated for two periods, which is $100(1 + .01)^2 = \$102.01$. Interest on the third month's $100 payment is accumulated for one period, or $100(1 + .01)^1 = \$101.00$. There is no interest on the fourth month's payment, but it must be added to the total amount due:

$$\$100 + 4100(1 + .01)^1 + 100(1 + .01)^2 + \$100(1 + .01)^3 = \$406.04$$

In the above example the amount of an ordinary annuity is seen as a geometric progression. The formula for the sum of a geometric progression is derived in Appendix A. The formula is:

$$S = \frac{a - ar^n}{1 - r}$$

where:

S = sum of a geometric progression
a = first term of the progression
r = common ratio
n = number of terms

For the above example the amount due of the annuity is:

$$S = \frac{\$100 - \$100(1.01)^4}{1 - (1.01)} = \$406.04$$

This example serves as a basis for understanding and deriving the formula for the amount due of an ordinary annuity (simple and certain):

$$S = R\left[\frac{(1 + i)^n - 1}{i}\right]$$

where:

> S = amount of an ordinary annuity
> R = size of each periodic payment
> i = interest rate per period
> n = number of periods

Proof.   The general expression for the amount due is:

$$S = R + R(1 + i) + R(1 + i)^2 + \cdots + R(1 + i)^{n-1}$$

This forms a geometric progression where the first term is R and the common ratio is $(1 + i)$. Substitution of these values in the formula for the sum of a geometric progression gives:

$$S = \frac{a - ar^n}{1 - r} = \frac{R - R(1 + i)^n}{1 - (1 + i)} = R\left[\frac{1 - (1 + i)^n}{-i}\right]$$

$$S = R\left[\frac{(1 + i)^n - 1}{i}\right]$$

Example 2:   Find the amount of an ordinary annuity where R = $100 with a yearly interest rate of 12% and monthly payments are made for one year.

Solution.

$$S = R\left[\frac{(1 + i)^n - 1}{i}\right] = \$100\left[\frac{(1 + .01)^{12} - 1}{.01}\right]$$

From Table 2:

$$S = 100\left[\frac{1.12682503 - 1}{.01}\right] = \$1{,}268.25$$

Example 3:   Find the periodic interest (i) for an ordinary annuity where S = $1,268.25 and R = $100 with monthly payments for one year.

Solution.

$$S = R\,\frac{(1 + i)^n - 1}{i}$$

$$\$1{,}268.25 = \$100 \; \frac{(1+i)^{12} - 1}{i}$$

$$\frac{(1+i)^{12} - 1}{i} = 12.6825$$

Solution 1.   Solving for i is a complex problem in this situation. Tables giving the amount due for ordinary annuities are used in such a case. Although no annuity tables accompany this text, the value for:

$$\frac{(1+i)^{12} - 1}{i}$$

can be found in a complete table giving appropriate values for i. If the amount due table were available, it would show that:

$$\frac{(1+.01)^{12} - 1}{.01} = 12.6825$$

and it would follow that the monthly interest is $i = .01 = 1\%$, and the yearly rate is 12%.

Solution 2.   Interest rates can vary so widely that annuity tables of the form:

$$\frac{(1+i)^{n} - 1}{i}$$

would not accurately give exact interest. In such cases a short computer program can be written to test various interest values in the expression:

$$\frac{(1+i)^{12} - 1}{i}$$

and to determine when the quotient equals 12.6825.

Present Value of an Ordinary Annuity

The present value of an ordinary annuity is found by totaling the present values of the periodic payments by using:

$$P = S(1+i)^{-n}$$

The present value of an ordinary annuity can be regarded as the unique principal that will compound to the amount of the annuity.

Example 4:   Find the present value of an ordinary annuity where R = $100, with a yearly interest rate of 12% where monthly payments are made for four months.

	1 month	2 months	3 months	4 months
0	$100	$100	$100	$100

Solution.   The present value of the first payment is:

$$100(1 + .01)^{-1} = .99009901$$

The present value of the second payment is:

$$100(1 + .01)^{-2} = .98029605$$

The present value of the third payment is:

$$100(1 + .01)^{-3} = .97059015$$

The present value of the fourth payment is:

$$100(1 + .01)^{-4} = .96098034$$

These results can be written as a geometric progression:

$$100(1 + .01)^{-1} + 100(1 + .01)^{-2} + 100(1 + .01)^{-3} + 100(1 + .01)^{-4} = \$390.20$$

The present value of the annuity is regarded as the unique principal that will compound to the amount of the annuity. For this example:

$$S = P(1 + i)^4 = \$390.20(1 + .01)^4 = \$406.04$$

The formula for the present value of the ordinary annuity is:

$$A = R \left[\frac{1 - (1 + i)^{-n}}{i} \right]$$

where:

A = present value of the ordinary annuity
R = size of each periodic payment

i = interest rate per period

n = number of periods

Proof.   In general the present value of the ordinary annuity can be written as a geometric progression:

$$A = R(1 + i)^{-1} + R(1 + i)^{-2} + \cdots + R(1 + i)^{-n}$$

The first term is $R(1 + i)^{-1}$, and the common ratio is $(1 + i)^{-1}$. By substitution into the formula for the sum of a geometric progression we obtain:

$$S = \frac{a - ar^n}{1 - r}$$

$$A = \frac{R(1 + i)^{-1} - R(1 + i)^{-1}(1 + i)^{-n}}{1 - (1 + i)^{-1}}$$

$$A = R\left[\frac{(1 + i)^{-1} - (1 + i)^{-n-1}}{i/(1 + 1)}\right] = R\left[\frac{1 - (1 + i)^{-n}}{i}\right]$$

Example 5:   Find the present value of an ordinary annuity where R = $100 and payments are made monthly for four months with a yearly interest rate of 12% (use Table 3).

Solution.

$$A = R\left[\frac{1 - (1 + i)^{-n}}{i}\right] = \$100\left[\frac{1 - (1 + .01)^{-4}}{.01}\right]$$

$$A = \$100\left[\frac{1 - .96098034}{.01}\right] = \$390.20$$

Periodic Payments: Mortgage Payments

The present value formula for the ordinary annuity can be used to determine the periodic house mortgage payment. The payment is R and the cost of the house is the present value, A. The formula for the periodic payment is obtained by solving the present value formula for R. Given that:

$$A = R\left[\frac{1 - (1 + i)^{-n}}{i}\right]$$

then the *periodic payment* is given by:

$$R = \frac{iA}{1 - (1 + i)^{-n}}$$

where:

R = size of each periodic payment
A = present value or cost of the house
i = interest rate per period
n = number of periods

Example 6:   A $40,000 house is being mortgaged at 12% a year for 20 years with monthly payments. Find the size of each payment (use Table 3).

Solution.

$$R = \frac{iA}{1 - (1 + i)^{-n}}$$

$$R = \frac{(.01)(40,000)}{1 - (1 + .01)^{-240}} = \frac{400}{1 - [(1 + .01)^{-60}]^4}$$

$$R = \frac{400}{1 - (.55044962)^4} = \frac{400}{.908194} = \$440.43$$

The numerator (iA) represents the amount of interest on the first payment. The payment R = $440.43 means that on the first payment $400 goes on interest and $40.43 goes toward the principal. A procedure could be set up to obtain a complete payment schedule for all 240 payments. The total amount paid for the $40,000 mortgage in the 20-year period is:

$$(440.43)(240) = \$105,703.20$$

PROBLEMS 6-5

*1. Find the amount due for the following ordinary annuities where the periodic monthly payments are $100 and the yearly interest rate is 12% for the following time intervals:

*a. 2 years   c. 6.5 years   e. 20 years
b. 4 years   d. 10 years

2. Find the size of each monthly payment for an ordinary annuity if the yearly interest rate is 12% and the amount due in two years is $3371.63.

3. Find the amount due for an ordinary annuity where the periodic monthly payment is $100 and the yearly interest rate is 8.25% for a time interval of 2.5 years.

*4. Find the present value of an ordinary annuity where $R = \$100$, the yearly interest rate is 12%, with monthly payments for time intervals of:

 *a. 2 years   b. 4 years   c. 20 years

*5. Find the monthly house mortgage payment for a house that cost $50,000 for a yearly interest rate of 12% where payments are made:

 *a. over a 20-year period

 b. over a 30-year period

What is the total amount paid over the time intervals? What is the interest on the first payment?

6-6 ANNUITY DUE

The *annuity due* is a series of equal payments made at the beginning of each payment interval. The formula for the amount of an annuity due is:

$$S = (1 + i) \ R \left[\frac{(1 + i)^n - 1}{i} \right]$$

where:

  S = amount of the annuity due
  R = size of each periodic payment
  i = interest per period
  n = number of periods

Proof. The amount of an annuity due with n terms can be presented as:

$$S = R(1 + i)^1 + R(1 + i)^2 + \cdots + R(1 + i)^n$$

This expression can be factored to give:

$$S = (1 + i)[R + R(1 + i) + R(1 + i)^2 + \cdots + R(1 + i)^{n-1}]$$

The bracketed term is the amount of an ordinary annuity.

Example 1: Find the amount for the annuity due with $R = \$100$ made monthly for 4 months with a yearly interest rate = 12%.

Solution.

$$S = (1 + .01) \ 100 \left[\frac{(1 + .01)^4 - 1}{.01} \right] = \$410.10$$

Present Value of an Annuity Due

The formula for the present value of an annuity due is:

$$A = R + R \left[\frac{1 - (1 + i)^{-(n-1)}}{i} \right]$$

where:

  A = present value of an annuity due
  R = periodic payment
  i = interest rate per period
  n = number of periods

PROBLEMS 6-6

*1. Find the amount of the annuities due for the time intervals given below. The monthly payment is \$100, and the yearly interest rate is 12%.

  *a. 2 years   b. 4 years   c. 20 years

  2. Find the amount of an annuity due if the monthly payment is \$100, the yearly interest rate is 12%, and the time interval of 3.5 years.

  3. Find the present value of an annuity due if the monthly payment is \$100, the yearly interest rate is 12%, and the time interval is 3 years.

6-7   DEPRECIATION

Straight-Line Method

The concept of depreciation is based on the fact that certain assets of a business have a limited number of years of useful life. A commonly used method of determining annual depreciation is the *straight-line* method based on the formula:

$$\text{depreciation} = \frac{\text{cost} - \text{trade-in value}}{\text{years of useful life}}$$

For example, if a piece of equipment cost $2,400 and has a trade-in value of $400 in five years the depreciation per year for five years is $400. The depreciation schedule is:

Year	Depreciation	Book value
0	$ 0	$2,400
1	400	2,000
2	400	1,600
3	400	1,200
4	400	800
5	400	400 (scrap value)
	$2,000	

Sum-of-the-Years Method

The straight-line method of depreciation requires that a fixed amount be depreciated each year; the *sum-of-the-years* technique permits a larger amount of depreciation to be taken at the outset of the depreciation schedule.

Let D be the total depreciation for n years and let S represent the sum of the years. The sum of the years forms an arithmetic progression, and the sum is:

$$S = 1 + 2 + \cdots + n = \frac{n(n+1)}{2}$$

which can be verified by using the formula for the sum of an arithmetic progression that is derived in Appendix A. The *sum-of-the-years* depreciation schedule is:

Year	Depreciation
0	
1	$\dfrac{Dn}{S}$
2	$\dfrac{D(n-1)}{S}$
3	$\dfrac{D(n-2)}{S}$
.	.
.	.
.	.

k	$\dfrac{D(n-k+1)}{S}$	depreciation for year k
.	.	
.	.	
.	.	
$n-1$	$\dfrac{D(2)}{S}$	
n	$\dfrac{D(1)}{S}$	

D represents the total depreciation. In the above schedule the sum of the entries in the depreciation column equals D:

$$\text{total depreciation} = \frac{D}{S} + \frac{2D}{S} + \frac{3D}{S} + \cdots + \frac{nD}{S}$$

$$= \frac{D}{S}(1 + 2 + 3 + \cdots + n) = \frac{DS}{S} = D$$

Example 1: An item worth \$2,400 is to be depreciated over five years. The scrap value of the item is \$400. The sum-of-the-years schedule is:

Year	Depreciation	Book value
0	—	\$2,400.00
1	$2,000\left(\dfrac{5}{15}\right) = 666.66$	1,733.33
2	$2,000\left(\dfrac{4}{15}\right) = 533.33$	1,200.00
3	$2,000\left(\dfrac{3}{15}\right) \doteq 400.00$	800.00
4	$2,000\left(\dfrac{2}{15}\right) = 266.66$	533.33

5	$2,000\left(\dfrac{1}{15}\right) = 133.33$	400.00

$$\text{Total} = \$2,000.00$$

The sum of the depreciation column forms an arithmetic progression that accumulates to the necessary total depreciation over the five years:

$$\text{total depreciation} = 2,000\left(\frac{5}{15}\right) + 2,000\left(\frac{4}{15}\right) + 2,000\left(\frac{3}{15}\right) + 2,000\left(\frac{2}{15}\right)$$

$$+ 2,000\left(\frac{1}{15}\right)$$

$$= 2,000\left(\frac{5}{15} + \frac{4}{15} + \frac{3}{15} + \frac{2}{15} + \frac{1}{15}\right) = 2,000(1) = \$2,000$$

Example 2:   An item worth $25,000 is to be depreciated over 10 years. The scrap value of the item is $2,000. Find the depreciation for (a) the second year and (b) the eighth year using the formula:

$$D_k = D\left(\frac{n - k + 1}{S}\right)$$

where:

D_k = the depreciation for year k

n = total number of years

s = sum of years

D = total depreciation

Solution.

$$D_2 = \frac{10 - 2 + 1}{55}\ (23,000) = \left(\frac{9}{55}\right)(23,000) = \$3,763.64$$

where:

$$s = \frac{n(n + 1)}{2} = \frac{10(11)}{2} = 55$$

$$D_8 = \frac{10 - 8 + 1}{55} = \left(\frac{3}{55}\right)(23,000) = \$1,254.55$$

Fixed-Rate-on-Diminishing-Book-Value Method

One of the most sophisticated mathematical methods of depreciation is the *fixed rate on diminishing book value*. The formula for the fixed rate is derived by assuming that a fixed rate (r) can be taken on the current book value to obtain the depreciation for that year. At the end of the useful life of the item, the book value will equal the trade-in value. In theory this method is similar to the sum-of-the years technique.

The formula to determine the fixed rate (r) can be derived from the fixed rate depreciation schedule where (r) represents the fixed rate. The fixed rate depreciation schedule is:

Year	Depreciation	Book value
0	0	C (cost)
1	Cr	$C(1-r)$
2	$C(1-r)r$	$C(1-r)^2$
3	$C(1-r)^2 r$	$C(1-r)^3$
.	.	.
.	.	.
.	.	.
n	$C(1-r)^{n-1}r$	$C(1-r)^n$

$C(1-r)^n$ represents the trade-in value T.

The fixed rate can be found by solving for r:

$$T = C(1-r)^n$$

$$\frac{T}{C} = (1-r)^n$$

$$\sqrt[n]{\frac{T}{C}} = 1 - r$$

$$r = 1 - \sqrt[n]{\frac{T}{C}}$$

The formula for the fixed rate is:

$$r = 1 - \sqrt[n]{\frac{T}{C}}$$

where:

   r = fixed rate

   n = number of years of useful life

   T = trade-in value

   C = cost

Example 3:   Find the fixed rate used to depreciate a piece of equipment that is worth $2,400 and has a trade-in value of $400 at the end of five years. Set up a depreciation schedule and compare it with the straight-line method.

Solution.

$$r = 1 - \sqrt[n]{\frac{T}{C}}$$

$$r = 1 - \sqrt[5]{\frac{400}{2400}}$$

$$r = 1 - .699 = .301$$

Alternate Solution:

$\sqrt[5]{\dfrac{400}{2400}}$ can be found by using logs:

$$\log \sqrt[5]{\frac{400}{2400}} = \log \left(\frac{400}{2400} \right)^{1/5} = \frac{1}{5} (\log 400 - \log 2400)$$

$$= \frac{1}{5} (2.6021 - 3.3802) = -.1556$$

Making the mantissa positive equals .8444 − 1. The antilog is .669; thus, r = .301. The depreciation schedule is:

Year	Depreciation	Book value
0	0	$2,400.00
1	$ 722.81	1,677.19
2	505.12	1,172.06
3	352.99	819.07
4	246.68	572.39
5	172.40	400.00
	$2,000.00	

The trade-in value is $400.00.

The column of depreciations is obtained by taking the fixed rate ($r = .301$) of the current book value:

.301(2400)	$ 722.81
.301(1677.19) =	505.12
.301(1172.06) =	352.99
.301(819.07) =	246.68
.301(572.39) =	172.40
	$2,000.00

PROBLEMS 6-7

*1. Set up a depreciation schedule by using both the straight-line method and sum-of-the-years method for a piece of equipment that is worth $3,600 and has a scrap value of $600 at the end of six years.

2. Set up a depreciation schedule by using the fixed-rate method for a piece of equipment that is worth $3,600 and has a scrap value of $600 at the end of six years.

3. Use the sum-of-the-digits method to find the depreciation for the sixth year of a piece of equipment worth $4,600 with a useful life of 10 years and a scrap value of $600.

4. Use the fixed-rate method to find the depreciation for the sixth year of a piece of equipment worth $4,600 with a useful life of 10 years and a scrap value of $600.

Appendix A

ALGEBRA REVIEW

A-1 REAL NUMBER SYSTEM

A real number is found on the number line which is a boundless straight line in the plane:

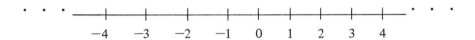

Real numbers can be broken down into two mutually exclusive sets, rational numbers and irrational numbers.

Rational numbers can be expressed as fractions (one integer divided by another) and by division result in an infinite repeating decimal (e.g., $1/3 = .3333 \ldots$). They are termed "rational," because their repeating decimal representations follow a logical or "rational" pattern.

Irrational numbers cannot be expressed as fractions and thus do not have a repeating decimal representation (e.g., $\sqrt{3} = 1.732 \ldots$). They are termed "irrational," because they have an "irrational" pattern.

A number such as $\sqrt{-4}$ does not exist on the number line and thus is not real. It exists only in the imagination and therefore is called an *imaginary number*. The imaginary unit is expressed by $i = \sqrt{-1}$.

To convert a number to *percent* (hundredths), multiply the number by 100:

Number	*Percent*
$1/2 = .5$	50%
$1/3 = .333 \ldots$	$33.333 \ldots \%$
1	100%
2.5	250%
$.005$	$.5\%$

To convert a percent to a number, divide the number by 100:

Percent	Number
50%	.5
250%	2.5
.5%	.005

A-2   BASIC ASSUMPTION OF ALGEBRA

The basic assumption of algebra states that identical operations must be performed on both sides of an equation. Regarding the four basic operations (addition, subtraction, multiplication, and division), the basic assumption of algebra can be expressed as:

If $a = b$, then $a + c = b + c$

If $a = b$, then $a - c = b - c$

If $a = b$, then $ac = bc$

If $a = b$, then $a/c = b/c$ $(c \neq 0)$

For example:

Equation	Solution	Reason
$2x = 8$	$x = 4$	Division by 2
$\dfrac{3}{5} x = 7$	$x = \dfrac{35}{3}$	Multiplication by $\dfrac{5}{3}$
$2x - 4 = 6$	$x = 5$	Addition of 4, followed by division by 2

The *rule of signs* states that when we multiply (or divide) two quantities, the result is positive if both quantities are positive, and the result is also positive if both quantities are negative. But if one quantity is negative and the other is positive, the result of multiplying (or dividing) is negative. For example:

$(-2)(-3) = 6$

$\dfrac{-4}{-2} = 2$

$\dfrac{-8}{4} = -2$

We must be concerned with two *algebraic violations*: (1) Division by zero is undefined or meaningless; and (2) the square root (or any even root) of a negative number is unobtainable and exists only in the imagination.

A-3   BASIC OPERATIONS WITH FRACTIONS

	Operation	*Examples*
Rule 1.	$\dfrac{a}{b} + \dfrac{c}{d} = \dfrac{ad + bc}{bd}$	$\dfrac{2}{3} + \dfrac{4}{5} = \dfrac{10 + 12}{15} = \dfrac{22}{15}$
Rule 2.	$\dfrac{a}{b} - \dfrac{c}{d} = \dfrac{ad - bc}{bd}$	$\dfrac{2}{3} - \dfrac{4}{5} = \dfrac{-2}{15}$
Rule 3.	$\dfrac{a}{b} \cdot \dfrac{c}{d} = \dfrac{ac}{bd}$	$\left(\dfrac{2}{3}\right)\left(\dfrac{4}{5}\right) = \dfrac{8}{15}$
Rule 4.	$\dfrac{\dfrac{a}{b}}{\dfrac{c}{d}} = \dfrac{ad}{bc}$	$\dfrac{\dfrac{2}{3}}{\dfrac{4}{5}} = \left(\dfrac{2}{3}\right)\left(\dfrac{4}{5}\right) = \dfrac{10}{12}$
Rule 5.	$\dfrac{-a}{b} = \dfrac{a}{-b} = -\dfrac{a}{b}$	$\dfrac{-2}{3} = \dfrac{2}{-3} = -\dfrac{2}{3}$

Rule 6.   The rule of *proportion* can be demonstrated by the diagram:

$$\dfrac{a}{b} \overset{=}{\underset{\nwarrow\nearrow}{}} \dfrac{c}{d}$$

The double-arrowed diagonals mean that multiplication can be performed in any sequence along the diagonals. The rule of proportion can be proved by using the basic assumption of algebra and is helpful in solving equations:

$$\dfrac{2}{3} \overset{=}{\underset{x}{}} \dfrac{7}{2}$$

$$x = \dfrac{21}{4}$$

In the case of a common denominator Rules 1 and 2 can be simplified:

$$\frac{a}{b} \pm \frac{c}{b} = \frac{a \pm c}{b}$$

$$\frac{8}{3} + \frac{7}{3} = \frac{15}{3} = 5$$

Fractions such as $\frac{a}{b}$ will be expressed in the convenient typographical form as a/b. In the prior examples we assume that the denominators are not 0.

The following examples demonstrate the use of the six basic rules in solving equations.

Example 1:   Solve the following equation for x: $x/2 = 7/2 + 3/5$.

Solution.

$$\frac{x}{2} = \frac{7}{2} + \frac{3}{5}$$

$$\frac{x}{2} = \frac{41}{10} \quad \text{(rule 1)}$$

$$x = \frac{82}{10} \quad \text{(rule of proportion)}$$

Example 2:   Solve the following equation for x: $(2/x) - 3 = -5x$ $(x \neq 0)$.

Solution.

$$\frac{2}{x} + \frac{5}{x} = 3 \text{ (basic assumption of algebra)}$$

$$\frac{7}{x} = 3 \text{ (rule 1 with common denominators)}$$

$$\frac{7}{3} = x \text{ (rule of proportion)}$$

Example 3:   Solve the following equation for x:

$$\frac{2}{x-2} - \frac{3}{2-x} = 5; \; x \neq 2$$

Solution.

$$\frac{2}{x-2} + \frac{3}{x-2} = 5 \text{ (rule 5)}$$

$$\frac{5}{x-2} = 5 \text{ (rule 1)}$$

$$5 = 5(x-2) \text{ (rule of proportion)}$$

$$5 = 5x - 10 \text{ (multiplication)}$$

$$3 = x \text{ (basic assumption of algebra)}$$

Example 4:   Solve the following equation for x:

$$\frac{2x-4}{3} = \frac{6x+2}{4}$$

Solution.

$$8x - 16 = 18x + 6 \text{ (rule of proportion)}$$

$$-22 = 10x \text{ (basic assumption of algebra and collecting like terms)}$$

$$\frac{-22}{10} = x \text{ (rule of proportion) or } x = \frac{-11}{5}$$

Fractions can be added or subtracted by finding the lowest common demoninator. The lowest common denominator is the smallest number into which both denominators will divide. For example:

$$\frac{5}{3} + \frac{4}{6} = \frac{10}{6} + \frac{4}{6} = \frac{14}{6} = \frac{7}{3}$$

$$\frac{2}{x} + \frac{3}{xy} = \frac{2y}{xy} + \frac{3}{xy} = \frac{3+2y}{xy}$$

A-4   EXPONENTS AND RADICALS

Operation	*Examples*

Rule 1. $x^n = x \cdot x \cdot x \cdot \ldots \cdot x$
(n times where n is a positive integer)

$2^3 = (2)(2)(2) = 8$

Rule 2. $\sqrt[n]{x} = a$ (a is the nth root of x if $a^n = x$)

$\sqrt[2]{16} = \sqrt{16} = 4$
$\sqrt[3]{8} = 2$

Rule 3. $x^{1/n} = \sqrt[n]{x}$

$16^{1/4} = \sqrt[4]{16} = 2$

Rule 4. $x^{-n} = \dfrac{1}{x^n}$ (forms the reciprocal)

$2^{-3} = \dfrac{1}{2^3} = \dfrac{1}{8}$; $4^{-1} = \dfrac{1}{4}$

Rule 5. $x^0 = 1 \, (x \neq 0)$

$5^0 = 1; \; -5^0 = 1$

Rule 6. $x^{a/b} = \sqrt[b]{x^a} = (\sqrt[b]{x})^a$

$8^{2/3} = 4; \; 8^{-2/3} = \dfrac{1}{4}$

Rule 7. $(x^p)(x^q) = x^{p+q}$

$(x^3)(x^6) = x^9$

Rule 8. $\dfrac{x^p}{x^q} = x^{p-q}$

$\dfrac{x^7}{x^3} = x^4$

Rule 9. $(x^p)^q = x^{pq}$

$(x^2)^3 = x^6$

Rule 10. $(xy)^p = x^p y^p$

$(xy)^4 = x^4 y^4$

Rule 11. $\sqrt[n]{xy} = \sqrt[n]{x}\sqrt[n]{y}$

$\sqrt[3]{(8)(27)} = 6$

Rule 12. $\sqrt{\dfrac{x}{y}} = \dfrac{\sqrt[n]{x}}{\sqrt[n]{y}}$

$\sqrt[3]{\dfrac{27}{8}} = \dfrac{3}{2}$

The *hierarchy of operations* in mathematics is accepted as: (1) exponentiation (done first), (2) multiplication or division (done second), and (3) addition or subtraction (done third). For example: $4 + 3 \cdot 2^2 = 16$. The use of parentheses can override the hierarchy of operations. For example, $(4 + 3 \cdot 2)^2 = 100$.

A-5   FACTORING

Factoring is breaking down an algebraic expression into products. The distributive law which states that $a(b + c) = ab + ac$, enables us to do this. For example, $2x^2 y + 4xz = 2x(xy + 2z)$.

The FOIL method demonstrates the technique of multiplying two factors $(a + b)$ and $(c + d)$:

$$(a + b)(c + d) = ac + ad + bc + bd$$

The sequence of steps can be expressed as multiplying the *F*irst terms in each expression, multiplying the *O*uter terms in each expression, multiplying the *I*nner terms in each expression, and multiplying the *L*ast terms in each expression. By using the FOIL method in reverse, certain algebraic expressions can be factored.

Example 1:

$x^2 - 4x + 3 = (x - 1)(x - 3)$
$x^2 - 4 = (x - 2)(x + 2)$
$x^2 + 4$ (does not factor)
$x^2 + x + 2$ (does not factor)
$2x^2 + 5x + 2 = (2x + 1)(x + 2)$
$x^3 - 5x^2 + 6 = x(x - 2)(x - 3)$

Division of algebraic expressions is analogous to division of arithmetic expressions and sometimes can result in factors. If division of arithmetic expressions results in a remainder of 0, then factors are obtained. For example, $21/7 = 3$ implies that 21 factors to $(7)(3)$, whereas $22/7 = 3 + 1/7$ implies that neither 7 nor 3 is a factor of 22. The same logic can be applied when factoring algebraic expressions:

$$
\begin{array}{r}
x^2 - 6x + 5 \\
x - 2 \enclose{longdiv}{x^3 - 8x^2 + 17x - 10}
\end{array}
$$

$x^3 - 2x^2$	(subtract)
$-6x^2 + 17x - 10$	
$-6x^2 + 12x$	(subtract)
$5x - 10$	
$5x - 10$	(subtract)
0	

The remainder of 0 indicates that $(x - 2)$ and $(x^2 - 6x + 5)$ are factors of $x^3 - 8x^2 + 17x - 10$. Thus, $x^3 - 8x^2 + 17x - 10 = (x - 2)(x - 1)(x - 5)$.

A *polynomial* is an algebraic expression in which the exponents of the variable are all positive integers. The degree of the polynomial is determined by the largest exponent. In general if $(x - r)$ is a factor of an nth-degree polynomial with leading coefficient of 1, then r must divide the constant term. This does not mean that every r that divides the constant term has $(x - r)$ as a factor but instead gives the candidates for those factors that must be tested by division. Moreover, an nth-degree polynomial can have n factors at most.

Example 2:   The candidates for factors of $x^2 - 5x + 6$ are:

$$(x \pm 1), (x \pm 2), (x \pm 3), (x \pm 6)$$

By elimination:

$$x^2 - 5x + 6 = (x - 2)(x - 3)$$

Example 3:   The candidates for factors of $x^3 + 2x^2 - x - 2$ are:

$$(x \pm 1), (x \pm 2)$$

By division:

$$x^3 + 2x^2 - x - 2 = (x - 1)(x^2 + 3x + 2) = (x - 1)(x + 1)(x + 2)$$

A-6   FINDING THE ZEROS OF EQUATIONS

The zeros of equations are found by setting an expression equal to 0 and then by finding the value or values (if any) that satisfy the equation. For example, $x - 2 = 0$ has one solution, or zero, namely $x = 2$, which is found by using the basic assumption of algebra. In the simplest case the basic assumption of algebra can be used directly to solve equations. However, in the case where the expression can be factored, the following algebraic fact is used: If $ab = 0$, then $a = 0$ and/or $b = 0$. For example:

$$x^2 - 4x + 3 = 0$$
$$(x - 1)(x - 3) = 0$$
$$x - 1 = 0 \text{ or } x = 1$$
$$x - 3 = 0 \text{ or } x = 3$$

A-7 INEQUALITIES AND ABSOLUTE VALUES

The notation $|x|$ denotes the absolute value of x and is defined to be x if x is positive and $-x$ if x is negative. For example:

$$|5| = 5; \ |{-5}| = 5$$

The notation $a < b$ means that "a is less than b." Interpreting this on the number line shows that a is to the left of b. A more formal definition of $a < b$ is that "a is less than b if there is a positive value m such that $a + m = b$."

Other notations involving inequalities include:

$a \leqslant b$ (a is less than or equal to b)

$a > b$ (a is greater than b)

$a \geqslant b$ (a is greater than or equal to b)

$a < x < b$ (x is between a and b)

$|x| < a$ (x is between a and $-a$; a is positive)

$|x| > a$ (x is greater than a or x is less than $-a$; a is positive)

The rules for dealing with inequalities are similar to those of equalities with the exception that when both sides of an inequality are multiplied (or divided) by a negative quantity, the sense of the inequality is reversed. For example:

$$5 + 3p > 20; \ p > 5$$
$$20 - 2p > 10; \ p < 5$$
$$20 > 20 - 2p > 10; \ 0 < p < 5$$

A-8 SUBSCRIPTS AND DELTA NOTATION

The notation x_k (k is a positive integer) denotes "x subscript k" of simply "x sub k." Subscript notation is convenient; we can use the same variable symbol throughout a problem while we change subscripts and thus indicate different variables. For example, $p_1, p_2, p_3 \ldots$ could indicate different values for the variable p.

The upper-case Greek letter delta, Δ, is a universally accepted mathematical symbol that means "change in." Together with subscript notation, the delta notation makes it possible to express changes concisely. Much of mathematical economics involves analyzing the change in economic variables, so these notations are used frequently.

Example 1:   If $p_1 = 1$ while $D_1 = 18$ and $p_2 = 3$ while $D_2 = 14$, then:

$$\Delta p = 2$$
$$\Delta D = -4$$
$$\frac{\Delta D}{\Delta p} = -2$$

Example 2:   If $p_1 = 3$ while $S_1 = 14$ and $p_2 = 6$ while $S_2 = 23$, then:

$$\Delta p = 3$$
$$\Delta S = 9$$
$$\frac{\Delta S}{\Delta p} = 3$$

Example 3:   If $p_1 = 2$ while $D_1 = 5$ and $p_2 = 4$ while $D_2 = 5$, then:

$$\Delta p = 2$$
$$\Delta D = 0$$
$$\frac{\Delta D}{\Delta p} = \frac{0}{2} = 0$$

Example 4:   If $p_1 = 2$ while $D_1 = 7$ and $p_2 = 2$ while $D_2 = 9$, then:

$$\Delta p = 0$$
$$\Delta D = 2$$
$$\frac{\Delta D}{\Delta p} = \frac{2}{0} \text{ (undefined)}$$

A-9   SUMMATION NOTATION

The upper-case Greek letter sigma, Σ, means "to sum." If X represents a set of numbers, then ΣX means to find the sum of set X. A set of numbers is frequently enclosed by braces and the elements separated by commas. For example, if set X is given by $X = \{2, 4, 6\}$, then:

$$\Sigma X = 2 + 4 + 6 = 12$$

ΣX^2 means to square each individual element of set X and then to find the sum. For example, if set X is given by $X = \{2, 4, 6\}$, then:

$$\Sigma X^2 = 4 + 16 + 36 = 56$$

$(\Sigma X)^2$ means to find the sum of set X and square the result. For example, if set X is given by $X = \{2, 4, 6\}$, then:

$$(\Sigma X)^2 = (12)^2 = 144$$

If each element of a set X has a matching element in set Y, then ΣXY means to multiply corresponding elements and then find their sum. For example, matching elements of sets X and Y are:

X	Y	XY
2	1	2
4	2	8
6	3	18
	ΣXY	= 28

If sets X and Y have the same number of elements, then:

$$\Sigma(X + Y) = \Sigma X + \Sigma Y$$

For example, if $X = \{2, 4, 6\}$ and $Y = \{1, 2, 3\}$, then:

$$\Sigma(X + Y) = \Sigma X + \Sigma Y = (2 + 4 + 6) + (1 + 2 + 3) = 18$$

For a constant k and a set X, $\Sigma kX = k\Sigma X$. For example, if $X = \{2, 4, 6\}$, then:

$$\Sigma 10X = 10\Sigma X = 10(2 + 4 + 6) = 120$$

Summation notation can be stated more formally by the use of subscripts. If a set X contains N elements $x_1, x_2, x_3, \ldots, x_N$, then:

$$\sum_{k=1}^{N} X_k = x_1 + x_2 + x_3 + \ldots + x_N$$

where $\displaystyle\sum_{k=1}^{N} X_k$ represents the entire set of elements from $k = 1$ to $k = N$. The subscript k is the *index*.

A-10   LIMITS AND THE CONSTANT e

The concept of a *limit* is based on the problem of analyzing an expression as a variable *approaches* a quantity (as opposed to when a variable actually equals a quantity). Here we examine the idea of a limit on an intuitive basis. It will be further developed in Chapters 1, 2, and 3. The concept of a limit forms the basis of calculus and is treated in Chapter 4.

The following example demonstrates the conventional limit notation: Suppose that we wish to find the limit of the fraction $1/x$ as x "approaches" 5. We can state that "as x approaches 5, the fraction $1/x$ approaches $1/5$." In limit (lim) notation, the expression is:

$$\lim_{x \to 5} \frac{1}{x} = \frac{1}{5}$$

Further examples to determine limits include:

$$\lim_{x \to 2/3} \frac{1}{x} = \frac{3}{2}$$

$$\lim_{x \to 0} \frac{1}{x} = \text{undefined (division by 0 is undefined)}$$

$$\lim_{x \to \infty} \frac{1}{x} = 0 \text{ (division of a constant by } \infty \text{ becomes infinitesimal)}$$

Note: Before you attempt to find the limit, make certain that the expression is reduced to lowest terms.

Example 1:

$$\lim_{x \to 3} \frac{x^2 - 9}{x - 3} = 6$$

Solution.

$$\frac{x^2 - 9}{x - 3} = \frac{(x + 3)(x - 3)}{(x - 3)} = (x + 3)$$

Cancellation is permitted, provided that $x \neq 3$. (In this problem x approaches but is not equal to 3, so the cancellation is permitted.) Notice that if x were allowed to equal 3 in the original expression, the limit could not be found, because the expression would be in the indeterminant form 0/0. It follows that:

$$\lim_{x \to 3} \frac{x^2 - 9}{x - 3} = \lim_{x \to 3} (x + 3) = 6$$

Now the question of why we allow x to "approach" 3 instead of allowing it to equal 3 arises, because the result would be the same. The answer to this question is found in Chapter 4. At this point it is sufficient to state that in many important circumstances it is not possible to evaluate an expression directly; the value must be "approached." This is demonstrated by the following definition of the constant e.

The constant $e = 2.71828 \ldots$ is obtained by carrying out the sequence $(1 + 1/n)^n$ for $n = 1, 2, 3, 4 \ldots$ indefinitely. This can be expressed as:

$$e = \lim_{n \to \infty} \left(1 + \frac{1}{n}\right)^n = 2.71828 \ldots$$

The table below gives some approximations of e. Notice that as n grows larger, a closer approximation evolves:

n	$\left(1 + \dfrac{1}{n}\right)^n$
1	2.0000
2	2.2500
.	.
.	.
.	.
10	2.5937
.	.
.	.
.	.
100	2.7048
.	.
.	.
.	.
1,000	2.7169
.	.
.	.
.	.
10,000	2.7181

A-11   GEOMETRIC AND ARITHMETIC PROGRESSIONS

A *geometric progression* is a set of numbers in which each one after the first is obtained from the preceding one by multiplying by a fixed number called the *common ratio*. If the first term of the progression is a and the common ratio is r, then the sum of n terms of a geometric progression is:

$$S_n = a + ar + ar^2 + ar^3 + \ldots + ar^{n-1}$$

A formula to find the sum of the geometric progression consisting of n terms is:

$$S_n = \frac{a - ar^n}{1 - r}$$

If the common ratio satisfies $|r| < 1$, then r^n approaches 0 as the number of terms (n) approaches infinity. The sum of the infinite geometric progression becomes:

$$S = \frac{a}{1 - r}$$

The formula for the sum of a geometric progression with n terms can be derived:

$$S_n = a + ar + ar^2 + ar^3 + \ldots + ar^{n-1}$$

$$rS_n = ar + ar^2 + ar^3 + ar^4 + \ldots + ar^n$$

$$S_n - rS_n = a - ar^n$$

$$S_n = \frac{a - ar^n}{1 - r}$$

Example 1:   Use the formula to find the sum of the first five terms of the following geometric progression:

$$S_5 = 2 + 6 + 18 + 54 + 162$$

Solution.

$$S_5 = \frac{2 - (2 \cdot 3^5)}{1 - 3} = 242$$

Example 2:   Find the sum of the infinite geometric progression:

$$S = 1 + \frac{1}{2} + \frac{1}{4} + \frac{1}{8} + \ldots$$

$$S = \frac{1}{1 - \frac{1}{2}} = 2$$

An *arithmetic progression* is a sequence of numbers generated by adding a fixed number to each term to derive the following term. The fixed term is called the *common difference*. The formula to find the sum of an arithmetic progression is:

$$S_n = \frac{n}{2} [2a + (n - 1)d]$$

where S_n is the sum of n terms, a is the first term, d is the common difference, and n is the number of terms.

The nth term is given by the formula:

$$a_n = a + (n - 1)d$$

where a_n represents the nth term.

The formula is derived in the following manner:

$$S_n = a + (a + d) + (a + 2d) + \ldots + [a + (n - 1)d]$$

$$S_n = [a + (n - 1)d] + \ldots + a$$

Adding the above equations results in:

$$2S_n = n[2a + (n - 1)d]$$

$$S_n = \frac{n}{2} [2a + (n - 1)d]$$

Example 3:   Find the sum of the following arithmetic progression:

$$S_{10} = 1 + 2 + 3 + \ldots + 10$$

Solution.   In this example $a = 1, n = 10$, and $d = 1$.

$$S_n = \frac{n}{2}\ [2a + (n-1)d] = S_{10} = \frac{10}{2}\ (2+9) = 55$$

Example 4:   Find the sum of the following arithmetic expression:

$$S_{10} = 4 + 8 + 12 + \ldots + 40$$

Solution.   In this example $a = 4, n = 10$, and $d = 4$.

$$S_{10} = \frac{10}{2}\ (8+36) = 220$$

A-12   LOGARITHMS

A logarithm is an exponent. In the expression $x = b^y$ the *logarithm* (or exponent) is y and the base is b. The expression $x = b^y$ is equivalent to the expression $\log_b x = y$. The purpose of multiple notations for exponents is that when the term "log" is used, it will suggest the use of tables as an aid to calculation. For example:

Exponential form	*Logarithmic form*
$2^3 = 8$	$\log_2 8 = 3$
$2^{-3} = \dfrac{1}{8}$	$\log_2 \dfrac{1}{8} = -3$
$10^0 = 1$	$\log_{10} 1 = 0$
$e^1 = e$	$\log_e e = 1$

Note: When base 10 is used (common logs), the base is not indicated: $\log x = y$. When base e is used (natural logs), the notation is: $\ln x = y$.

The three laws of exponents and their respective laws of logarithms (with examples of each law) are:

$$b^m b^n = b^{m+n} \text{ (law of exponents); } 2^3 2^4 = 2^7$$

$$\boxed{\log_b A \cdot B = \log_b A + \log_b B \text{ (law of logarithms)}}$$

$$\log_2 8 \cdot 16 = \log_2 8 + \log_2 16 = 3 + 4 = 7$$

$$\frac{b^m}{b^n} = b^{m-n} \text{ (law of exponents)}; \quad \frac{2^4}{2^3} = 2^1$$

$$\log_b \frac{A}{B} = \log_b A - \log_b B \text{ (law of logarithms)}$$

$$\log_2 \frac{16}{8} = \log_2 16 - \log_2 8 = 4 - 3 = 1$$

$$(b^m)^n = b^{mn} \text{ (law of exponents)}; \quad (2^2)^3 = 2^6$$

$$\log_b A^n = n \log_b A \text{ (law of logarithms)}; \quad (\log_2 4)^3 = 3 \log_2 4 = 3 \cdot 2 = 6$$

The *common log* of a number can be expressed by:

$$\log N = c + m$$

In this expression c is the *characteristic* and m is the *mantissa*. The characteristic is an integer (positive, negative, or 0) that characterizes the size of the number (obtained by direct examination of the number N). The mantissa is the fractional part of the logarithm and is found by using the tables of common logs. The mantissa is a positive fraction between 0 and 1.

A-13   COUNTING PROBLEMS

Fundamental Principle

The *fundamental principle* in counting states that if an event can occur in m different ways and if, after this has occurred, another event can occur in n different ways, then $m \times n$ represents the number of ways that both events can occur in order. The following examples are illustrative.

Tossing a die twice (or two dice once) yields 36 different outcomes: $m \times n = (6)(6) = 36$. The fundamental principle can be generalized to any number of events. Tossing three dice once yields 216 different outcomes: $(6)(6)(6) = 216$. The probability of obtaining two kings in drawing two cards from an ordinary deck with replacement after the first draw is:

$$\left(\frac{4}{52}\right)\left(\frac{4}{52}\right) = \frac{16}{2704} = .0059 = .59\%$$

where the chance (probability) of obtaining a king in a single draw is 4/52.

Factorial Notation

Factorial n is defined as:

$$n! = n(n-1)(n-2) \ldots 1$$

where n is a positive integer. For example:

$$4! = 4 \cdot 3 \cdot 2 \cdot 1 = 24$$

$$1! = 1$$

$$\frac{4!}{2!} = \frac{4 \cdot 3 \cdot 2 \cdot 1}{2 \cdot 1} = 12$$

By special definition, $0! = 1$.

Permutation

A set specified by order, which consists of r distinct elements, is a *permutation* of the r elements. For example, the first three letters of the alphabet form six permutations: $abc, acb, bac, bca, cab, cba$.

The number of permutations of n things taken r at a time is given by:

$$\boxed{{}_nP_r = \frac{n!}{(n-r)!}}$$

The number of permutations of the letters a, b, and c taken three at a time is:

$$_3P_3 = \frac{3!}{0!} = 6$$

The number of permutations of the letters a, b, c, and d taken two at a time is:

$$_4P_2 = \frac{4!}{2!} = 12$$

Combination

A set of r distinct elements is a *combination* of r elements. For a permutation, order is important, but for the combination order is not important. For example, the number of combinations of the letters a, b, and c taken three at a time is 1. The number of combinations of n things taken r at a time is given by:

$$_nC_r = \frac{n!}{r!(n-r)!}$$

The number of combinations of the letters a, b, and c taken two at a time is:

$$_3C_2 = \frac{3!}{2!1!} = 3$$

Combination of the letters a, b, and c taken zero at a time results in the null set:

$$_3C_0 = \frac{3!}{0!3!} = 1$$

A-14   BINOMIAL THEOREM

The *binomial theorem* gives the expansion of $(a + b)^n$, where n is a positive integer. The theorem can be derived inductively by examples:

$$(a+b)^1 = \quad\quad\quad a + b$$
$$(a+b)^2 = \quad\quad a^2 + 2ab + b^2$$
$$(a+b)^3 = \quad a^3 + 3a^2b + 3ab^2 + b^3$$
$$(a+b)^4 = a^4 + 4a^3b + 6a^2b^2 + 4ab^3 + b^4$$

·

·

·

In the above expansion the exponent of a decreases, while the exponent of b increases. The expansion of $(a + b)^n$ contains $(n + 1)$ terms, and the sum of the exponents for any given term is n. The coefficients in the expansion of $(a + b)^n$ form a pattern known as Pascal's triangle:

$$
\begin{array}{ccccccc}
 & & & 1 & 1 & & \\
 & & 1 & 2 & 1 & & \\
 & 1 & 3 & 3 & 1 & & \\
1 & 4 & 6 & 4 & 1 & &
\end{array}
$$

·

·

·

Any number in this triangle can be found by adding the two numbers immediately over the number.

These coefficients can also be generated by using $_nC_r$:

$$_1C_0 = 1 \qquad _1C_1 = 1$$

$$_2C_0 = 1 \qquad _2C_1 = 2 \qquad _2C_2 = 1$$

$$_3C_0 = 1 \qquad _3C_1 = 3 \qquad _3C_2 = 3 \qquad _3C_3 = 1$$

$$\cdot$$

$$\cdot$$

$$\cdot$$

In general, $(a + b)^n = a^n + {_nC_1}a^{n-1}b + {_nC_2}a^{n-2}b^2 + \ldots + b^n$.

Appendix B

TABLES

Table 1   Common Logarithms

N	0	1	2	3	4	5	6	7	8	9
10	0000	0043	0086	0128	0170	0212	0253	0294	0334	0374
11	0414	0453	0492	0531	0569	0607	0645	0682	0719	0755
12	0792	0828	0864	0899	0934	0969	1004	1038	1072	1106
13	1139	1173	1206	1239	1271	1303	1335	1367	1399	1430
14	1461	1492	1523	1553	1584	1614	1644	1673	1703	1732
15	1761	1790	1818	1847	1875	1903	1931	1959	1987	2014
16	2041	2068	2095	2122	2148	2175	2201	2227	2253	2279
17	2304	2330	2355	2380	2405	2430	2455	2480	2504	2529
18	2553	2577	2601	2625	2648	2672	2695	2718	2742	2765
19	2788	2810	2833	2856	2878	2900	2923	2945	2967	2989
20	3010	3032	3054	3075	3096	3118	3139	3160	3181	3201
21	3222	3243	3263	3284	3304	3324	3345	3365	3385	3404
22	3424	3444	3464	3483	3502	3522	3541	3560	3579	3598
23	3617	3636	3655	3674	3692	3711	3729	3747	3766	3784
24	3802	3820	3838	3856	3874	3892	3909	3927	3945	3962
25	3979	3997	4014	4031	4048	4065	4082	4099	4116	4133
26	4150	4166	4183	4200	4216	4232	4249	4265	4281	4298
27	4314	4330	4346	4362	4378	4393	4409	4425	4440	4456
28	4472	4487	4502	4518	4533	4548	4564	4579	4594	4609
29	4624	4639	4654	4669	4683	4698	4713	4728	4742	4757
30	4771	4786	4800	4814	4829	4843	4857	4871	4886	4900
31	4914	4928	4942	4955	4969	4983	4997	5011	5024	5038
32	5051	5065	5079	5092	5105	5119	5132	5145	5159	5172
33	5185	5198	5211	5224	5237	5250	5263	5276	5289	5302
34	5315	5328	5340	5353	5366	5378	5391	5403	5416	5428
35	5441	5453	5465	5478	5490	5502	5514	5527	5539	5551
36	5563	5575	5587	5599	5611	5623	5635	5647	5658	5670
37	5682	5694	5705	5717	5729	5740	5752	5763	5775	5786
38	5798	5809	5821	5832	5843	5855	5866	5877	5888	5899
39	5911	5922	5933	5944	5955	5966	5977	5988	5999	6010
40	6021	6031	6042	6053	6064	6075	6085	6096	6107	6117
41	6128	6138	6149	6160	6170	6180	6191	6201	6212	6222
42	6232	6243	6253	6263	6274	6284	6294	6304	6314	6325
43	6335	6345	6355	6365	6375	6385	6395	6405	6415	6425
44	6435	6444	6454	6464	6474	6484	6493	6503	6513	6522
45	6532	6542	6551	6561	6571	6580	6590	6599	6609	6618
46	6628	6637	6646	6656	6665	6675	6684	6693	6702	6712
47	6721	6730	6739	6749	6758	6767	6776	6785	6794	6803
48	6812	6821	6830	6839	6848	6857	6866	6875	6884	6893
49	6902	6911	6920	6928	6937	6946	6955	6964	6972	6981
50	6990	6998	7007	7016	7024	7033	7042	7050	7059	7067
51	7076	7084	7093	7101	7110	7118	7126	7135	7143	7162
52	7160	7168	7177	7185	7193	7202	7210	7218	7226	7235
53	7243	7251	7259	7267	7275	7284	7292	7300	7308	7316
54	7324	7332	7340	7348	7356	7364	7372	7380	7388	7396

Table 1   Common Logarithms (Continued)

N	0	1	2	3	4	5	6	7	8	9
55	7404	7412	7419	7427	7435	7443	7451	7459	7466	7474
56	7482	7490	7497	7505	7513	7520	7528	7536	7543	7551
57	7559	7566	7574	7582	7589	7597	7604	7612	7619	7627
58	7634	7642	7649	7657	7664	7672	7679	7686	7694	7701
59	7709	7716	7723	7731	7738	7745	7752	7760	7767	7774
60	7782	7789	7796	7803	7810	7818	7825	7832	7839	7846
61	7853	7860	7868	7875	7882	7889	7896	7903	7910	7917
62	7924	7931	7938	7945	7952	7959	7966	7973	7980	7987
63	7993	8000	8007	8014	8021	8028	8035	8041	8048	8055
64	8062	8069	8075	8082	8089	8096	8102	8109	8116	8122
65	8129	8136	8142	8149	8156	8162	8169	8176	8182	8189
66	8195	8202	8209	8215	8222	8228	8235	8241	8248	8254
67	8261	8267	8274	8280	8287	8293	8299	8306	8312	8319
68	8325	8331	8338	8344	8351	8357	8363	8370	8376	8382
69	8388	8395	8401	8407	8414	8420	8426	8432	8439	8445
70	8451	8457	8463	8470	8476	8482	8488	8494	8500	8506
71	8513	8519	8525	8531	8537	8543	8549	8555	8561	8567
72	8573	8579	8585	8591	8597	8603	8609	8615	8621	8627
73	8633	8639	8645	8651	8657	8663	8669	8675	8681	8686
74	8692	8698	8704	8710	8716	8722	8727	8733	8739	8745
75	8751	8756	8762	8768	8774	8779	8785	8791	8797	8802
76	8808	8814	8820	8825	8831	8837	8842	8848	8854	8859
77	8865	8871	8876	8882	8887	8893	8899	8904	8910	8915
78	8921	8927	8932	8938	8943	8949	8954	8960	8965	8971
79	8976	8982	8987	8993	8998	9004	9009	9015	9020	9025
80	9031	9036	9042	9047	9053	9058	9063	9069	9074	9079
81	9085	9090	9096	9101	9106	9112	9117	9122	9128	9133
82	9138	9143	9149	9154	9159	9165	9170	9175	9180	9186
83	9191	9196	9201	9206	9212	9217	9222	9227	9232	9238
84	9243	9248	9253	9258	9263	9269	9274	9279	9284	9289
85	9294	9299	9304	9309	9315	9320	9325	9330	9335	9340
86	9345	9350	9355	9360	9365	9370	9375	9380	9385	9390
87	9395	9400	9405	9410	9415	9420	9425	9430	9435	9440
88	9445	9450	9455	9460	9465	9469	9474	9479	9484	9489
89	9494	9499	9504	9509	9513	9518	9523	9528	9533	9538
90	9542	9547	9552	9557	9562	9566	9571	9576	9581	9586
91	9590	9595	9600	9605	9609	9614	9619	9624	9628	9633
92	9638	9643	9647	9652	9657	9661	9666	9671	9675	9680
93	9685	9689	9694	9699	9703	9708	9713	9717	9722	9727
94	9731	9736	9741	9745	9750	9754	9759	9763	9768	9773
95	9777	9782	9786	9791	9795	9800	9805	9809	9814	9818
96	9823	9827	9832	9836	9841	9845	9850	9854	9859	9863
97	9868	9872	9877	9881	9886	9890	9894	9899	9903	9908
98	9912	9917	9921	9926	9930	9934	9939	9943	9948	9952
99	9956	9961	9965	9969	9974	9978	9983	9987	9991	9996

Table 2 $(1 + i)^n$ (for $i = 1\%$)

n	1%	n	1%	n	1%
1	1.01000000	36	1.43076878	71	2.02683100
2	1.02010000	37	1.44507647	72	2.04709931
3	1.03030100	38	1.45952724	73	2.06757031
4	1.04060401	39	1.47412251	74	2.08824601
5	1.05101005	40	1.48886373	75	2.10912847
6	1.06152015	41	1.50375237	76	2.13021975
7	1.07213535	42	1.51878989	77	2.15152195
8	1.08235671	43	1.53397779	78	2.17303717
9	1.09368527	44	1.54931757	79	2.19476754
10	1.10462213	45	1.56481075	80	2.21671522
11	1.11566835	46	1.58045885	81	2.23888237
12	1.12682503	47	1.59626344	82	2.26127119
13	1.13809328	48	1.61222608	83	2.28388390
14	1.14947421	49	1.62834834	84	2.30672274
15	1.16096896	50	1.64463182	85	2.32978997
16	1.17257864	51	1.66107814	86	2.35308787
17	1.18430443	52	1.67768892	87	2.37661875
18	1.19614748	53	1.69446581	88	2.40038494
19	1.20810895	54	1.71141047	89	2.42438879
20	1.22019004	55	1.72852457	90	2.44863267
21	1.23239194	56	1.74580982	91	2.47311900
22	1.24471586	57	1.76326792	92	2.49785019
23	1.25716302	58	1.78090060	93	2.52282869
24	1.26973465	59	1.79870930	94	2.54805698
25	1.28243200	60	1.81669670	95	2.57353755
26	1.29525631	61	1.83486367	96	2.59927293
27	1.30820888	62	1.85321230	97	2.62526565
28	1.32129097	63	1.87174443	98	2.65151831
29	1.33450388	64	1.89046187	99	2.67803349
30	1.34784892	65	1.90936649	100	2.70481383
31	1.36132740	66	1.92846015		
32	1.37494068	67	1.94774475		
33	1.38869009	68	1.96722220		
34	1.40257699	69	1.98689442		
35	1.41660276	70	2.00676337		

Table 3 $(1 + i)^{-n}$ (for $i = 1\%$)

n	1%	n	1%	n	1%
1	0.99009901	36	0.69892495	71	0.49338105
2	0.98029605	37	0.69200490	72	0.48849609
3	0.97059015	38	0.68515337	73	0.48365949
4	0.96098034	39	0.67836967	74	0.47887078
5	0.95146569	40	0.67165314	75	0.47412949
6	0.94204524	41	0.66500311	76	0.46943514
7	0.93271805	42	0.65841892	77	0.46478726
8	0.92348322	43	0.65189992	78	0.46018541
9	0.91433982	44	0.64544546	79	0.45562912
10	0.90528695	45	0.63905492	80	0.45111794
11	0.89632372	46	0.63272764	81	0.44665142
12	0.88744923	47	0.62842301	82	0.44222913
13	0.87866260	48	0.62026041	83	0.43785063
14	0.86996297	49	0.61411921	84	0.43351547
15	0.86134947	50	0.60803882	85	0.42922324
16	0.85282126	51	0.60201864	86	0.42497350
17	0.84437749	52	0.59605806	87	0.42076585
18	0.83601731	53	0.59015649	88	0.41659985
19	0.82773992	54	0.58431336	89	0.41247510
20	0.81954447	55	0.57852308	90	0.40839119
21	0.81143017	56	0.57280008	91	0.40434771
22	0.80339621	57	0.56712879	92	0.40034427
23	0.79544179	58	0.56151365	93	0.39638046
24	0.78756613	59	0.55595411	94	0.30245590
25	0.77976844	60	0.55044962	95	0.38857020
26	0.77204796	61	0.54499862	96	0.38472297
27	0.76440392	62	0.53960358	97	0.38091383
28	0.75683557	63	0.53426097	98	0.37714241
29	0.74934215	64	0.52897126	99	0.37340832
30	0.74192292	65	0.52373392	100	0.36971121
31	0.73457715	66	0.51854844		
32	0.72730411	67	0.51341429		
33	0.72010307	68	0.50833099		
34	0.71297334	69	0.50329801		
35	0.70591420	70	0.49831486		

Table 4   The Exponential Function

x	e^x	e^{-x}	x	e^x	e^{-x}	x	e^x	e^{-x}
0.0	1.000	1.000	3.5	33.12	0.030	7.0	1,096.6	0.0009
0.1	1.105	0.905	3.6	36.60	0.027	7.1	1,212.0	0.0008
0.2	1.221	0.819	3.7	40.45	0.025	7.2	1,339.4	0.0007
0.3	1.350	0.741	3.8	44.70	0.022	7.3	1,480.3	0.0007
0.4	1.492	0.670	3.9	49.40	0.020	7.4	1,636.0	0.0096
0.5	1.649	0.607	4.0	54.60	0.018	7.5	1,808.0	0.00055
0.6	1.822	0.549	4.1	60.34	0.017	7.6	1,998.2	0.00050
0.7	2.014	0.497	4.2	68.69	0.015	7.7	2,208.3	0.00045
0.8	2.226	0.449	4.3	73.70	0.014	7.8	2,440.6	0.00041
0.9	2.460	0.407	4.4	81.45	0.012	7.9	2,697.3	0.00037
1.0	2.718	0.368	4.5	90.02	0.011	8.0	2,981.0	0.00034
1.1	3.004	0.333	4.6	99.48	0.010	8.1	3,294.5	0.00030
1.2	3.320	0.301	4.7	109.95	0.009	8.2	3,641.0	0.00027
1.3	3.669	0.273	4.8	121.51	0.008	8.3	4,023.9	0.00025
1.4	4.055	0.247	4.9	134.29	0.007	8.4	4,447.1	0.00022
1.5	4.482	0.223	5.0	148.4	0.0067	8.5	4,914.8	0.00020
1.6	4.953	0.202	5.1	164.0	0.0061	8.6	5,431.7	0.00018
1.7	5.474	0.183	5.2	181.3	0.0055	8.7	6,002.9	0.00017
1.8	6.050	0.165	5.3	200.3	0.0050	8.8	6,634.2	0.00015
1.9	6.686	0.150	5.4	221.4	0.0045	8.9	7,332.0	0.00014
2.0	7.389	0.135	5.5	244.7	0.0041	9.0	8,103.1	0.00012
2.1	8.166	0.122	5.6	270.4	0.0037	9.1	8,055.3	0.00011
2.2	9.025	0.111	5.7	298.9	0.0033	9.2	9,897.1	0.00010
2.3	9.974	0.100	5.8	330.3	0.0030	9.3	10,938	0.00009
2.4	11.023	0.091	5.9	365.0	0.0027	9.4	12,088	0.00008
2.5	12.18	0.082	6.0	403.4	0.0025	9.5	13,360	0.00007
2.6	13.46	0.074	6.1	445.9	0.0022	9.6	14,765	0.00007
2.7	14.88	0.067	6.2	492.8	0.0020	9.7	16,318	0.00006
2.8	16.44	0.061	6.3	544.6	0.0018	9.8	18,034	0.00006
2.9	18.17	0.055	6.4	601.8	0.0017	9.9	19,930	0.00005
3.0	20.09	0.050	6.5	665.1	0.0015			
3.1	22.20	0.045	6.6	735.1	0.0014			
3.2	24.53	0.041	6.7	812.4	0.0012			
3.3	27.11	0.037	6.8	897.8	0.0011			
3.4	29.96	0.033	6.9	992.3	0.0010			

Appendix C

ANSWERS TO SELECTED PROBLEMS

PROBLEMS 1-1, page 3

1.
Domain (x)	*Range (y)*
a. all real x	all real y
b. all real x	$y \geqslant 0$
c. all $x \neq 0$	all $y \neq 0$
d. all real x	$y \geqslant 2$
e. all real x	$y \geqslant 0$
f. all real x	$y \leqslant 0$
g. $x \geqslant 0$	$y \geqslant 0$
h. $x \neq 2$	$y \neq 0$
i. $x \geqslant 2$	$y \geqslant 0$
j. all real x	$y \geqslant 0$

2. $f(0) = 4, f(3) = 10, f(-4) = -4, f(a) = 2a + 4, f(a + b) = 2(a + b) + 4 = 2a + 2b + 4, f(x + \Delta x) = 2(x + \Delta x) + 4 = 2x + 2\Delta x + 4, g(0) = 0, g(-3) = 9, g(c) = c^2, g(a + b) = (a + b)^2 = a^2 + 2ab + b^2, g(x + \Delta x) = (x + \Delta x)^2 = x^2 + 2x\Delta x + \Delta x$

PROBLEMS 1-2, page 4

1. If a point lies on the y axis, then $x = 0$ (and conversely). If a point lies on the x axis, then $y = 0$ (and conversely).

PROBLEMS 1-3, page 6

1a.

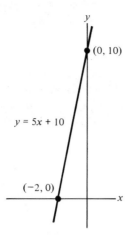

$y = 5x + 10$

b.

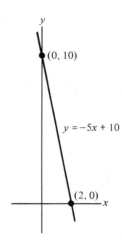

$y = -5x + 10$

c.

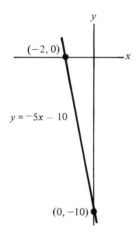

$y = -5x - 10$

d.

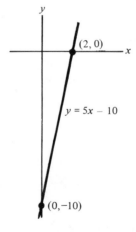

$y = 5x - 10$

3a.

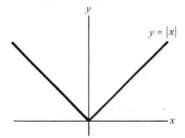

$y = |x|$

PROBLEMS 1-4, page 13

1. Slopes for Problem 1, Section 1-3:

	$\dfrac{\Delta y}{\Delta x}$	$\dfrac{\Delta x}{\Delta y}$
a.	5	1/5
b.	−5	−1/5
c.	−5	−1/5
d.	5	1/5
e.	5	1/5
f.	5	1/5
g.	5	1/5
h.	.25	4
i.	.25	4
j.	0	undefined
k.	0	undefined
l.	0	undefined
m.	undefined	0
n.	undefined	0
o.	undefined	0
p.	1	1
q.	−1	−1
r.	2/3	3/2

2. a. $7y - 10x = 1$ c. $x = 4$

   b. $y = 4$ d. $y + x = 2$

3. a. The table for $y = 4x + 10$ is:

x		y	
$\begin{array}{c}0\\1\end{array}\Big]\ \Delta x = 1$		$\begin{array}{c}10\\14\end{array}\Big]\ \Delta y = 4$	

$$\frac{\Delta y}{\Delta x} = \frac{4}{1}$$

$\begin{array}{c}2\\3\\4\end{array}\Big]\ \Delta x = 2$		$\begin{array}{c}18\\22\\26\end{array}\Big]\ \Delta y = 8$	

$$\frac{\Delta y}{\Delta x} = \frac{8}{2} = \frac{4}{1}$$

4. a. Given that $y = 8x$, then:

$$\frac{f(x + \Delta x) - f(x)}{\Delta x} = \frac{8(x + \Delta x) - 8x}{\Delta x} = \frac{8x + 8\Delta x - 8x}{\Delta x} = 8$$

b. Given that $y = 4x + 10$, then:

$$\frac{f(x + \Delta x) - f(x)}{\Delta x} = \frac{4(x + \Delta x) + 10 - (4x + 10)}{\Delta x}$$

$$= \frac{4x + 4\Delta x + 10 - 4x - 10}{\Delta x} = 4$$

PROBLEMS 1-5, page 15

1a.

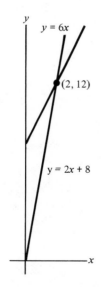

b.

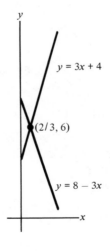

2. a.

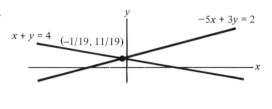

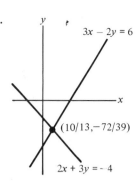

PROBLEMS 1-6, page 22

1. $y = 100 - 20x$

x (quantity)	y (price)
0	100
1	80
2	60
3	40
4	20
5	0

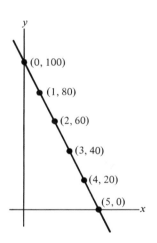

2. $y = 200 - 2x$

5. a. $\dfrac{\Delta y}{\Delta x} = -2, \quad \dfrac{\Delta x}{\Delta y} = \dfrac{-1}{2}$

   b. $\dfrac{\Delta y}{\Delta x} = -3, \quad \dfrac{\Delta x}{\Delta y} = \dfrac{-1}{3}$

6. a.

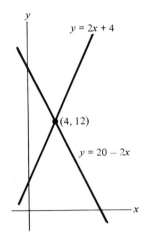

$y = 2x + 4$

(4, 12)

$y = 20 - 2x$

PROBLEMS 1-7, page 27

1. a. $y = 20 - 2x$

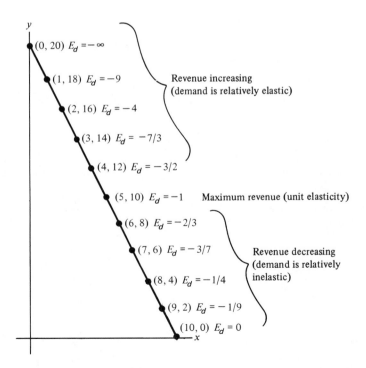

(0, 20) $E_d = -\infty$

(1, 18) $E_d = -9$

Revenue increasing
(demand is relatively elastic)

(2, 16) $E_d = -4$

(3, 14) $E_d = -7/3$

(4, 12) $E_d = -3/2$

(5, 10) $E_d = -1$ Maximum revenue (unit elasticity)

(6, 8) $E_d = -2/3$

(7, 6) $E_d = -3/7$

Revenue decreasing
(demand is relatively
inelastic)

(8, 4) $E_d = -1/4$

(9, 2) $E_d = -1/9$

(10, 0) $E_d = 0$

2. a.

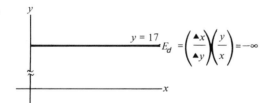

3. a.

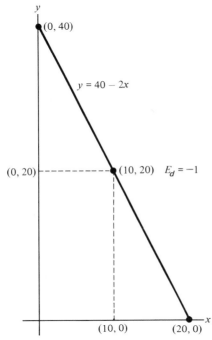

$$E_d = \left(\frac{-1}{2}\right)\left(\frac{y}{x}\right) = \left(\frac{-1}{2}\right)\left(\frac{40-2x}{x}\right) = -1$$

$$\frac{40-2x}{2x} = 1$$

$$40 - 2x = 2x$$

$$x = 10; \ y = 20$$

PROBLEMS 1-8, page 36

1. $y = \$5$

a. Price $(ATR; y)$	Quantity (x)	Total revenue $(TR = 5x)$	$MR = \dfrac{\Delta R}{\Delta x}$	$ATR = \dfrac{TR}{x}$ $= 5$
5	0	0		
5	1	5	5	5
5	2	10	5	5
5	3	15	5	5
5	4	20	5	5
.	.	.	.	.
.	.	.	.	.
.	.	.	.	.

b.

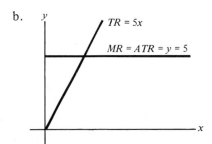

2. $y = 20 - 2x$

a. $ATR = \dfrac{TR}{x} = y = 20 - 2x$	Quantity (x)	$TR = xy = x(20 - 2x)$	$MR = \dfrac{\Delta R}{\Delta x}$
20	0	0	18
18	1	18	14
16	2	32	10
14	3	42	6
12	4	48	2
10	5	50	0
8	6	48	-2
6	7	42	-6
4	8	32	-10
2	9	18	-14
0	10	0	-18

b.

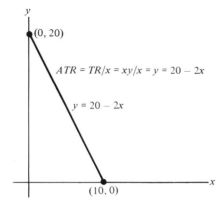

PROBLEMS 1-9, page 38

1. $E_d = \left(\dfrac{\Delta x}{\Delta y}\right)\left(\dfrac{y}{x}\right) = (-\infty)\left(\dfrac{y}{x}\right) = (-\infty)\left(\dfrac{10}{x}\right) = -\infty$. E_d is perfectly elastic, which

means that revenue is always increasing. The firm's revenue function is $TR = 10x$.

2. $y = 20 - 2x$

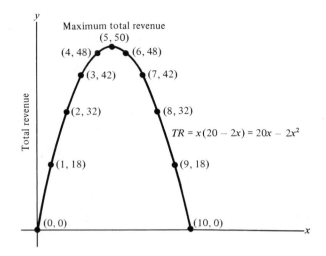

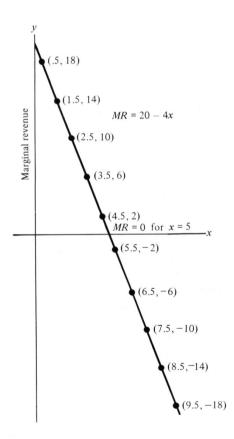

4. The equation representing demand is $y = a - x$ and $E_d = -1$ at the midpoint of the line, which is $(a/2, a/2)$. The point of intersection of demand with the guideline is found by solving $x = a - x$, which gives $x = a/2$ and $y = a/2$.

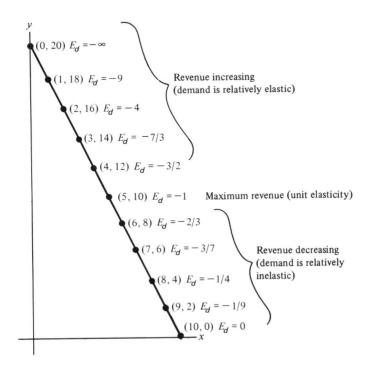

PROBLEMS 1-11, page 45

1. a.

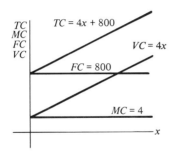

2.

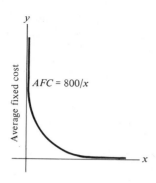 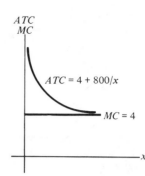

7. In a purely competitive firm marginal revenue must be greater than marginal cost in order to reach a break-even point and to assume positive profits. This means that the slope of revenue is greater than the slope of cost. Therefore, revenue will intersect cost.

PROBLEMS 1-12, page 48

1. a.

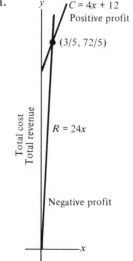

b.

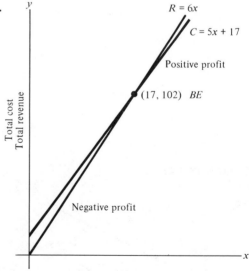

Find BE by solving

$24x = 4x + 12$ or $x = 3/5$.

Find BE by solving

$5x + 17 = 6x$ or $x = 17, y = 102$.

4. a.

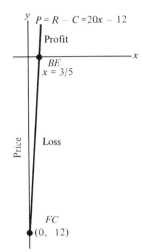

b.

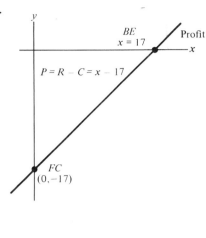

5. a.

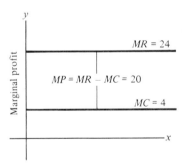

b.

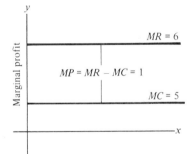

7. a. $X_{BE} = \dfrac{FC}{MR - MC} = \dfrac{12}{24 - 20} = \dfrac{3}{5}$

b. $X_{BE} = \dfrac{FC}{MR - MC} = \dfrac{17}{6 - 5} = 17$

PROBLEMS 1-13, page 55

1. a.
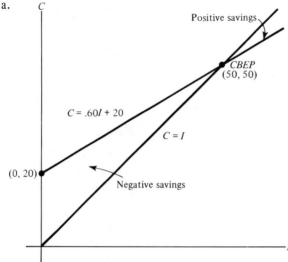

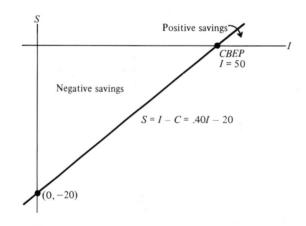

2. a.
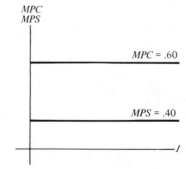

4. a. $M = \dfrac{1}{1 - MPC} = \dfrac{1}{.40} = 2.5 = 250\%$

PROBLEMS 1-14, page 60

1. a. $x = \dfrac{\begin{vmatrix} 4 & 1 \\ 18 & -1 \end{vmatrix}}{\begin{vmatrix} 2 & 1 \\ 3 & -1 \end{vmatrix}} = \dfrac{22}{5}$

$y = \dfrac{\begin{vmatrix} 2 & 4 \\ 3 & 18 \end{vmatrix}}{\begin{vmatrix} 2 & 1 \\ 3 & -1 \end{vmatrix}} = \dfrac{-24}{5}$

j. $x = \dfrac{\begin{vmatrix} -3 & 1 & 2 \\ 1 & 2 & -4 \\ -3 & 2 & -4 \end{vmatrix}}{\begin{vmatrix} 1 & 1 & 2 \\ 3 & 2 & -4 \\ -1 & 2 & -4 \end{vmatrix}} = \dfrac{32}{32} = 1$

$y = \dfrac{\begin{vmatrix} 1 & -3 & 2 \\ 3 & 1 & -4 \\ -1 & -3 & -4 \end{vmatrix}}{32} = \dfrac{-80}{32} = \dfrac{-5}{2}$

$z = \dfrac{\begin{vmatrix} 1 & 1 & -3 \\ 3 & 2 & 1 \\ -1 & 2 & -3 \end{vmatrix}}{32} = \dfrac{-24}{32} = \dfrac{-3}{4}$

2. a. $1 \begin{vmatrix} 4 & 5 \\ 2 & 5 \end{vmatrix} - 2 \begin{vmatrix} 3 & 5 \\ 3 & 5 \end{vmatrix} + 3 \begin{vmatrix} 3 & 4 \\ 3 & 2 \end{vmatrix} = -8$

5. $\begin{vmatrix} a & b \\ a & b \end{vmatrix} = ab - ab = 0$

6. $\begin{vmatrix} a & b \\ c & d \end{vmatrix} = ad - bc; \quad \begin{vmatrix} c & d \\ a & b \end{vmatrix} = bc - ad$

PROBLEMS 1-15, page 66

1. The objective function to maximize is $P = 60x + 30y$, and the slope is between the slopes of the restraints. Therefore, profit is maximized at the point (2, 10). Maximum profit is: $P = 60(2) + 30(10) = \$420$.

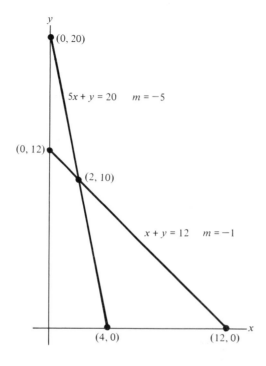

2. The objective function to maximize is $P = 30x + 60y$, and the slope of the objective function is $m = -(1/2)$, which means that profit is maximized at the point (0, 12). Maximum profit is: $P = 30(0) + 60(12) = \$720$.

3. The objective function to maximize is $P = 80x + 10y$, and the slope of the objective function is $m = -8$, which means that profit is maximized at the point (4, 0). Maximum profit is: $P = 80(4) + 10(0) = \$320$.

PROBLEMS 1-16, page 74

1. a.

X	Y	XY	X^2	Y^2
0	0	0	0	0
1	2	2	1	4
2	4	8	4	16
3	6	18	9	36
4	8	32	16	64
10	20	60	30	120

$$r = \frac{100}{\sqrt{1000}} = 1 \text{ (points lie exactly on a straight line)}$$

$$b = \frac{0}{50} = 0$$

$$m = \frac{100}{50} = 2$$

The best-fitting line is $y = 2x$.

b.

X	Y	XY	X^2	Y^2
0	2	0	0	4
1	3	3	1	9
2	5	10	4	25
3	5	15	9	25
4	6	24	16	36
10	21	52	30	99

$$r = .96$$

$$b = \frac{110}{50} = 2.2$$

$$m = \frac{50}{50} = 1$$

The best-fitting line is $y = x + 2.2$.

PROBLEMS 2-1, page 79

1.

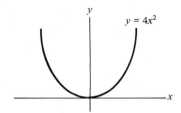

$y = 4x^2$

2.

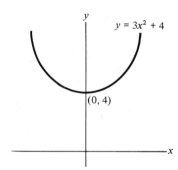

$y = 3x^2 + 4$

$(0, 4)$

3.

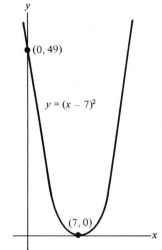

$(0, 49)$

$y = (x - 7)^2$

$(7, 0)$

4.

$y = (x - 5)^2 + 2$

(0, 27)

(5, 2)

PROBLEMS 2-2, page 84

1. a. $x^2 - 10x + 16 = (x - 8)(x - 2) = 0$; $x = 8, x = 2$

   b. $x^2 + 10x + 16 = (x + 2)(x + 8) = 0$; $x = -2, x = -8$

   c. $x^2 + 6x - 16 = (x + 8)(x - 2) = 0$; $x = -8, x = 2$

2. a. $x = \dfrac{-8 \pm \sqrt{40}}{4} = \dfrac{-4 \pm \sqrt{10}}{2}$

   b. $x = \dfrac{-8 \pm \sqrt{88}}{4} = \dfrac{-4 \pm \sqrt{22}}{2}$

3. a. $y = x^2 - 10x + 16$

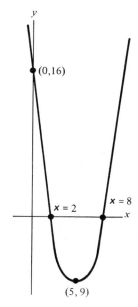

b. $y = x^2 + 10x + 16$

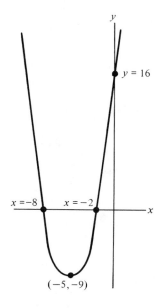

4. $y = (x - 5)(x - 7) = x^2 - 12x + 35$

5. The three points determine three equations in three unknowns:

$3 = 4a + 2b + c$

$10 = 9a + 3b + c$

$21 = 16a + 4b + c$

The solutions are $a = 2$, $b = -3$, $c = 1$, and $y = 2x^2 - 3x + 1$.

PROBLEMS 2-3, page 86

1. a.

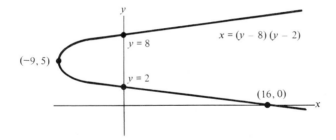

PROBLEMS 2-4, page 87

1. a.

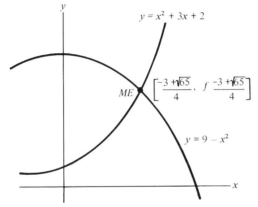

PROBLEMS 2-5, page 93

1. $y = 5, TR = 5x, MR = 5, ATR = y = 5, E_d = -\infty$ (perfectly elastic)

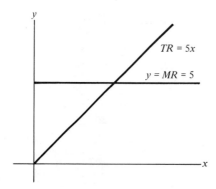

Chapter 3

PROBLEMS 3-1, page 98

1. a.

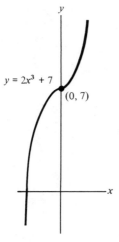

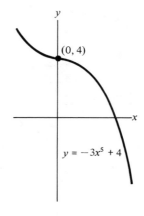

2. a.

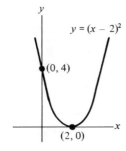

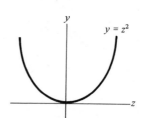

PROBLEMS 3-2, page 101

1. a.

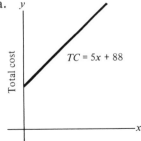

$TC = 5x + 88$

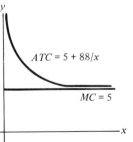

$ATC = 5 + 88/x$

$MC = 5$

$AFC = 88/x$

2.

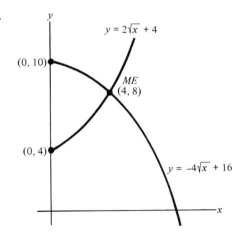

$y = 2\sqrt{x} + 4$

$(0, 10)$

ME
$(4, 8)$

$(0, 4)$

$y = -4\sqrt{x} + 16$

PROBLEMS 3-3, page 106

2. a.

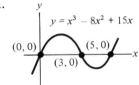

$y = x^3 - 8x^2 + 15x$

$(0, 0)$

$(5, 0)$

$(3, 0)$

3. a.

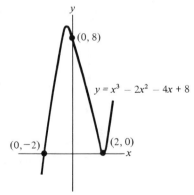

$y = x^3 - 2x^2 - 4x + 8$

(0, 8)

(0, −2)   (2, 0)

PROBLEMS 3-4, page 110

1.

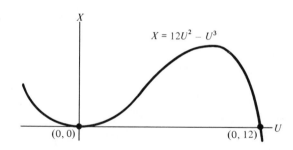

$X = 12U^2 - U^3$

(0, 0)   (0, 12)

PROBLEMS 3-5, page 116

1.

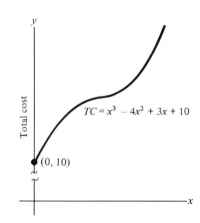

$TC = x^3 - 4x^2 + 3x + 10$

(0, 10)

2.

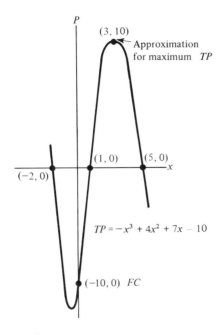

P

(3, 10)

Approximation
for maximum TP

(1, 0)

(5, 0)

x

(−2, 0)

$TP = -x^3 + 4x^2 + 7x - 10$

(−10, 0) FC

PROBLEMS 3-6, page 117

1. a.

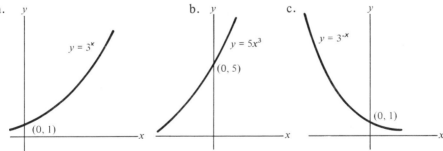

y

$y = 3^x$

(0, 1)

x

b. y

$y = 5x^3$

(0, 5)

x

c.

y

$y = 3^{-x}$

(0, 1)

x

PROBLEMS 4-1, page 128

1. a. $y' = \lim\limits_{\Delta x \to 0} \dfrac{c - c}{\Delta x} = 0$

d. $y' = \lim\limits_{\Delta x \to 0} \dfrac{2(x + \Delta x)^2 - 2x^2}{\Delta x} = 4x^2$

PROBLEMS 4-2, page 132

1. a. $y' = m$
   b. $y' = -9$
   c. $y' = -8x + 8$
   d. $y' = 12 - 2x$

2. a. $\dfrac{dy}{dx} = -3; \quad \dfrac{dx}{dy} = \dfrac{-1}{3}$

3. a. $\dfrac{dz}{dw} = 3$

   b. $\dfrac{dz}{dw} = 8w - 8$

4. The derivative of the sum is: $\dfrac{d}{dx}(6x + 4x) = \dfrac{d}{dx}(10x) = 10$

   The sum of the derivatives is: $[f'(x) = 6] + [g'(x) = 4] = 10$

6. a. $f'(x) = 4x, f'(0) = 0, f'(1) = 4, f'(2) = 8, f'(-1) = -4, f'(-2) = -8$

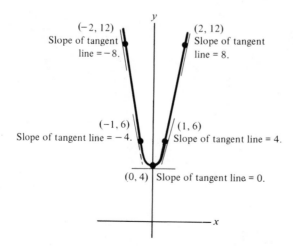

(−2, 12)
Slope of tangent line = −8.

(2, 12)
Slope of tangent line = 8.

(−1, 6)
Slope of tangent line = −4.

(1, 6)
Slope of tangent line = 4.

(0, 4) Slope of tangent line = 0.

PROBLEMS 4-4, page 146

1. a. $y' = 4x^3$, and for positive values of x, y' is positive, which means that $f(x)$ increases. For negative values of x, y' is negative, which means that $f(x)$ decreases. For $x = 0$, $y' = 0$, which means that $f(x)$ levels off.

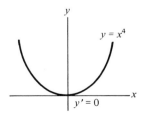

b. $y' = 3x^2$, which means that y' is positive and that $f(x)$ is increasing for all values of x except $x = 0$, in which case $y' = 0$ and $f(x)$ levels off.

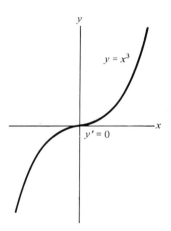

c. $y' = 2x - 4$, which means that y' is positive for x greater than 2 and $f(x)$ increases. For x less than 2, y' is negative and $f(x)$ decreases. For $x = 2$, $y' = 0$ and $f(x)$ levels off.

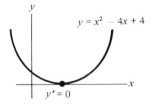

2. a. $R = 12x - 3x^2$ and $R' = 12 - 6x$, which means that R' is positive for x less than 2, which means that $R = f(x)$ increases. R' is negative for x greater than 2, which means that case $R = f(x)$ decreases. $R' = 0$ for $x = 2$, which means that $R = f(x)$ levels off at $x = 2$.

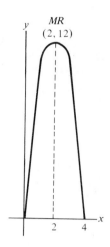

3. a. $C = (x^3/3) - x^2 + 4x + 10$ and $C' = x^2 - 2x + 4$. For all positive values of x, C' is positive, which means that $C = f(x)$ is always increasing. C' is a parabola concave up with vertex at $(1, 3)$. The graph of C' appears in the first quadrant, and if the total cost function is to be a third-degree polynomial that always increases, marginal cost must appear concave up and must be positive (that is, it must appear in the first quadrant). In a later problem we will prove that the vertex of C' must lie in the first quadrant also.

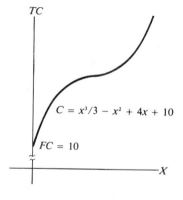

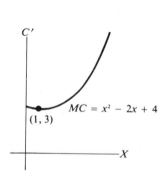

5. For $P = (-x^3/3) + x^2 + 15x - 10, P' = -x^2 + 2x + 15$. Maximum profit is found by solving $P' = 0$ or $x^2 - 2x - 15 = 0$, which gives $x = -3$ and $x = 5$.

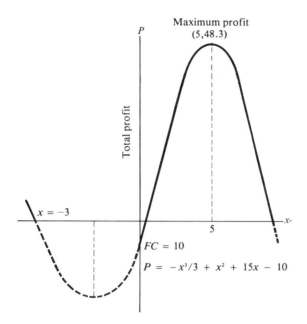

8. a. $y = 16 - x^2$ and $y'' = -2$, which means that $y = f(x)$ is concave down.

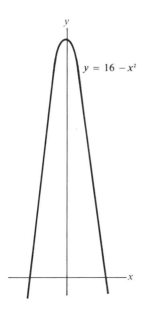

b. $y = -x^3 + 27$ and $y'' = -6x$, which means that $y = f(x)$ is concave up for negative values of x and concave down for positive values of x.

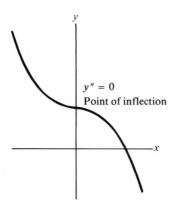

PROBLEMS 4-5, page 154

1. $y = 16 - x^2$

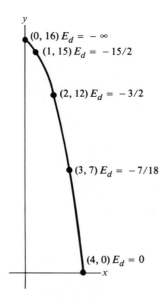

3. a. For $y = 1/x^2$, $dy/dx = -2/x^3$ and $dx/dy = -x^3/2$, which gives:

$$E_d = \left(\frac{-x^3}{2}\right)\left(\frac{1/x^2}{x}\right) = \frac{-1}{2}$$

PROBLEMS 4-6, page 173

1. $MPC = .5 + 1/(4\sqrt{I})$. For $I = 4$, $MPC = 62.5\%$ and $MPS = 37.5\%$. The multiplier is $M = 2.666\ldots$. For $I = 9$, $MPC = 58\ 1/3\%$ and $MPS = 41\ 2/3\%$. The multiplier is $M = 2.4$. For $I = 16$, $MPC = 56.25\%$ and $MPS = 43.75\%$. The multiplier is $M = 2.28$.

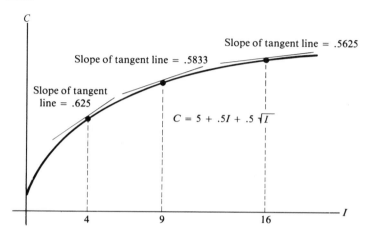

4. a.   b.

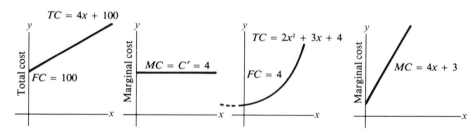

5. Minimum ATC occurs for $ATC' = 2 - (18/x^2) = 0$ or $x = 3$. ATC intersects MC at minimum ATC: $2x + 8 + (18/x) = 4x + 8$ or $x = 3$.

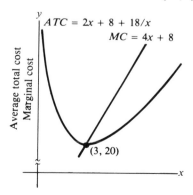

8. a.

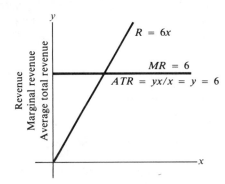

b.

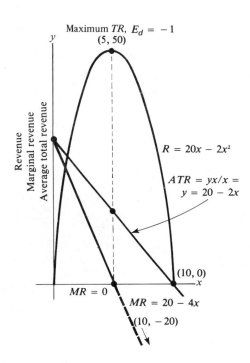

9. a. For $y = 20 - 2x$, $R = 20x - 2x^2$ and $MR = 20 - 4x$. $E_d = -1$ at the midpoint of the line $y = 20 - 2x$, so $E_d = -1$ for $x = 5$. $MR = 0$ at $x = 5$. If demand is relatively elastic, an increase in price will result in a decrease in revenue (a decline in price will cause an increase in revenue). If demand is relatively inelastic, a decrease in price will cause a decrease in total revenue (an increase in price will cause an increase in total revenue).

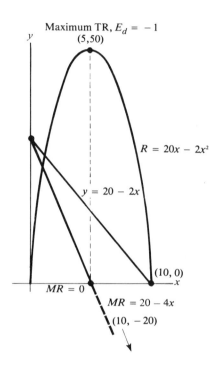

10. a. Demand is relatively elastic from both the demand expressions y_1 and y_2 at the "kink."

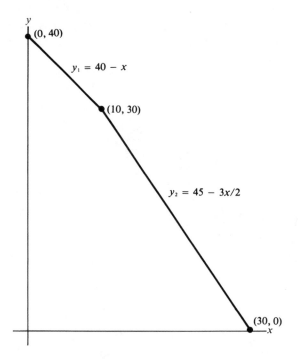

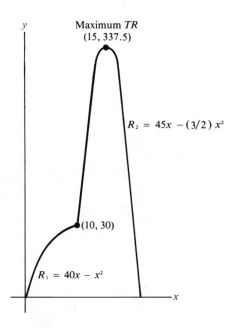

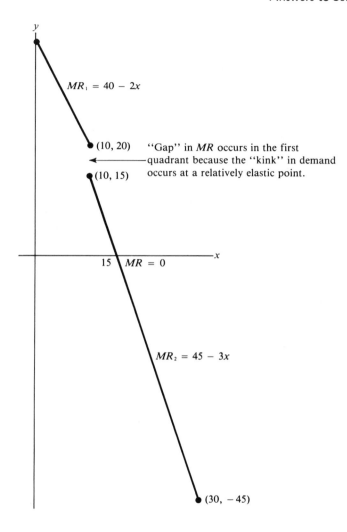

$MR_1 = 40 - 2x$

(10, 20)

(10, 15)

"Gap" in MR occurs in the first quadrant because the "kink" in demand occurs at a relatively elastic point.

15    $MR = 0$

$MR_2 = 45 - 3x$

(30, −45)

11. a.

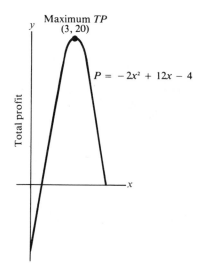

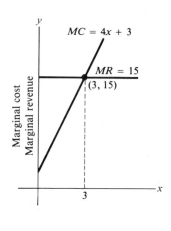

d.

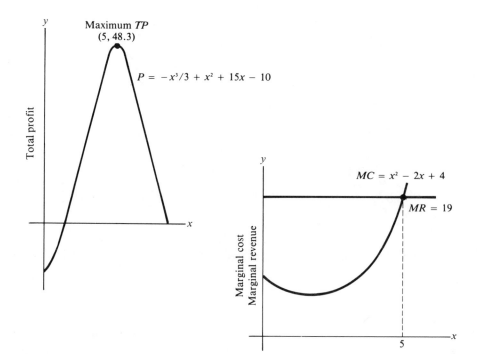

PROBLEMS 4-7, page 180

1. a.

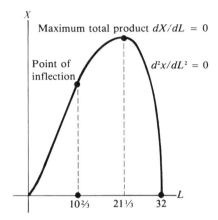

X

Maximum total product $dX/dL = 0$

Point of inflection

$d^2x/dL^2 = 0$

$10\frac{2}{3}$ $21\frac{1}{3}$ 32

L

PROBLEMS 4-8, page 185

1. $EOQ = \sqrt{\dfrac{(2)(7200)(20)}{3(.20)}} = 693$

PROBLEMS 4-9, page 193

1. a. $\displaystyle\int 6 = 6x + c$

c. $\displaystyle\int 3x - 4 = \dfrac{3x^2}{2} - 4x + c$

e. $\displaystyle\int \dfrac{13}{x^2} = 0$

h. $\displaystyle\int (8w^2 + 3)\, dw = \dfrac{8w^3}{3} + 3w + c$

3. a. $\displaystyle\int MR = \int 10 - 2x = 10x - x^2 = TR$

4. a. $\displaystyle\int MC = \int 4 = 4x + 10 = TC$

PROBLEMS 4-10, page 196

1. a.

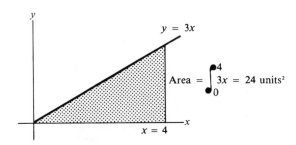

Area $= \int_0^4 3x = 24$ units^2

b.

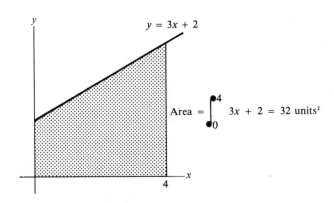

Area $= \int_0^4 3x + 2 = 32$ units^2

PROBLEMS 4-11, page 199

1. a. $y = (3x + 10)^4$; $y' = 4(3x + 10)^3 (3) = 12(3x + 10)^3$

2. a. $y = (x^2)(x^3)$; $y' = x^2(3x^2) + x^3(2x) = 5x^4$

3. a. $y = \dfrac{x^5}{x^3}$; $y' = \dfrac{x^3(5x^4) - x^5(3x^2)}{(x^3)^2} = 2x$

4. a. $x^2 + y^2 = 36$; $2x + 2yy' = 0$; $y' = \dfrac{-x}{y}$

PROBLEMS 5-1, page 202

2. a. $\displaystyle\sum_{j=1}^{50} a_{10,j}$

PROBLEMS 5-2, page 209

1. $\begin{pmatrix} 1 & -7 & 4 \\ 0 & 3 & 4 \end{pmatrix} + \begin{pmatrix} 2 & 4 & -6 \\ 1 & -3 & 5 \end{pmatrix} = \begin{pmatrix} 3 & -3 & -2 \\ 1 & 0 & 9 \end{pmatrix}$

6. $2\begin{pmatrix} 5 & 6 \\ -1 & 3 \end{pmatrix} - 2\begin{pmatrix} 3 & -4 \\ 3 & 7 \end{pmatrix} = \begin{pmatrix} 4 & 20 \\ -8 & -8 \end{pmatrix}$

7. $\begin{pmatrix} -3 & 4 \\ -5 & 2 \end{pmatrix} \cdot \begin{pmatrix} 3 & 7 \\ 1 & -5 \end{pmatrix} = \begin{pmatrix} -5 & -41 \\ -13 & -45 \end{pmatrix}$

10. $\begin{pmatrix} 3 & 5 \\ 4 & 9 \end{pmatrix} \cdot \begin{pmatrix} 0 & 0 \\ 0 & 0 \end{pmatrix} = \begin{pmatrix} 0 & 0 \\ 0 & 0 \end{pmatrix}$

16. $\begin{pmatrix} 1 & 2 \\ 5 & 7 \\ 3 & 8 \end{pmatrix} \cdot \begin{pmatrix} 7 \\ 6 \end{pmatrix} = \begin{pmatrix} 19 \\ 77 \\ 69 \end{pmatrix}$

21. $\begin{pmatrix} 1 & 2 \\ 2 & 4 \\ 3 & 6 \\ 4 & 8 \end{pmatrix}$

PROBLEMS 5-3, page 215

1. a. $\begin{pmatrix} \dfrac{1}{37} & \dfrac{5}{37} \\[2mm] \dfrac{7}{37} & \dfrac{-2}{37} \end{pmatrix}$

2. a. $\dfrac{1}{32} \cdot \begin{pmatrix} -16 & 32 & 0 \\ 16 & -40 & 8 \\ 0 & 12 & -4 \end{pmatrix}$

PROBLEMS 5-4, page 226

1. a. $\begin{pmatrix} x \\ y \end{pmatrix} = \text{INV} \begin{pmatrix} 2 & -1 \\ 3 & 1 \end{pmatrix} \cdot \begin{pmatrix} 4 \\ 6 \end{pmatrix} = \begin{pmatrix} 2 \\ 0 \end{pmatrix}$

2. a. $\begin{pmatrix} x \\ y \\ z \end{pmatrix} = \text{INV} \begin{pmatrix} 1 & 1 & 1 \\ 3 & 2 & 1 \\ 4 & 3 & 1 \end{pmatrix} \cdot \begin{pmatrix} 6 \\ 10 \\ 13 \end{pmatrix} = \begin{pmatrix} 1 \\ 2 \\ 3 \end{pmatrix}$

3. $\begin{pmatrix} 2 & -3 & | & 4 \\ 4 & 3 & | & 8 \end{pmatrix} \cdot \begin{pmatrix} 1 & 0 & | & 2 \\ 0 & 1 & | & 0 \end{pmatrix}$

PROBLEMS 5-6, page 237

1. Initial table:

$$\begin{pmatrix}
x & y & s_1 & s_2 & P & \text{Constants} \\
1 & 1 & 1 & 0 & 0 & 12 \\
5 & 1 & 0 & 1 & 0 & 20 \\
\hline
-60 & -30 & 0 & 0 & 1 & 0
\end{pmatrix}$$

$x = 2, y = 10$, maximum profit = \$420

PROBLEMS 6-1, page 243

1. a. $I = Prt = \$1000(.10)\left(\dfrac{140}{365}\right) = \$38.26$

    $S = \$1038.26$

2. $P = \dfrac{I}{rt} = \dfrac{80}{.08} = \$1000$

PROBLEMS 6-2, page 248

1. a. $S = P(1 + i)^n = 1,000(1 + .01)^{12} = \$1,126.83$

2. a. $S = P(1 + i)^n = 1,000\left(\dfrac{1 + .12}{365}\right)^{730} = \$1,271.14$

4. $P = S(1 + i)^{-n} = 100,000(1 + .01)^{-36} = \$69,892.50$

PROBLEMS 6-3, page 252

2. a. $S = Pe^{rt} = 100e^{.10} = \$1,105.00$

4. $S = pe^{rt} = 1000e^{.5} = \$1,649.00$

PROBLEMS 6-4, page 256

1. a. $APR = (1 + i)^n - 1 = \left(\dfrac{1 + .10}{12}\right)^{12} - 1 = 10.47\%$

4. b. $APR = e^r - 1 = e^{.10} - 1 = 10.5\%$

5. $P = \dfrac{A}{1 - rt} = \dfrac{1,000}{1 - .06} = \$1,063.83$

    $APR = \dfrac{P - A}{At} = \dfrac{63.83}{500} = 12.766\%$

PROBLEMS 6-5, page 263

1. a. $S = R\left[\dfrac{(1+i)^n - 1}{i}\right] = (100)\left[\dfrac{(1+.01)^{24} - 1}{.01}\right] = \$2,697.35$

4. a. $A = (R)\left[\dfrac{1-(1+i)^{-n}}{i}\right] = (100)\left[\dfrac{1-(1+.01)^{-24}}{.01}\right] = \$2,124.30$

5. a. $R = \dfrac{iA}{1-(1+i)^{-n}} = \dfrac{.01(50,000)}{1-(1+.01)^{-240}} = \$550.54$

    Total amount paid in 20 years = \$132,129.60; Interest on first payment is \$500.

PROBLEMS 6-6, page 265

1. a. $S = (1+i)\left[\dfrac{(R)(1+i)^n - 1}{i}\right] = (1.01)\left[(100)\ \dfrac{(1+.01)^{24} - 1}{.01}\right] = \$2,724.32$

PROBLEMS 6-7, page 271

1. Straight-line method: Sum-of-the-years method:

Year	Depreciation	Book value		Year	Depreciation	Book value
0	0	3,600		0	0	3,600.00
1	500	3,100		1	857.14	2,742.86
2	500	2,600		2	714.29	2,028.57
3	500	2,100		3	571.43	1,457.14
4	500	1,600		4	428.57	1,028.57
5	500	1,100		5	285.71	742.86
6	500	600		6	142.86	600.00
	3,000				3,000.00	

INDEX